Woman in Islam

WIEBKE WALTHER

Woman in Islam

ABNER SCHRAM · MONTCLAIR

GEORGE PRIOR · LONDON

Translated from the German by C.S.V. Salt
© 1981 Edition Leipzig
Published in the United States of America in 1981
by Abner Schram Ltd., 36 Park Street, Montclair, N.J. 07042
Published in the United Kingdom in 1981 by
George Prior Associated Publishers Ltd.
37-41 Bedford Row, London WClR 4JH
ENGLAND
ISBN: 0-86043-554-7

Library of Congress Catalog Card Number: 80-67091
ISBN: 0 8390-0256-4
Designed by Volker Küster
Printed in the German Democratic Republic

Contents

Foreword

At the start of the 1980's,
more than 700 million people are estimated
to be followers of the Islamic faith, a great deal of them living
in traditional Islamic countries that increasingly occupy
the forefront of international interest.
The situation of half these many millions, the women of Islam, is a subject
which time and again in the last century and a half has caught the attention both of
non-Islamic authors, who
usually display a critical turn of mind, and of Moslem apologists.
This book examines the subject of woman in Islam from a largely historical standpoint.
Attention is focused on the main Islamic countries;
that is, the Arab world, Turkey, Iran, and Mogul India.
Islamism in Black Africa and East and Southeast Asia requires special treatment, and has
not been covered here. Even with
these limitations, it has been possible to touch only the surface of the wealth of material available.
Nevertheless in dealing
with the wide-ranging and diversified subject of woman in the traditional Islamic countries,
every effort has been made to draw a well-rounded picture, avoid
sweeping generalizations, and adequate- ly justify statements and conclusions.
Since the book has been written for a wide range of readers,
the usual technical transcription of Arabic, Persian, and Turkish names
and terms has been dropped in favor of one that takes account
of pronunciation, although the results are still only an approximation because
of differences in the phonetic systems. In the interests of easier recognition
by the expert, however, the customary transcription has been retained for the original titles of works
listed in the bibliography.
I would like to thank my Moslem colleagues in Egypt and Iraq who, in writing and
in conversations, readily answered the questions I put to them in the course of two study trips.
I respect and honor their views.
At the same time, I hope they will understand that I, as a non-Moslem, do not always
share them. This difference in viewpoint begins with the title.
In contrast to the
position of many Moslems today, orientalists see in Islam more than a religion;
they point out that unlike any other religion in the course of history,
Islam has penetrated and shaped the politics and culture of the countries
dominated by it and has molded the life of those who profess it.
Thus, in this book, "woman in Islam" encompasses not only
the position of women in religion
and religious law but also in social life,
history, and culture.

Introduction: Historical Background

In about the year 610, when he was some forty years of age, the merchant Mohammed, from an impoverished branch of the Qoraysh, principal tribe of the Arab trading city of Mecca, had a vision. His subsequent interpretation of this vision, which came after much reflection and searching for God, was that the archangel Gabriel had brought him a message from Allah. In the Arabia of the seventh century, Allah was the name given the supreme god of numerous divinities and demons. Arab theologians do not agree on what verses were the first to be heard by Mohammed, since the Koran (*Qor'ān*, "recitation") was only written down after Mohammed's death and arranged only according to the length of its *Suras* or chapters.

It is quite certain, however, that the first communications announced by Mohammed as the revealed word of Allah were a warning to the arrogant merchant caste of Mecca, a warning of the Day of Judgment and the End of the World. Mohammed's message urged the merchants to do good and pious deeds, to abandon polytheism, and to praise the goodness, mercy, justice, and power of Allah; later they also proclaimed the joys of Paradise awaiting the faithful.

These revelations were presented in rhyming prose, a stylistic form used by ancient Arabic soothsayers. Considered the word of God, the revelations were and are of such majesty that Moslems throughout the ages have regarded the Koran as a stylistically inimitable miracle, which, in the Orthodox view, must not be translated. Nonetheless they have been translated, and Arberry's translation of one of the oldest *Suras* conveys an impression of this form: "Recite: In the Name of thy Lord who created—created Man of a blood-clot.—Recite: And thy Lord is the Most Generous—who taught by the Pen—taught Man, that he knew not."* The

* Translated by A. J. Arberry. All other quotations from the Koran are taken from Richard Bell's *The Qur'ān* (Edinburgh: T. & T. Clark). Subsequent citations will be indicated by numbers in parentheses ( ), with the first number designating the *Sura*, the second the verses.

wealthy merchants of Mecca took no heed of Mohammed's message, since they made money not only out of the caravan trade but also out of the cult of the Ka'ba in Mecca, in which a black meteorite was revered, and which attracted numerous Bedouin tribes of the Arabian Peninsula as well. The merchants quickly scented a threat to their privileges and prosperity, however, and persecuted Mohammed and his early followers, treating them with scorn and contempt. Among these first followers were Mohammed's then wife, Khadija, of whom we will hear again, and members of Mecca's middle and lower classes.

The commercial aristocracy's pressure on the followers of the new faith became increasingly severe, and ultimately Mohammed was compelled to accept an invitation from the Arab tribes of Aus and Khazraj, dwelling at the date oasis of Yathrib some three hundred kilometers from Mecca. These two tribes were enemies and hoped to find a mediator in the founder of the new religion.

In 622, Mohammed and his followers made the migration *(hijra)* from Mecca to Yathrib, which was renamed Medina from the Arabic *Madinat an-nabiy*, "the city of the Prophet." This year of 622 marks the beginning of Islamic chronology, which, unlike the Roman calendar, is based on lunar years.

Mohammed now became the religious and political head of a community, and Islam, at least in concept, has preserved this unity of political and religious leadership throughout the centuries. His revelations from this period no longer possess the passion of the first *Suras* of Mecca. They contain rules designed to govern the life of the new community and the relationship between the *muhājirūn*, "the emigrants" from Mecca, and the *Ansār*, their "helpers" in Medina, for bonds of tribal membership, deriving from kith-and-kin relationships, were now to be replaced by the *umma*, the "community of the faithful." In modern Arabic, *umma* signifies "nation."

The *Suras* of Medina also deal with questions relating to Judaism and Christianity, since several Jewish tribes lived in Medina and Christians were to be found close by, princi-

This highly realistic Arab miniature of 1237 depicts the arrival of two travelers in a small town. Everything is shown: the mosque and minaret, various domestic animals at the waterside, hen and cock on the dome-shaped roofs of houses in what is probably the sūq or market. On the right is a view of the town gate and the guard with his long halberd. In front of it sits a woman with a distaff under her arm. The clothing of all the persons shown is decorated with the strips of lettering known as tirāz, as are the saddlecloths of the camels.

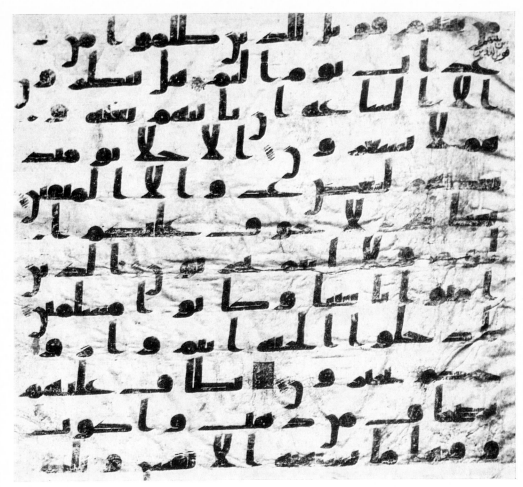

2
In the numerous wars of Islamic history—
excluding the early period in which they
took part in the fighting—women were
victims of the conquerors, as everywhere
else in the world. This miniature, showing the conquest of a city, possibly Bagdad, by the Mongols, in the thirteenth
century depicts military equipment in use
at the time. The ruler, scepter in hand,
stands at the city gate from which a pon-
toon bridge extends across the river. Only
the defenders of the city are seen, not their
adversaries.

3
This handwritten manuscript, dating
from the eighth century, was produced
more than two hundred years before Ko-
rans began to be artistically decorated with
colorful designs. Indeed, it is one of the
oldest surviving fragments of the Koran
in a rough lettering of early Kūfic. It contains verses of the 43rd Sura, and in the
lower third Verse 70: "Enter the Garden,
you and your spouses, in gala attire."

4
Small figures, such as this tin relief of a
woman worshiper of the Seljūq period, are
rarely found in Islamic art of earlier centuries. The woman wears rich ornamentation, including a crown in her hair.

5

A scene from a Persian romantic epic—a prince visiting a princess in her pavilion—shows the room's splendidly decorative interior. Not only are there colored tiles on the walls but also delicate murals, which, according to Islamic traditions, are not really permissible. On the floor, under the glittering golden throne of the king, is a brilliant red carpet.

One of the most delicate of all Islamic miniatures shows the arrival of Prince Humāy at the residence of Princess Humāyūn and her ladies. The golden crescent of the moon and the stars stand out against the blue of the night sky, but the blossoming shrubs and trees in the garden and the gowns of the ethereal figures shine forth with all the colors of daylight.

7

A miniature from a collection of legends of the Prophet. The Koran also contains the Old Testament story of Noah and the ark. Noah is shown with a nimbus of flames, since, according to the Koran, he is a prophet; his three sons and daughters are depicted here as Moslems of the second half of the sixteenth century. Animals can be recognized in the hull of the ship, and the water is rising over a dome and two minarets.

There are sorceresses, female demons, and good and wicked fairies in the literature of the Islamic countries, but Islam has never experienced anything like witch-hunting. Here is a scene from the Shāh-nāmeh, *the Iranian national epic: the killing of a sorceress.*

9

A colorful scene before the gate of an Indian city on a miniature painted in 1617 for the library of the Emperor Jahāngīr. In this miniature, we see a baker in his shop, a wood seller, a water carrier, gardeners at work and, screened by trees and a wall, women making lace at the side of a watercourse. Within the city, Koran readers can be identified on the roof of a house, in the interior of which two women are gesticulating while two others are talking in the harem garden. The guardian of the gate looks down from above.

pally among some Bedouin tribes of the Arabian Peninsula but also in areas bordering states with a higher level of civilization. Mohammed regarded himself as the last of a series of messengers of God to mankind, bringing perfection to his revelations to Jews and Christians. However, he acquired knowledge of the two religions in their popular form, which diverged on many questions from Orthodox doctrine. At first, Mohammed believed that the Jews of Medina would acknowledge him as a prophet. When this did not happen, his reaction was harsh. He also changed the direction of prayer from Jerusalem to the Ka'ba in Mecca, thus recognizing the Arab Ka'ba cult as a central element in the new faith.

Mohammed gradually acquired followers among the Bedouin tribes of the Arabian Peninsula. In the course of a number of traditional Bedouin raids for plunder, he achieved material benefits for his followers and ultimately was able to gain the upper hand over his adversaries among the merchant aristocracy of Mecca. In 630, Mohammed and his followers entered Mecca in triumph. When he died at Medina in 632, most of the Bedouin tribes and the inhabitants of the few cities in Western Arabia were followers of Islam, the new faith that was more appropriate than Christianity or Judaism to the social conditions prevailing in those areas at that time. In the centuries that followed, Islam has demonstrated a capacity to absorb new elements and to adapt to more highly developed social and cultural structures.

The governing maxim of the Islamic faith is: *La ilāha illā 'llāh wa-Muḥammad rasūl Allāh*, "There is no god but Allah, and Mohammed is the messenger of Allah." In contrast to Jesus in Christianity, who designated himself the Son of God, Mohammed said of himself, "I am only a human being like yourselves." (18:110) Mohammed is the instrument of revelation, of the divine message revealed in the Koran. The Koran has remained unchallengeable for Moslems even to the present time; a believer considers it to be self-evident that God does not err and the Koran is the word of God. Later, his community, probably following the example of the Christian view of Jesus, came to believe that Mohammed performed miracles. He regarded himself as the Seal of the Prophets; that is, the last in a line of prophets that included Adam, Abraham, Moses, and Jesus, all of whom had proclaimed divine doctrines, but he had brought God's message to the Arabs. This recognition of earlier prophets and above all of "book religions" like Christianity and Judaism, which like Islam possess holy scriptures, allowed Islam to be tolerant toward other religions in the Middle Ages. At times, in the history of Islam, Jews and Christians played a notable role in the public life of the Islamic countries. They were physicians, court secretaries, translators, and money chang-

ers. Nevertheless, they had to pay higher taxes, and in that respect at least were always second-class citizens.

Islam *(Islām)* means "surrender to God's will"; a believer is a Moslem, "one who surrenders to God's will." But the concept of Islam, the outward profession of this religion, also includes that of *imān*, "profound belief coming from the heart." Surrender to God's will presupposes *hosn az-zann*, the belief that God, Allah, is good and one can trust in God's knowing what is best for Man.

The duties that Islam imposes on the faithful are prayers five times a day in the direction of Mecca; these are not silent communications with God but a sequence of bows, prostrations, and the repetition of certain dogmas. The alms tax is to free the rich from excessive wealth and to express the financial responsibility they share for poorer citizens. In the month of Ramadān, the practicing Moslem must fast from dawn till dusk; in addition, he must make the pilgrimage to the Ka'ba in Mecca at least once in his lifetime.

In contrast to Christianity, Islam has no priests, no body of religious officials to undertake tasks that cannot be entrusted to ordinary members of the faith. Just as Mohammed was the political and religious leader in one person, his successors had a similar status and initially called themselves *Khalīfat rasūl Allāh*, "successor to the envoy of Allah." Of course, an *imām* or prayer leader had to perform his function in the various mosques, but he was not ordained the way a Catholic priest is, for instance.

Within a few decades of Mohammed's death, Arab troops —semi-nomads and religious warriors—had conquered the entire area surrounding them comprising states on a high level of civilization. They put an end to the Sassanid Empire in the East, and they conquered a large part of the area in the West occupied by the other great power of that time, Byzantium. It was not only religious fervor that gave strength to the Moslems in these conquests. Rich booty fell into their hands, and their success seemed to confirm for them not only the correctness of their doctrine but also their belief that Allah was on their side.

Whereas Abū Bakr, the first Khalif after Mohammed, still distributed the spoils equally among the Moslems, however, the next in line, Omar, introduced social distinctions determined by the intensity of one's profession of faith. Since this was difficult to assess, the degree of relationship to the Prophet and the date of conversion to Islam became the decisive criteria. Contrary to the Islamic doctrine of equality among all believers, an oligarchy emerged, and the first social protests occurred, these being expressed in religious schisms. Othmān, the third of the first four Khalifs whom Moslems up to now idealize as "the rightly guided," and his successor, Ali, were murdered. Ali's followers in Iraq formed the Shi'at Ali, the party of Ali, or the Shi'a, as it was called later, which recognizes only Ali and his descendants as legitimate claimants to the title of Khalif. At the present time, the Shi'ites live mainly in Lebanon, Iraq, South Yemen, Iran, and India. They account for about 10 percent of all followers of Islam. Most Moslems describe themselves as Sunnites, as people who regard the *Sunna* or "custom" of the Prophet as their model and remain true to the community of the faithful.

In 661, the Arab dynasty of the Omayyads came to power in the person of the Khalif Mo'āwiya, who made Damascus the capital. As a result, Central Arabia, with its two holy cities of Mecca and Medina, gradually returned to the status of a minor province.

When the rule of the Omayyads was ended in 750 by the Abbāsids, the *dār al-Islām* or "House of Islam" reached from the Pyrenees to the Valley of the Indus. In general, social relations in the conquered territories were left unchanged by the Arabs. Structures of an early feudal pattern continued to exist in countries with a higher level of civilization, whereas in the deserts and steppes of the Khalifat, Turkish, Arab, and Berber nomads relied on cattle breeding. The conquered people were mostly peasants, artisans, merchants, officials of the administrative apparatus (which the Arabs left intact), and great landowners, who, unlike the European feudal lords of the Middle Ages, lived in the cities, and not on their fiefs. All these people—for the most part Jews or Christians—enjoyed the protection of the Arab ruling class. They had to pay taxes, but this was nothing new, as they had always been required to do so when conquered by others in the past. Over time, increasing numbers of them embraced Islam, and, in accordance with Arab custom, they as "new Moslems," *mawāli* in Arabic, had to join an Arab tribe. Considerable dissatisfaction developed among these new Moslems, particularly in Iran, since they felt at a disadvantage in comparison with the Arab ruling class.

The Abbāsids, who traced their ancestry back to an uncle of Mohammed, skillfully exploited this situation to their own advantage. With their period of rule, beginning in 750, the Iranian element predominated in the Khalifat. Outwardly, the shift in the center of power toward the East was reflected in the founding by the second Abbāsid Khalif al-Mansūr in 762 of a new metropolis, Bagdad, not far from Ctesiphon, the old royal residence-city of the Sassanid rulers. Certain institutions and offices typical of the Sassanid Empire were now further developed, and a stabilization of the state apparatus, administration, court ceremonies, and jurisdiction took place. Translations provided access to the works of Greek and Indian science, medicine, mathematics, and philosophy. Stimulated by the cultural values of the various peoples belonging to the Islamic world—Spaniards, North Africans, Egyp-

tians, Syrians, Byzantines, Greeks, and Persians—there developed a flourishing civilization, the uniting bond of which was Islam and its language, Arabic. The cities became not only wealthy centers of culture, science, and art but also of trade, commodity production, and especially banking and finance. The ruling form of society was Oriental feudalism, the characteristic feature of which is that the State through its representative, the Khalif, acts as the supreme landowner. The broad upper and middle strata of the towns were based on trade and commerce, and did not emerge as a class with definite political aims, even though they were sometimes very active in the political sense. Islamic legislation makes no distinction between the urban and rural population.

The Abbāsids ruled until 1258, but after one hundred years of their rule local dynasties began to emerge in individual parts of their territory. As early as 756 an independent Moslem empire came into being in Spain under the Omayyads. Independent dynasties subsequently appeared in Morocco, Tunisia, and Egypt. In the tenth century, when local Iranian princes held power, there was a revival of the Persian language, and, with it, occurred an Iranian cultural renaissance in which the literature of the New Persian language flourished. Till then, even authors and poets of Iranian origin had used Arabic. At about the same time, a new ethnic element—the Turks—became significant in the Khalifat. Their power was ultimately consolidated in the dynasty of the Seljūqs, who captured Bagdad in 1055. Apart from the Omayyads in Spain and the Fātimids in Egypt, the local courts recognized the sovereignty of the Khalifs, and at first their existence did not adversely affect cultural developments in the Khalifat. Rather, patronage for the arts increased.

The wave of Mongolian conquests that swept over Bagdad in 1258 put an end to the Khalifat of the Abbāsids. In the following centuries, various centers of power emerged in the Islamic world. The Mamlūks in Egypt maintained the traditions of Arab-Islamic culture there and in Palestine and Syria until their realm was incorporated in 1516–17 in the Sultanate of the Ottoman Turks. By 1453, the Turks had conquered Constantinople and subsequently advanced across Southeast Europe as far as Vienna. In Iran, art and culture flourished once more under the Safavids (1502–1722). In 1526, Bābur, a descendant of Tīmūr the Lame, established the Mogul Empire in India. Southern Russia and present-day Soviet Central Asia was ruled by the Khans of the Golden Horde and the Chagatay.

In the fifteenth century, the Moslems were driven from the Iberian Peninsula; their domination of Sicily had ended even before. However, merchants and traders brought Islam to Southeast Asia and Africa. With the progressive decline in the power of the Islamic world, its individual centers, from the end of the eighteenth century on, increasingly came within the spheres of influence of the European colonial powers, which took control of some of them during the nineteenth century. In the first Balkan war (1912–13), those Balkan countries which were still under Turkish domination won back their independence. It was only after the First and the Second World Wars that national states emerged in the Islamic territories, most of them designating Islam as the state religion in their constitutions. The former regions of Islam in Central Asia have been Soviet republics for some decades and have followed a different pattern of social development.

In this examination of the position of women in Islam, it should be borne in mind that Islam was the uniting bond for different ethnic elements and cultural traditions. Despite an all-embracing religion, a variety of opinions was possible and thus differing viewpoints may be found. For example, a saying attributed to Omar, the second Khalif, is frequently quoted: "Take refuge in God from the evils caused by women, and beware (even) of the most pious of them!" [53, 158]* The theologian who quotes these words in his treatise on statecraft of the eleventh century says a few pages further on that the prosperity and population of the world depend on women and "it is a fact that all the trials, misfortunes, and woes which befall men come from women." [53, 172]

The words of the Spanish-Arab mystic Ibn Arabī (1165–1240) may be quoted as evidence of a contrary view: "Whoever knows the worth of women and the mystery reposing in them will not refrain from loving them; indeed, love for them is part of the perfection of a man knowing God for it is a legacy of the Prophet and a Divine love." [137, 480] And the Spanish-Arab philosopher Averroës (Ibn Roshd, 1126–1198), influenced by Plato's doctrines, courageously criticized in sharp words the attitude of Moslems of that time toward the female sex: "In these (our) states, however, the ability of women is not known, because they are only taken for procreation there. They are therefore placed at the service of their husbands and relegated to the business of procreation, child rearing, and breast feeding. But this denies them their (other) activities. Because women in these states are considered unfit for any of the human virtues, it often happens that they resemble plants. That they are a burden to the men in these states is one of the reasons for the poverty of these states." [140, 191]

Differing attitudes toward women are also reflected in the popular literature of Islamic countries. In Princess Arūs al-

Arā'is, the "bride of brides," the epitome of irresistible beauty and seduction is paired with unfathomable, murderous evil and corruption. [185, 7 ff.] On the other hand, the merchant's wife Marhūma in the Turkish *Book of Parrots*—in other sources she appears as Marjūma—is the personification of true marital love who defies even the worst trials and tribulations. And how in *Thousand and One Nights*, the Vizier's beautiful daughter Shehrāzād, with her fascinating narrative talent, astutely and patiently conquers her royal spouse's misogyny, born of adverse experience, is well known to everybody.

These various attitudes were determined by local, ethnic, religious, and social factors. Thus Arab women originally had a freer position than in Sassanid Persia, for instance, and the Turks never restricted the freedom of their women to the extent practiced by other peoples of the Near East. Admittedly, it is possible to give only an indication of these differences, partly on account of the limitations of space but also because of the lack of research to date. Too, a word must be said about the validity of our sources, which mainly reflect the urban society that characterized Islamic culture. There is relatively little information about the situation of the Bedouins and the peasants. Within urban society, it is above all the Court circles, the upper strata and their slaves, which are mentioned in the sources. The Moslem aristocracy considered all the other strata of the population without distinction as *āmma*, a "great mass" or even "mob," and looked down on them with contempt.

Around 800, a Vizier of the illustrious Iranian family of the Barmecids divided the Islamic society of that time into four "classes": "(1) rulers, who owe their leading position to merit; (2) Viziers, who are characterized by sagacity and intelligence; (3) persons of high rank, who owe their position to wealth; and (4) the middle class, who are associated with the first three by education. The remainder are dirty scum, a muddy brook, and low animals. Each of them thinks only of eating and sleeping." [115, 144]

Political rank, wealth, and finally education were thus the factors that determined one's status. Not even the numerous merchants and craftsmen are included, apart from those who were extremely rich.

The best documented sources regarding women deal with the wives of the Prophet, that is, with their relationship with Mohammed, since he was held to be the "fine example" for every good Moslem in all subsequent periods. In what the Arabs call *adab* literature, there are charming anecdotes about high-born ladies, poetesses, singers, and educated female slaves of the Court circles. Many of these tales, which are partly amusing and partly didactic in character, may be inventions of a later period, but they illustrate how the au-

* Numbers in brackets [ ] designate sources. The first numeral is the number in the Bibliography; the second indicates the page. Roman numerals refer to the volume.

thors imagined an above-average woman to be—always from a male viewpoint, of course. In any event, these little tales would not have had an effect if they had not reflected reality at least to some extent. Since they often provide us with a glimpse of "intimate life" of that time, as if through a gap in a curtain, one or another of the tales will be referred to occasionally in the pages that follow.

We do not have specific data about most of the individual women with whom we are concerned here, since a woman had to keep within the protected zone of the harem. The date of birth is known only in very few cases, as there were neither registry offices nor birth registers in the Islamic countries until a few decades ago. Variations as to the year of death are also frequent. The sources are mostly full of praise concerning the physical, intellectual, and ethical qualities of princesses and ladies of society in particular, with the criteria for beauty, wisdom, and virtuousness based, of course, on the time and setting in question.

Women from the common people are to be found in popular tales, such as the famous collection of *Thousand and One Nights (Arabian Nights)*. When we read that the mother of Alā ad-Dīn (Aladdin), famous for his magic lamp, says: "I toil away, day and night, spinning cotton to earn a few loaves of bread" [164, II, 656], we can conclude that this was probably the fate of many of the women of the urban proletariat. Only the imagination of the narrator allows such women to escape from their daily toil with the aid of magical devices.

Social utopias were also found in fairy tales: In the story of Prince Ahmed and the beautiful fairy Perī Bānū, there is the dream of female emancipation, which, even centuries later, has by no means been realized everywhere. In the fairy world of Perī Bānū, girls are at complete liberty to choose a partner for themselves and do not have to accept the man selected by their parents. This is why marriages there are happy, unlike those in the human world. Girls in the fairy-tale world can reveal their feelings to the man they love without having to wait until he courts them. Incidentally, in the cosmographic literature of the Arabs, there are islands which are inhabited and ruled exclusively by women.

From sociological works of recent decades, such as those about the Bedouin and fellah women of certain districts, conclusions may be drawn as to the conditions of life in the past, since it may be assumed that in the course of the centuries relatively little has changed in such markedly conservative ways of life. Finally, information about customs and conditions of life is also contained in the reports by European travelers from the sixteenth century on, although their accuracy and credibility vary.

To an even greater extent than literature perhaps, the art of the Islamic countries was a product of Court circles, and its function was to satisfy their predilection for pomp and luxury. It is well known that Islam, like Judaism and early Christianity, is characterized by hostility toward images. The Koran forbids the worship of idols by practicing Moslems, but it is only the literature based on sayings of the Prophet, written down from the eighth century on, which expressly prohibits the depiction of man and beast. It is stated there that whoever makes such pictures will be required on the Day of Judgment to breathe life into what he has created. [82, II, 55] This means that the artist has usurped a power of creation belonging to Allah alone. Thus there were no decorative figures in mosques or in copies of the Koran. The state of perfection attained in the calligraphy and geometrical and plant ornamentation found in the sacral structures of Islam and in Koran manuscripts is probably due to the constraints imposed by this attitude toward sacral art on the one hand and the desire for ornamentation that was nevertheless present on the other. Arabic writing, which was adopted from the Persians and the Turks, is exceptionally well suited to such artistry by reason of its flowing elegance.

Apart from the earliest period of Islam, scarcely any tableaux or large statues of Islamic art have survived. However, the ban on the pictorial representation of man and beast was not taken so seriously in secular buildings. In harem rooms and baths of Omayyad palaces in the Syrian desert, mural paintings have survived, and statues have also been found in one of the palaces. In the generously proportioned figures of women and in the depiction of rulers, riders, hunters, and musicians, there is evidence of the influence of Late Antiquity. In contrast, the Sassanid tradition predominates in the murals of the Khalif's palace at Samarra. (Text fig. p. 21) Traces of mural paintings have also been found in other regions of the Islamic world.

From about the eleventh century on, paintings in books started to appear. To begin with, scientific texts and especially translations of Greek and Syrian works into Arabic were illustrated; they were followed in the thirteenth century by illustrations of belletristic literature. Considerable realism is achieved by the miniatures from the Bagdad of the second half of the thirteenth century which appear in manuscripts of the *Maqāmāt*, "assemblies," of Harīrī, the polished narratives of the adventures of an educated vagabond. (Fig. 1)

From the middle of the thirteenth century, the Mongols contributed elements of Far Eastern origin, which survived in the miniature paintings of Iran. Subjects for the bookmaker's art in Iran were initially the *Shāh-nāmeh*, the Iranian "national epic," and later the romantic epics of the poet Nizāmī, his imitators, and Jāmī, who will be discussed later.

There were also other poetic works, mostly of a mystical character. From time to time, historical texts were decorated with miniature paintings, and from the fifteenth century on, this was also the case with legendary stories of the Prophet. (Fig. 7)

Painting schools emerged at the various courts and certain motifs were repeatedly depicted. The painter was regarded far less highly in the Islamic world of the Middle Ages than the calligrapher or the gilder. This is also the reason that few miniaturists are known to us by name. It only became customary in the sixteenth century for pictures to be signed. It was the calligrapher who determined the position and layout of a miniature painting by leaving a free page or by his arrangement of the text on the page.

Iranian miniatures of the Middle Ages are charmingly characterized by brilliant colors, by the entire lack of perspective in their naïve-sensual presentation, by dreamy, romantic landscapes, and often by boyishly delicate human figures. But precisely because certain subjects were taken up time and again and much was copied, they have only a limited value as documentary evidence.

From the twelfth century on, figures are suddenly found on metal and ceramic products. Since Islam prohibits the use of vessels of pure gold or silver—a proscription that was subsequently disregarded, however—silver was inlaid in a highly artistic manner on vessels of copper or brass (Fig. 54), while ceramic products were coated with lustrous gold. These decorations were greatly influenced by the miniature paintings of the same period as was the woven depiction of figures in fabrics and later in carpets. From the mid sixteenth century, portraits and pictures of individuals appeared in Iranian painting, possibly because the Courts no longer patronized artists on the same scale as before, and these were now dependent on less wealthy clients, who could collect only single sheets and not entire manuscripts as in the past.

Turkish miniature painting (Fig. 35) was more realistic than many of the Iranian paintings and, in addition, often contained elements of humor. In Mogul paintings, Persian and Indian influences are apparent in the evident attempt to apply perspective and three-dimensional representation. A notable realism can also be observed in most cases, everyday scenes being depicted and not just life at Court and in the towns.

From the beginning of the nineteenth century, European influence became increasingly apparent in the art of the Islamic countries. It is at this time that large statues and oil paintings appear.

Following this brief review, we can now turn to the position of women in a sphere that has been aptly described by a German orientalist as "the most decisive expresssion of Islamic thinking" and "the essential nucleus of Islam in general" [146, 1], this being Islamic law. On Islamic territory, it applied—and, in some respects, still applies—only to Moslems, and members of other religions were subject to their own jurisdiction. It was, however, free for Jews and Christians to consult a Moslem *qādī* if they wished to do so.

Woman in Islamic Law, in the Koran, and in Tradition

Islamic law, as described in broad outline here and as it concerns women, is still in force at the present time, although in most countries in a modified form that takes account of modern social conditions. Turkey, which was massively secularized under Kemal Atatürk, introduced Swiss civil law in 1926—but not without encountering some difficulties in the course of time.

In the Koran, it is stated in a context dealing with divorce: "... they (women) have the same right as is exercised over them, though the men have a rank above them." (2:228) In every religion, each age has its own interpretation of the Holy Scriptures; this is true in Islam, too. Thus liberal Moslems now take the view that the superiority of man over woman refers here only to his greater physical strength and to the responsibility he has toward women. A non-Moslem is inclined to interpret the quoted statement in a way that takes account of the time at which the Koran was written and of circumstances in Mohammed's life; even the first Islamic historians relate the revelations to circumstances in the life of the Prophet.

We would therefore say that the Koran retains the view prevalent in Antiquity and in the Ancient Orient of the essential superiority of men in relation to women. This is even clearer in another verse from the Koran: "The men are overseers over the women by reason of what Allah hath bestowed in bounty upon one more than another, and of the property which they have contributed; upright women are therefore submissive, guarding what is hidden in return for Allah's guarding (them); those on whose part ye fear refractoriness, admonish, avoid in bed, and beat; if they then obey you, seek no (further) way against them." (4:34/38) The economic superiority of man is thus clearly the basis for the superior status men enjoyed not only in the Arabian Peninsula of the seventh century but in many countries of the world down to the present day.

Without wishing to adopt the self-justifying attitude of many Moslems, it is recalled that August Bebel, only a hun-

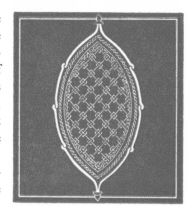

dred years ago, was able to write: "In common German law, women are still minors everywhere in relation to men; the man is the master whom she has to obey in marriage. Should she be disobedient, Prussian law gives the man of 'low estate' the right to punish his wife with moderate physical chastisement ... Since the force and number of the blows is prescribed nowhere, it is the man who sovereignly decides this." [20, 209]

The Koran is not the only source of Moslem law. Soon after the death of Mohammed, it was noticed that the prescriptions in the Koran did not suffice for the shaping of a life pleasing to God. And so a start was made with the collection of narratives (*hadîth*, in Arabic) of what Mohammed said, did, or even only silently approved in certain situations. The aim was to shape one's own life according to *Sunna* or "custom"; that is, the "fine example" of the Prophet. This included even such details as Mohammed's having said that it was better to eat and drink with the right hand than with the left since the left was used by the Devil. From the eighth century on, these *hadiths*—designated "traditions" by orientalists—were recorded in great compendiums. Six of these compendiums, especially those of Bokhāri (d. 870) and of Moslem (d. 875) became canonical.

However, if the *hadiths* are examined closely—for instance, those which reflect the attitude toward women—it soon becomes apparent that they contain a very wide range of views, some of which are even contradictory. In one place, Mohammed is reported to have said: "I have left no temptation behind which would be more harmful to my community than that which women represent for men." [82, V, 200] In another, the following saying is attributed to him as well: "The entire world is a joyous place but the most joyous thing in it is a virtuous woman." [82, II, 168]

In the traditions, there are anecdotes referring to towns that had not even been captured or founded during Mohammed's lifetime and to factions that emerged only after his death. It may therefore be assumed that this literature does indeed include the *Sunna* of the Prophet, but reflects to a greater extent the different trends and opinions in the Moslem community in the first two centuries after Mohammed. The representatives of differing views and factions wanted to stabilize a social structure consisting of the most diverse elements. They hoped to arrive at a standard of general validity by attributing to the Prophet Mohammed modes of behavior and values which they considered religiously and ethically appropriate. As proof of the authenticity of such traditions, the isnād, "chain of authorities," was provided; they were the names of those who claimed to have heard this tradition from another. Consequently, the ultimate authority had always to be one of the companions of Mohammed or one of the members of his family.

Since the Moslems realized at a fairly early stage that not everything said in the traditions to have originated with Mohammed could, in actual fact, have been said by him personally, the successive narrators were the subject of criticism. Just as the collection of traditions became an independent branch of knowledge with its representatives traveling through the Islamic countries to hear traditions from authorities in the various regions, another branch of knowledge developed concerned with the collection and investigation of the biographies of those handing down these traditions. This was called "the Science of the Men" in Arabic, although a fairly large number of the traditions are attributed to women, for example, to Ā'isha, Mohammed's favorite wife. The last volume of the collection of traditions of Ahmed Ibn Hanbal, for example—numbering six volumes in all—contains only traditions attributed to a female authority.

The Koran and the Sunna are thus the two principal sources of Islamic law, at least for the Sunnites. The Shi'ites accept only those traditions which go back to Mohammed's cousin and son-in-law Ali and his descendants. Nevertheless, Shi'ite law in most cases differs but little from Sunnite law, since the content of the traditions considered correct by both groups is often identical and only the sources are different.

It soon became apparent, however, that passages in both the Koran and in the literature of the traditions permitted different interpretations. Another authority was needed, and this was found in the ijmā', as it is known, this being the "universal agreement, the concurrent opinion of all Moslem scholars alive at the same time in a certain period" [92, 46] concerning a certain problem. This consensus was not established by any sort of commission, such as a council or a synod, but had to emerge by itself. In the course of Islamic history, institutions and even doctrinal opinions have been sanctioned by ijmā' which did not exist in early Islam, for example, the Khalifat, which of course appeared only after Mohammed's death, the veneration of saints, and the doctrine of the infallibility and freedom from sin of the Prophet, which conflicts with the message of the Koran. The validity of the ijmā' is justified by the well-known tradition: "My community shall never agree upon an error."

Finally, the fourth source of Islamic law is the establishment of analogies (qiyās, in Arabic); in actual fact a method of arriving at a verdict in law. In those cases which are to be found neither in the Koran nor in the Sunna nor in the ijmā', an independent decision was made on the analogy of examples contained in the sources. However, there were differences of opinion as to the extent to which analogies could be used. In the course of time, four different schools of law developed in Sunnite Islam, and these acknowledged each other as alternatives: the Hanafī, Māliki, Shāfi'ī, and Hanbali. They are to be found in various regions of the Islamic world, but they do not vary very much in their dogmas.

Since Islamic law deals with the entire life of Moslems from a religious perspective, it includes moral judgments as well. There are "Recommended," "Indifferent," and "Reprehensible" categories as well as "Mandatory" and "Forbidden." This provides ample scope for differences of opinion. However, there is agreement that the application of the category in question is dependent on the circumstances that led to it. These categories do not apply in penal law.

In addition to provisions concerning family law and penal law, Islamic law (shari'a) also contains prescriptions concerning the religious duties of Moslems. The role of women in Moslem observance is examined here.

A number of verses in the Koran are addressed both to men and women. Sura 33:35 reads as follows:

The self-surrendering men and the self-surrendering women, the believing men and the believing women, the obedient men and the obedient women, the truthful men and the truthful women, the enduring men and the enduring women, the submissive men and the submissive women, the almsgiving men and the almsgiving women, the fasting men and the fasting women, the continent men and the continent women, the Allah-remembering men and the Allah-remembering women—for them Allah has prepared forgiveness and a mighty reward.

Contrary to the belief that was widespread in Christendom for centuries, the Koran does not assert that women have no soul. They have the same claim to a place in Paradise as men (see 40:8). However, the woman-hating elements among the pious of the first few centuries, whose numbers evidently increased after contact with Christian asceticism in particular, circulated a tradition that was frequently quoted in later years. Mohammed is reported to have said: "I stood at the gates of Paradise, most of those who entered there were poor, and I stood at the gates of Hell, most of those who went in there were women." [82, V, 209f.] This is also explained: "Who tell secrets when they confide in someone, are too obstinate when they request something and are ungrateful when they receive it." [82, V, 137]

Still, the Koran does not regard Eve as the seductress of Adam; that is, as responsible for the expulsion of Man from Paradise and for his toilsome existence on Earth, as she is presented in the Old Testament, but considers that Satan led both of them astray. (2:34; 7:19ff.)

The religious duties imposed by Islam on the faithful apply to women just as much as to men, apart from the few restrictions concerning special physiological features of women. Like the sick, menstruating women are required to make up for corresponding days of fast later and are likewise freed from certain rituals of pilgrimage and from prayer. This is linked with concepts concerning the religious uncleanliness of a menstruating woman, a view widely held by many peoples in earlier times. From these few restrictions, the woman haters among the Moslems developed a body of arguments that they claimed established the inferiority of women in the religious sphere. In the same way, they asserted that women were intellectually inferior, pointing out that their testimony was considered to have half the value of a man's. [24, 6, 6] A woman should make a pilgrimage only if accompanied by her husband or a male relative. Opinions are divided as to whether and how long an unaccompanied woman should travel; they vary between not at all and two to three days.

Apart from the obligatory prayers at the mosque on Friday, the Islamic day of rest, Moslems can say their prayers just as well at home as in the mosque. A large number of traditions indicates that in the first centuries of Islam, women took full advantage of their right to pray in the mosque. There are, however, traditions calling on them not to decorate and perfume themselves for their prayers in the mosque. A recommendation that was regularly observed by women entering the mosque for prayer was that they should pray separately from men and place themselves in a row behind them. This is similar to the practice in Orthodox Jewish places of worship where, down to the present day, women have their own gallery; likewise, in some village churches of Germany symbols on the pews indicate that men and women used to sit separately. The purpose of these arrangements was certainly to prevent men and women from being distracted by each other in an unseemly manner in a House of God.

But even at a relatively early period, efforts must have been made to prevent women from attending prayers in a mosque since traditions warn the Moslems against their doing so. With the social degradation of women that accompanied the economic and political decline of the Islamic countries, they were increasingly deprived of the right to pray in a mosque.

A woman of any self-respect was expected not even to leave the house once she was married, unless she was obliged to. An example of this is to be found in the trilogy of the well-known Egyptian novelist Nagīb Mahfūz (b. 1911), which is set in Cairo in the first half of the twentieth century. Amīna, the wife of a middle-class merchant, has never left the house since her marriage except in a closed carriage to visit her mother. Encouraged by her sons, the representatives of a new generation, she satisfies her greatest wish during the First World War while her husband is away and visits the Hosayn Mosque, situated not far from her house. When her husband learns of this, he repudiates her, the mother of his five children, the wife who had shown him obedient affection for many years and who had never failed to meet his every wish. Even in the 1960's, it was reported by a sociologist that in small towns in Morocco women did not enter the mosques, most of them because they were not familiar with the prayer ritual. Those familiar with it were afraid that people might say they went into the mosque only to meet their lovers. They dared to visit a mosque only in the large towns where nobody knew them. [106]

However, in a few Islamic countries, women were allowed to participate in prayers in a mosque for important religious celebrations. The Turkish authoress Halidé Edib tells in her memoirs of how, as a child in the 1880's, she accompanied her nurse to a mosque in Istanbul for ceremonial prayer at the end of the month of fasting. She also relates how a sensitive Moslem sees Islamic prayer, the outward ritual of which appears so strange to a non-Moslem:

> *The Imam stood in front of the mihrab, his back to the people, and opened the prayer. It is wonderful to pray led by an Imam. He chants aloud the verses you usually repeat in lonely prayer. You bow, you kneel, your forehead touches the floor. Each movement is a vast and complicated rhythm, the rising and falling controlled by the invisible voices of the several muezzins. There is a beautiful minor chant. The refrain is taken up again and again by the muezzins. There is a continual rhythmic thud and rustle as the thousands fall and rise. The rest belongs to the eternal silence.* [39, 72]

Only in large harems, however, have women performed the office of the *imām*, the prayer leader; that is, before an exclusively female congregation.

It should be noted here, however, that women played a notable role in the religious life of the Islamic countries, especially in mysticism. But this is a subject that will be examined later.

Now to family law. It is taken for granted that a distinction must be drawn between Islamic law as such and the

10

A man and a woman accuse each other before the qādī. A scribe records their complaints.

11

The rogue Abū Zayd from the Maqāmāt of Harīrī has disguised himself as a woman, and is trying to sell his son as a slave. The buyer is gesticulating, and the black slaves sitting on a bench are obviously involved in the bargaining. On the upper floor of the roofed building, the weighing of money seems to be in progress.

12
Carved wooden ornaments with geometrical
designs and inscriptions decorate this
prayer niche in a mosque in honor of Sayyida Roqayya, revered as a saint, from
the Egypt of the Fātimid period.
Two lines of Kūfic lettering at the upper
edge state that it was made at the order of
the wife of the Fātimid Khalif al-Āmir.

13
The decorative lettering on the sacred buildings of Islam is not only an ornamental
element but also conveys messages to the
faithful. Here a verse from the Koran
states that Allah has promised gardens in
Paradise for devout men and women.

14
Not figures but geometrical ornamentation and inscriptions on colored tiles or
bricks were and still are used as decoration for sacred buildings. This is a
detail from the mosque attributed to
Bībī Khānum, a sister of Tīmūr Leng,
in Samarkand; it is believed to have
been destroyed by an earthquake in the
fifteenth century.

15

This is how a Persian miniaturist of the sixteenth century imagined Mohammed's first meeting with Khadīja, who was to become his wife. As a sign of the saintliness which was later attributed to him, the Prophet is surrounded by a nimbus of flames. He is also wearing a veil, which completely hides his face.

16

According to the Koran—this is a miniature from a later collection of legends about the prophets—Jesus was not born in a stable. Mary was overcome by labor pains under a palm tree, which provided her with fresh dates to eat and under which there flowed a streamlet with cool, clear water. (19: 23 ff.) The Holy Child is also surrounded by a nimbus of flames since Islam regards Jesus as a prophet, too. He is wrapped in the manner that was probably customary for infants at that time in Iran.

17

The shari'a allowed a man to take up to four wives at the same time, provided he treats them justly and as many concubines as he wished from among his slaves. Thus rulers and other powerful personages could establish large harems in which close watch was kept over the women.

18

With the artful faces of children, Adam and Eve leave the garden of Paradise. Two guards and a virgin of Paradise watch them go; others observe them from a building. In the foreground, a peacock and a snake symbolize human vanity. In the Koran, it is not Eve who seduces Adam; rather, Satan, at the front of the picture, leads both of them astray.

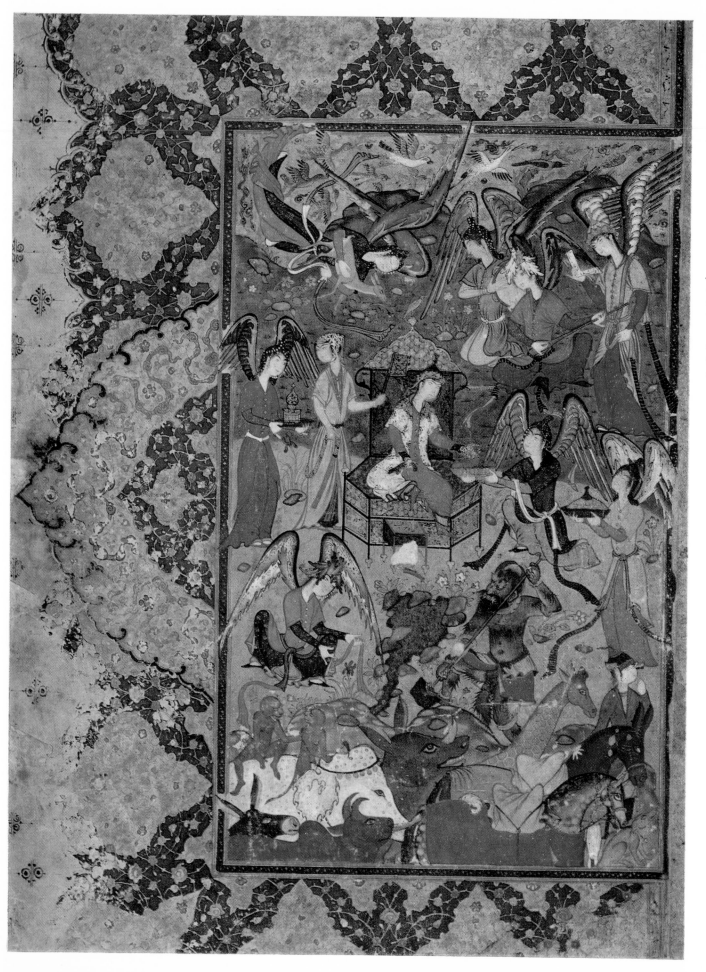

19
The Queen of Saba is mentioned in the Koran without any of the negative comments subsequently made about women rulers. In this miniature, she is painted as an Iranian princess of the sixteenth century with the tāj-kulāh, the "crown hat," on her head, and she is surrounded by winged genies bearing refreshments or playing music. In the foreground, from the realm of fantasy, are Satan and a herd of steeds, which, according to the Koran, were created by Allah from divine spirits and which obey the orders of Salomo, the Queen's lover.

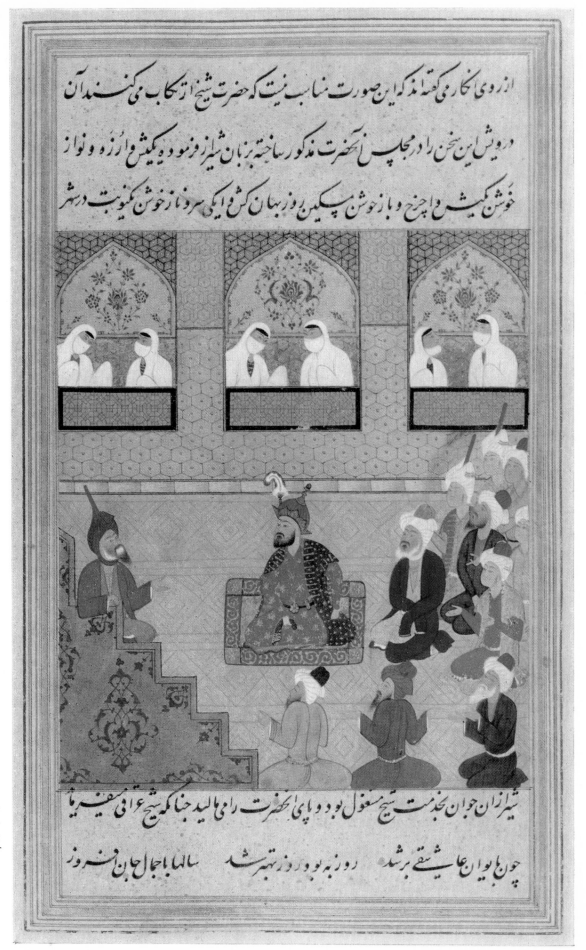

20

Among the Sūfis, the Islamic mystics, women were more highly esteemed than in Orthodox Islam. A Persian miniature from the mid sixteenth century shows women taking part in a service in a mosque from a position in a gallery of their own, as prescribed by the Sunna.

21

A scene from a popular novel. Men stoning an adulterous pair. On the right, a second scene: the Abyssinian who seduced the woman is sitting in a crate.

law that is applied in actual fact in the Islamic countries. "Tell me, what thing we ever did, which was permitted by law?" to quote the protest of a prince of Mosul in the eleventh century when he was reproached with being married to two sisters at the same time. [14, 17f.] Expressed in particularly crass terms though this may be, a great deal of literature on legal loopholes exists, showing that ways and means were always being sought to lessen or circumvent the application of the sometimes strict prescriptions. It was certainly not just pettifoggers who indulged in this but also celebrated jurists, who were famous for their skill in interpreting rules in a pragmatic manner.

One of the punishments laid down in the Koran, flagellation for drinking wine or other alcoholic beverages, was certainly seldom, if ever, applied. At any rate, lyrics praising wine have existed in Arabic since the second Islamic century. Persian poets such as Omar Khayyām and Hāfiz lauded wine drinking as a form of opposition to Orthodox Islam.

In any case, it was probably always true that people felt themselves bound most of all by the provisions in Islamic law concerning the family. As already noted, the Koran explicitly stresses the superiority of men over women, and in actual fact women are legally at a disadvantage in many respects. Down to the present time, for example, the evidence of two women is considered equivalent to that of one man in countries with Islamic law. Nevertheless, Islamic law led to an improvement in the position of women when compared with the pre-Islamic period, especially as regards the laws of succession and marriage. In the pre-Islamic period there was no question of a woman's being an heir, since property had to stay in the tribe. Under Islamic law, she inherits half of what male members of the family receive.

Marriage is recommended to the faithful in Islam both in the Koran (24:32) and in the *Sunna*, but it is not a sacrament as in the Catholic Church. Nevertheless, according to the Koran, it still has a certain sacral character since it speaks of a "firm compact" (4:25/21) between husband and wife. The same expression is used in the Holy Scriptures of the Moslems for the alliance of Allah with Mohammed and with the prophets of the other scripture religions. In Islam, marriage is based on a civil law contract, which, according to the prescription in the Koran, as in Roman law, did not yet have to be in written form in the first centuries. The parties to the contract are the bridegroom and the bride's guardian *(wālī)*, her closest male relative, usually her father or her brother or, if need be, even the judge himself. Two free male witnesses or one male and two female witnesses must be present. The *Sunna* recommends that the bride should not be married without her consent. However, silence is sufficient indication of agreement in the case of a virginal bride, since she is consid-

ered to be too shy or timid to say so for herself. When the girl is a minor, her guardian can also force her into marriage, but she has the right to annul this as soon as she is of age. The Mālikī, Shāfi'ī, and Hanbali even permit an adult woman to be forced by her guardian to contract marriage. On the other hand, the Hanafī allow an adult woman to arrange her own marriage on condition that she chooses a man of her own rank and fixes an adequate dowry.

According to a large number of traditions, Mohammed recommended that anyone wishing to marry a girl or woman should see her first. However, the content of some of these traditions indicates that at the time they appeared or were handed down this was certainly not or no longer customary and resistance was encountered. In one tradition, for example, the narrator reproaches a man who attempts to look at the girl with the words: "You, a companion of the Prophet, will do this?!" The other replies that Mohammed had advised this. [82, IV, 225] All the traditions end with the appearance of the girl being pleasing to the narrator and with his marrying her. In this manner, the narrator certainly wished to reinforce his argument.

An important part of the marriage contract is the fixing of the dowry (*mahr* or *sadāq*, in Arabic). To begin with, the *mahr* was not a purchase price, as was often said, but a kind of compensation the bridegroom had to give to the parents of the bride for the loss to the tribe of the sons the woman would bear. The evidence for this is that the *mahr* was not paid—and this is still so among Bedouins today—when the girl married her cousin on her father's side; that is, remained in the tribe. The *sadāq* was the wedding gift the girl received. As early as the time of Mohammed, there was no longer any distinction between these two terms. The *mahr* or the *sadāq* was given to the bride, and symbolized the status that she had. In Europe, it was customary for centuries for parents to give a daughter a dowry when she got married. This frequently led to the bride's being considered an unavoidable adjunct to property one could acquire only by marriage. When in the Islamic Orient even today the man is required to give the woman a dowry on marriage, the European form of "marriage for money" is excluded at all events. The Islamic custom, on the other hand, gives the parents of the bride the opportunity to refuse their daughter to an unwelcome suitor by making excessively high demands.

The *mahr* was, and mostly still is, used for the purchase of furnishings for the household and clothing for the wife. In earlier times it even consisted of such articles. The various schools of law quote different minimum and maximum figures for the dowry. However, marriage deeds that have survived indicate that the top limit could be greatly exceeded. The origin and rank of the bride, her age or rather her youth, her beauty, in short whether or not she was a desirable match, determined the size of the dowry.

In the early Islamic community, it was obviously considered right that an impoverished suitor should have the possibility of marriage by fixing a dowry appropriate to his circumstances. Thus one tradition tells of a man who wanted to marry but possessed nothing he could give to the woman as dowry. Mohammed decided that he should have her for the sections of the Koran he knew by heart. [24, 67, 14] Incidentally, this woman had offered herself in marriage to the Prophet himself, and it is said that she was not the only one who did this. This is evidence of the magnetism Mohammed must have had for those around him. It is also evidence of a self-confidence on the part of women in Ancient Arabia that is totally lacking not only among Islamic women of later centuries but also in young Central European girls even today. They are taught that it is seemly for a woman to behave in a passive and shy manner toward men. There are reports of other women who were married to Mohammed but who said, when he came to them in the bridal chamber: "I take refuge from you in God." At this, so it is said, he had them sent back to their families without delay. [87, VIII, 100ff.] This, too, shows that at the time of Mohammed Arab women were assertive enough to make no secret of their wishes or disinclination.

It was often agreed in the marriage contract that a part of the dowry was to be paid only in the event of divorce so as to protect the wife from hasty action by her husband. Payment in installments was also possible if a fairly large initial payment was made at the time of the wedding.

Islam allows a man to be married to more than one wife at the same time. Opinions differ as to whether polygyny was prevalent on the Arabian Peninsula before the time of Mohammed. Recent European research [158, 62, 81; 176, 274ff.] indicates that there is no unequivocal evidence of this, at least as far as Mecca and Medina are concerned. Admittedly, early Islamic historians tell of a man having several wives, but they also list the various husbands of many women. These early historians assume that for the women it was a question of marriages contracted one after the other, as was true in later periods. However, this could equally well have been the case for men. It is a fact that in other countries of the Middle East, such as Iran, there were polygynous marriages in the pre-Islamic period. It is just as certain that in pre-Islamic Arabia very loose sexual mores were the rule. It was actually through Islam that the institution of marriage contracts was first introduced to the Arabian Peninsula.

The verse in the Koran, from which for centuries the right of man to a polygynous marriage has been derived, reads as follows: "If ye fear that ye may not act with equity in regard to the orphans, marry such of the women as seem good to you, double or treble or fourfold—but if ye fear that ye may not be fair, then one (only) or what your right hands possess; that is more likely to secure that ye be not partial . . ." (4:3) Modern Moslems often interpret this verse as essentially an exhortation in favor of monogamy since at another place in the Koran it is said that a man who is married to several wives at the same time cannot be equally just to all of them. (4: 128/129) However, the first part of the verse permits the conclusion that here Mohammed was concerned with the maintenance of widows and, in particular, the daughters of men killed in battle during the early years of Islam. Mohammed, who was himself an orphan, often regarded himself as the advocate of the weak and underprivileged. Consequently, at a time when marriage represented the only possibility of providing for a woman, the Koran recommends marriage to widows and female orphans. This assumption is supported by the fact that the verse quoted probably dates from the time immediately after the battle of the Moslems against the Meccans at Okhod in which many Moslems lost their lives. Mohammed himself set an example for his community and married two widows of slain Moslems. Indeed, in most of his marriages, if not in all of them, he is said to have also had the solidarity of his community in mind.

At the same time, Islamic law requires a man to provide each of his wives with a household of her own. Thus polygyny was usually the privilege of the prosperous who, in addition to their wives, could also select any number of concubines from among their slaves.

As impediments to marriage, Islamic law lists similar situations and conditions that preclude marriage in many other societies, for example, too close a blood relationship or relationship by marriage (4: 26ff.) or "by suckling." Furthermore, the law prescribes that a man may not be married to two sisters at the same time. A Moslem woman may not marry a non-Moslem, but a Moslem man is permitted to marry a Jewish or a Christian woman. The man should not be of a lower rank than the woman, but the converse—except for the Shi'ites—is permissible.

After the death of her husband, a free woman must observe a period of mourning of four months and ten days. After a divorce, she must wait three months before remarrying. Men, however, are permitted to remarry immediately. The waiting period for the woman was introduced by Mohammed so that it could be determined whether the woman was expecting a child so that the paternity could be established without doubt. When the woman was pregnant, she could marry again only after the birth of the child.

As in the pre-Islamic period, extreme youth was no bar to marriage, at least not in the Islam of the Middle Ages. Mohammed himself married his favorite wife Ā'isha, the daughter of one of his closest associates, the subsequent first Khalif Abū Bakr, when she was six years old. When she came to him, she was nine and, according to the tradition, still played with dolls. It was later laid down that a mentally healthy Moslem became marriageable with puberty, but there is a difference of opinions as regards age.

The duties of the man in marriage include providing his wife or wives with shelter, food, and clothing. If she is accustomed to being waited on, he must provide her with a female servant. At least according to the law, the wife cannot be required to contribute to the upkeep of the household by doing work or by a financial contribution. However, among the poor, she would certainly have been obliged to do so. In Islamic marriage, there is no joint ownership of property. The wife can therefore freely dispose of her own property and in this respect is in a substantially more favorable position than European women have enjoyed for centuries. According to the early tradition, the duties of the wife include feeling responsible for the household of her husband and those belonging to it.

Traditions of later periods, it is true, give the husband the highest authority not only over the wife's possessions, but also over her sexual behavior toward him, over her decision to fulfill her religious duties or even over simply leaving the house. [see 120, IV, 411 f.] They thus contradict the *shari'a* but doubtless reflect the customs of later centuries.

The Koran has this to say about the relations between husband and wife in marriage: "Amongst His signs is that He hath created for you of your own species spouses that ye may dwell with them, and hath set love and mercy between you." (30:20) One of the few marriage deeds that has survived, dating from Egypt of the thirteenth century, contains the recommendation that the husband should "make his relations with her (his wife) pleasant" and that she is under the same obligation toward him. [35, 170] Traditions urge the man to treat his wife well, as in the following, which refers to the concept prevalent in the Ancient Orient that woman was created from one of the ribs of man: "Treat the women well for woman was created from a rib and the most curved part of the rib is the top part. Should you try to bend it straight, you will destroy it but if you leave it as it is, it remains curved. So treat the women well!" [24, 60, 1] A modern woman would surely object to this attitude of lofty male superiority, but it should be recalled, for instance, that there were still arguments in central Germany in the seventeenth century as to whether women were human beings at all. [74]

The ideal concept of a good Moslem wife is to be found in a tradition that relates how Mohammed answered the question of how the best wife should behave: "Who pleases him when he looks at her, obeys him when he commands, and does not oppose him in things which he rejects for her and for himself." [82, II, 25] She should thus be pretty and submissive, although later chapters will show that intelligent women especially were often prepared to accept anything but this ideal of submission to the will of a man.

The Arabic expression that is often translated by the word "adultery" really means something more than that, namely, any sexual relations between a woman and a man who are not bound to each other by a legal marriage and, as long as slavery existed, intimate relations between a man and a slave who did not belong to him. All this in Islam is punishable for man and woman alike.

In *Sura* 24:2, it is stated: "The fornicatress and the fornicator—scourge each of them with a hundred stripes; let no pity affect you in regard to them in the religion of Allah, if ye have come to believe in Allah and the Last Day." A number of the faithful should be present as witnesses of this punishment. At a relatively early stage, it became the custom, deriving from Jewish penal law, to stone the adulterous pair and not to flog them. The application of such a harsh punishment was greatly restricted, however, by the requirement specified at another place in the Koran (4:19) that four witnesses must be able to testify to the adultery. Since they were required to have witnessed the act itself, it must have been difficult in most cases to find the necessary witnesses. A man who accuses a woman of infidelity and cannot provide four witnesses of this is to receive eighty strokes of the lash for slander. To avoid this punishment, however, he can repeat his allegation four times, calling on Allah to witness the truth of it. His wife can defend herself by likewise swearing four times that her husband has lied. After this fourfold oath, the two of them must call on Allah to curse them should they not have told the truth. (24:6–9)

It was an episode that took place in Mohammed's own family that led to this severe punishment for libel. Mohammed usually drew lots before he set out on a military expedition to determine which of his wives should accompany him. Thus it happened on one of his campaigns against a Bedouin tribe that he took along his wife Ā'isha, who was thirteen years old at the time and accompanied the train in a closed litter on the back of a camel. One evening, while the people were preparing to set off again, Ā'isha went away from the others to answer a call of nature. On the way back, she said later, she noticed that she had lost her necklace and retraced her steps once more. When she at last got back to the camp, she found that Mohammed and his band had already departed. At that time, Ā'isha was a slight little person—she herself said it was a result of the frugal diet of the Moslems—and the

*Calligraphic illuminated page
with the* basmala.

men who placed her litter on the camel did not even realize that she was not in it. Ā'isha wrapped herself in her robe and lay down in the desert sand, hoping that the others would return when they noticed that she was missing. A young man then appeared, one of the followers of Mohammed, who for some reason had also been left behind by the others. Ā'isha did not yet wear a veil; so he recognized her immediately and tried to talk to her. But, she subsequently related, she gave him no answer. He placed her on his camel and led the animal. When they ultimately caught up with the others on the following morning, her absence had not yet been noticed. But now the storm broke. All those to whom the young woman was a thorn in the flesh because she was so greatly favored by Mohammed and also those who bore ill will toward him contributed to the gossip about her. As Ā'isha later said, she was the last to hear of all this. She only noticed that Mohammed was not so friendly to her as hitherto. She fell ill and with Mohammed's permission returned to her parents to be looked after. Mohammed, deeply wounded and confused, asked others for their advice. A variety of opinions was expressed. The harshest was that of his cousin Ali, who was perhaps goaded by his wife, Fātima, Mohammed's daughter, who may have resented the privileged position of her youthful stepmother. "There are women enough," he said, "you could make another her successor," a remark for which Ā'isha never forgave him, as future events showed. But, in the end, Mohammed decided in favor of Ā'isha. He visited her at her parents' house to urge her to show

regret, but she wept and refused since this would have been an admission of guilt. It was then revealed to Mohammed that all the rumors were "slander" and that those who had spread them were "liars," and it was this revelation which led to the provisions described above. Some of those whose words had been especially harsh received eighty strokes of the lash. The wise Ā'isha subsequently remarked that hitherto she had considered herself too slight and insignificant for Allah to have revealed on her account a verse of the Koran which was then recited in the mosque and used in prayer; she had only hoped that God would reveal her innocence to Mohammed by a dream. [84, 736 ff.]

A large group of the Shi'a also recognized another form of marriage, which was still general in the early years of Islam until it was prohibited by Khalif Omar, who was of strict morality. This was the *mut'a*, which is generally translated as "temporary marriage" or "marriage of enjoyment." A Shi'ite was allowed to contract a "marriage" for a certain period. This usually happened when a man was traveling, since it was not customary for a wife to accompany her husband. The sole purpose of such a "marriage" was to enable a man to satisfy his sexual desires in a legal manner but not to found a household or produce children. Nevertheless, when a child resulted from such a union, it enjoyed equal rights under the law of succession with children from other marriages.

All other forms of "marriage" practiced in Arabia up to the time of Mohammed, were done away with by Mohammed. These included, for instance, the custom whereby a man whose wife had remained childless would send her for a short time to another, preferably one of high social rank, so that she might conceive, or the group marriage of several men with one woman, or a form of marriage in which a son inherited his stepmother from his dead father or his sister-in-law from his deceased brother so that they would be looked after.

In Islam, the death of one of the two partners in a marriage signifies the end of that marriage. However, a marriage might also be dissolved by the *talāq*, the repudiation of the wife by the husband. Islamic law permits every man in a healthy mental state to do this without having to give any reason for it and without consulting a judge. However, there are traditions which describe the *talāq* as an act hateful to Allah.

The form of the *talāq* that emerged as customary until the law was modified in many Islamic countries in recent decades was as follows: The man pronounces the formula of repudiation—variations in the choice of words exist—twice, either in immediate succession, or with a month between. At that point, he can still revoke. Only after the third time is the divorce valid. It is laid down in the Koran that at the time of divorce the husband must provide for a wife who is suckling a child until it is weaned; this can extend to a period of two years. (2:233)

If the man desires to remarry the woman, although he has repudiated her three times, there is a provision which perhaps seems odd at first sight. However, the original idea behind it was certainly to protect the wife from a hasty step the husband might take. According to this provision a wife who has been repudiated must first marry another and be repudiated by him in turn before she can go back to her first husband. (2:230) This led many men, usually those who were not believed to possess excessive virility, to make themselves available—in return for a fee—for fictitious marriages, after which they would quickly repudiate the women who then could remarry their original husbands. In a pleasant little story, the Egyptian author Mahmūd Taymūr (1894–1973) features such a "good sheikh," to whom men entrust their repudiated wives in the belief that he is too unworldly to touch them. In the end, however, he falls in love with one of these women and does not wish to give her back.

There is only a limited number of ways in which a wife can free herself from her husband. The *khol'*, or redemption, was adopted from heathen practice and consists in the wife's purchasing her freedom from her husband by the payment of a certain sum—frequently equivalent to the dowry. However, the wife or her guardian can also have included in her marriage contract a clause specifying that she can oblige her husband, under certain conditions, to pronounce the *talāq*,

for example if he strikes her or wishes to take a second wife. Nevertheless, the extent to which a woman can take advantage of this possibility in actual fact depends to a very great degree first on her self-confidence and secondly on the social position of divorced women in general. In Moslem India, for instance, this type of marriage contract was widespread in the 1950's, but in Egypt, I was informed in the spring of 1977 by several sources, including a deputy of the Minister of Justice, only a few women had the courage to have a marriage contract prepared in this form. In certain instances, for example, when she can prove that her husband is not able to provide for her, is impotent, or is suffering from a mental disorder, an adult woman can demand that a judge dissolve the marriage.

The provisions determining whether children are regarded as legitimate, apart from those actually born during a marriage—according to Hanafite law every child born within two years of the dissolution of the marriage is legitimate—are to be explained by the medical knowledge, or rather lack of medical knowledge, of the time. The mother has the right of custody for girls until they are of age or until they marry and for boys until puberty or the age of seven years. However, the father is the legal guardian of the children, and he is obliged by law to maintain them only when they are poor. Thus the mother usually returns with the children she has to look after to her family, who maintains her.

One of the numerous anecdotes of classical Arab literature tells of how a mother fought before a judge for her son, who was claimed by the father, the child probably having attained the age of seven years.

She said: "This is my son. He was born from my body, he directs his little steps to my lap, and my breast has suckled him. I look on him when he awakes and watch over him when he lays himself down at night. I have been doing that for years, and now that he is weaned, has gained in strength, and his good qualities are welcome, his father wants to take him from me and bring him up far from me." The judge then said to the husband: "You have heard the words of your wife, what do you have to answer them with?" The man replied: "She has spoken the truth, but I carried him in me before she carried him, and I placed him in her before she put him in the world. I will teach him knowledge and the power of a wise decision." The judge turned to the woman: "What is your answer to this, woman?" She replied: "He is right in what he says. But he carried him when he weighed almost nothing whereas he weighed so much in me that he almost dragged me to the ground. When he (the husband) passed him on, he experienced pleasure, but I bore him in the awareness of all tortures." Her words were pleasing to the judge, and he ordered the man: "Give her her son for she has more right to him than you." [19, 6 ff.]

If this little story is to be believed, judges were certainly led by the well-chosen words of a clever woman to turn a blind eye to legal regulations and to show more humanity than was provided for by the law.

In Islamic law, slaves occupied a special position in a certain sense. Like Judaism and Christianity, Islam did not do away with slavery, which existed as an institution throughout the Ancient Orient. It did attempt, however, to improve the conditions in which the slaves lived.

In the Koran the setting free of slaves is recommended as a meritorious act (4: 36), and traditions refer to slaves as the "brothers" of Moslems and advise the latter to treat them well and to provide for their maintenance. Only those captured as infidels in war or born into slavery could be slaves in Islam. For a debtor, for example, to sell his children or others or even himself into slavery was prohibited by law, but it probably happened on occasion. Incidentally, the slave trade with countries of the Islamic faith was a flourishing and profitable business for centuries for the Christian countries of the Mediterranean area.

In law, slaves were regarded as objects. Good-looking and well-educated female slaves often served as valuable gifts with which to obtain the favor of high-ranking persons. In fact, under certain conditions, both male and female slaves could rise to very influential positions and achieve great prosperity. There were, for instance, slave dynasties, such as the Mamlūks in Egypt. Clever and adroit slaves were often employed in shops and in trade. There was no industrial slavery.

Basically, slaves were under legal incapacity, but they had certain rights as persons. With the consent of their master, they were allowed to marry, but only among the Mālikī were they allowed to marry up to four female slaves, two being the maximum fixed by the other schools of law. However, a slave owner could force his slaves to marry. A female slave could marry a free Moslem; the children of such marriages were slaves. But she could not marry her own master unless he first set her free. In this case, her children were equally free. Slaves could be used as concubines by their masters but only by them; slaves could not be forced into prostitution, as had obviously been the case often in pre-Islamic Arabia. A free Moslem woman evidently did not have the right to concubinage with one of her slaves. According to the Mālikī, the female slave had the right to share the nights of her master with his free wife on an equal basis, but other schools of law allowed her only one night in every three.

In other respects, too, certain conditions and responsibilities which Islamic family law imposed upon free persons were restricted as far as slaves were concerned. The punishment for immorality and for slander in connection with immorality, for example, was only half of that fixed for a freeman.

The period a widowed or divorced female slave was required to wait before remarrying was shorter than for a free person. A slave could repudiate his wife but could take her back only after one *talāq* had been pronounced. The owner of a female slave who was married, no matter whether her husband was free or a slave, did not have the right to make her his concubine. Nor was this allowed when a female slave was owned by several men. The owner of a female slave who had borne her master a child was no longer entitled to sell her, give her away, or use her as a pledge after the birth of the child, and she became free on her master's death. In law, the children of legal concubines had exactly the same status as the children of free wives. As will subsequently be seen, this provision was of great importance in the further development of Islamic society.

Beginning in the more progressive Islamic countries, at about the middle of the nineteenth century decrees were issued for the restriction of slavery. Most Islamic countries officially ended slavery in the constitutions adopted after the First World War. In conservative countries of the Arabian Peninsula, such as Saudi Arabia and Bahrein, slavery was ended only some 30 years ago.

It is thus evident that the *shari'a* draws social distinctions between men and women and between free persons and slaves. However, all free women are equal before the law, whatever social stratum they belong to.

In the 33rd *Sura* of the Koran, dating from the time spent by Mohammed as the respected head of the Islamic community in Medina, there are special provisions concerning the position within the young Moslem community to be held by the wives of the Prophet, by then nine. The same *Sura* emphasizes Mohammed's right to special provisions as compared with all other Moslems, who were permitted to have four legal wives at most. It is unlikely that those around the Prophet would have criticized the special privileges he claimed for himself. They probably considered it self-evident that an exceptional person like Mohammed should enjoy special rights. In the same 33rd *Sura*, the additional name of "Mother of the Faithful" is given to the wives of Mohammed, and they are forbidden to marry again after his death.

Much has been written and said about the wearing of the veil by women in Islam. Basically, there is no binding prescription for this in Islamic law, but there are suggestions, as in the 33rd *Sura*, which says: "O prophet, say to thy wives, and thy daughters, and the womenfolks of the believers, that they let down some (part) of their mantles over them; that is more suitable for their being recognised and not insulted." (33: 59)

A verse from another *Sura*, which is quoted as evidence of the exhortation to women to veil themselves, reads:

Say to the believing women that they cast down their eyes and guard their private parts and show not their ornaments, except so far as they (normally) appear, and let them throw their scarves over their bosoms and not show their ornaments except to their husbands or their fathers or the fathers of their husbands or to their sons or the sons of their husbands, or their brothers or the sons of their brothers or the sons of their sisters, or their womenfolks, or those in their possession (i.e. slaves) ... (24: 31)

At neither of these two places is there any specific mention of veiling the face, only of a certain more general covering. The second of the two verses quoted seems to assume that certain parts of the body were visible anyway. Opponents of veiling as, for example, the freethinker Jāhiz in the ninth century [49, 57ff.], have pointed out too, that while on a pilgrimage, one of the "pillars" of the Islamic faith—in the state of *ihrām*, as it is called—men and women are required to uncover face and hands.

It is known that noble ladies of the trading city of Mecca wore veils even before Islam. In one tale, set in the market place of the Ancient Arabian city of Okaz, a group of jaunty youths struck up a conversation with a young girl from another tribe. The young lady was veiled and wore a gown with a train. Full of admiration, they bade her reveal her face, but this favor she refused them. One of the youths then approached her from behind and, without her noticing it, fastened her train to the neck of her robe—the others probably distracting her attention by talking to her. When she stood up, she unwittingly revealed her naked back to the rowdy throng. The layabouts hooted with laughter and mocked her: "She refused to let us look at her face, now we can see her back." This demeaning treatment of a young woman caused a bloody feud. [104, 15ff.] Incidentally, the story also indicates that women of that time, even though they were veiled, could converse freely with men.

The veil already existed in countries that were conquered by the Moslems, such as Persia. In the Ancient Orient, among the Assyrians and Babylonians, the veil was a symbol of class distinctions. It was the right of free women to wear it. In contrast the slave who did this was liable to be punished. In this way an early Arabian historian explains *Sura* 33: 59 that Mohammed's wives had been annoyed by his opponents in Medina when they left the house at night in order to relieve nature because they took unveiled women for slaves. [87, 126ff.]

The custom of wearing the veil spread quickly, at least in the upper circles of society. In the countryside, among the Bedouins and wherever women had to perform heavy physical toil, the veil was more of a nuisance, and the custom of wearing it has never been strictly observed. The veiling of female slaves was likewise not taken seriously, and the Koran permits old women a less strict covering. (24: 59)

If we wish to use miniatures as documentary evidence then we must conclude that even high-ranking ladies, not only in the urban society of Iraq in the thirteenth century (Fig. 26), but also that of Iran in the fifteenth century (Fig. 6), did not always strictly adhere to the wearing of veils. We often find examples of distinguished ladies without veils meeting with freemen who were not related to them, at least in their own gardens and palaces, but not only there (Fig. 10). Certainly these miniatures are illustrations to literary texts but one may assume that the painters used facts existing which were familiar to them from their environment. Moreover, reports by Europeans traveling there confirm these observations, in any case for Iran in the fifteenth century. [64, 171f.] When visiting the mosque (Fig. 20, 107) and also when the lady aristocrats mixed with the people (Fig. 33), the hair and the lower part of the face were certainly always covered. If on the other hand ladies from princely houses appear without veils on Indian miniatures of the Mogul period, then we know that these ladies did not sit for the portraits themselves but that one of the female slaves did it for them.

It may also be noted that at times men, too, wore veils, for instance, social revolutionaries who appeared in the garb of a prophet. One such was the leader of the Zanj insurrection by black slaves used for the drainage of swamps in Southern Iraq in the second half of the ninth century. In most later miniatures, the Prophet Mohammed is shown with a veil over his face, but it is unlike the veil worn by women, as the eyes are not exposed. (Fig. 15)

Closely connected with the veil is the exclusion of women from public life in Islam. This is founded on a verse in the Koran which clearly refers to the wives of the Prophet: "... When ye ask them (i.e. the wives of the Prophet) for any article, ask them from behind a curtain; that is purer for your hearts and for theirs." (33: 53; see also 33: 55)

It is reported in an Arab historical work dating from the ninth century that this revelation originated at the marriage of Mohammed to the beautiful Zaynab Bint Jahsh, former wife of his adopted son Zayd Ibn Hāritha. Mohammed had once seen Zaynab in her undergarments as he was about to enter Zayd's house and had coveted her from then on. Zayd, who was very much attached to his adoptive father, wanted to divorce her immediately so that Mohammed could marry her, but Mohammed did not want to accept Zayd's offer. On the other hand, Zaynab had married Zayd against her will and now displayed a clear lack of affection for him. In the end, her marriage with Mohammed took place. The tradition reports that toward the end of the wedding feast the guests showed no signs of departing. Mohammed impatiently left the room several times and went out into the courtyard, hoping that he would finally be left alone with his new bride. But this was not the case. It was now that the verse quoted above was revealed to him. [87, VIII, 74 ff.] This shows that Zaynab's attractiveness for her guests—at the time she was in her mid or even late thirties—was considered to have been very great.

It was the custom in Sassanid Persia for high-ranking persons to be hidden from the sight of ordinary mortals by a curtain. We do not know whether Mohammed was aware of this. However, even the first Omayyad Khalif Mo'āwiya was often separated from his subjects by a curtain—especially when he was not in full control of his senses on account of an excessively high intake of alcohol. In later times, some of the Islamic dynasties, such as the Fātimids in Egypt, evolved their own ceremonial in this connection. Thus, to begin with, the veil and the curtain were symbols of honor and rank.

The restriction of women to the domestic area, which grew out of the use of the veil and curtain, and their exclusion from public life, which was paralleled by increasing limitations on their opportunities for education, proved to have unfavorable consequences for the social position of women and for the development of the whole of society in the Islamic countries in the course of later centuries.

Women's organizations in the various countries have made a special plea for the reformation of the *shari'a*, but more will be said about this in the final chapter. We will now examine the daily life of women in the Islamic countries of the past.

Life in Family and Society

In most cases, the birth of a girl caused the mother less joy than that of a boy. Even before anything was said to her or the child shown to her, she could guess that she had given birth to a daughter from the fact that the women attending her at the birth did not rejoice aloud and praise Allah as soon as the child arrived but kept their voices low as they whispered to each other. [78, 255] This applied to all levels of society, from the Bedouins and the peasants to the lower, middle and upper classes in the towns and even to Court

circles. The wealthy did not consider the arrival of a baby girl an excuse for an elaborate feast of joy, as was customary at the birth of a son. The reason for this was essentially a practical one; existence was an uncertain matter in those times, and a son could contribute to the maintenance of the family. Among the Bedouins, he could even help in defense against enemies, but a girl could not. Furthermore, when a girl married, she left her own family to live with her husband's and, with the sons she bore, added to its strength. Among the Bedouins of pre-Islamic Arabia, it even happened that baby girls were buried alive soon after birth in the sand of the desert. This was strictly forbidden by the Koran, which also censured a father for scowling at the birth of a daughter and being resentful of his fate. (16:60f.)

The name of the child was chosen by the parents. The standard names for girls in most of the Islamic countries even today include names from the family of the Prophet—such as that of his mother Āmina, of his wives Khadija, Ā'isha, and Zaynab, of his daughters Fātima, Umm Kulthūm, and Roqayya. Like everywhere else, the names elected were and still are subject to fashion, family traditions, local, and social factors. Either directly after the birth or, in many places, seven days later, a teacher of religion came to the parents' dwelling and whispered the chosen name, the call to prayer, and the Islamic creed in the child's ear. With this, the child was received into the community of the faithful and, according to superstitious beliefs, was protected from being harmed by evil spirits.

Beyond this a child's hair should be shorn on the seventh day and a sacrificial animal be slaughtered in his honor, so it was stipulated in the *Sunna*. Here, too, the lesser esteem in which girls were held becomes evident. For a boy child two wethers were slaughtered, for a girl child only one or the offering was even omitted. The meat of the sacrificial animal was given to the poor. The faithful were also asked to weigh the shorn hair of the child and to offer the equivalent of the weight in the form of silver or gold as alms. This custom certainly originated from Ancient Arabic paganism but was approved of by Mohammed.

There is a whole series of little poems in classical Arabic literature which reveal the various feelings aroused by the birth of a girl.

An Arab poetess indicates how a daughter was regarded in the family:

How can I help it that she is a girl?
She washes my hair and is a credit to me,
She brings me the veil that has fallen down,
And when she is bigger and is eight,
She will look splendid in a gown from Yemen.
I will marry you to Marwān or Mo'āwiya,
Noble men, for a high dowry certainly.
[174, 221]

Concern about the future of a little girl could also give rise to such pessimistic verses as these:

Is Wasnā not like a pearl,
At least in the soft little gown of silk.
But her loveliest gown is a spotless shroud
In which she is wrapped on the bier
And when she is hurriedly buried,
Our heart leaps and jumps with joy.
[174, 223]

This concern in the world of Islam, which is basically well-disposed toward children, is expressed in yet another way:

If I did not have any little daughters,
Small and delicate like chicks covered in down,
The Earth would offer me space enough
To seek my livelihood,
Yet our children are for us
As if our hearts were wandering on Earth:
If only a breath of wind touches one of them,
We find no peace from pain.
[174, 224]

The Arab poet Bashshār Ibn Bord (d. 784) mourns the death of a daughter in the following poem:

O little daughter, whom I did not want,
You were scarcely five when Death took you.
I had loved you so dearly,
That sorrow broke my heart.
Yes, you were better than a son,
Who soon begins to drink and at night pays whores.
[Ibid.]

It would seem that even at that time the education of sons was not without problems.

The little girl grew up in the women's quarters of the house or in the women's part of the tent. The Arabic name for the former is *harim* while the Persian-Indian designation for it is *zenāneh*. The word *harim* has come to us, via Turkish, in the form "harem," and is associated with a great deal of fantasy about voluptuous extravagance and sensual pleasures. In fact, the Arabic word *harim* designated a holy and inviolable place, since, according to the Arab concept, it was through his female relatives that the honor of a man could be most profoundly violated. The part of the house where the female members of the family and the household lived, the harem, was normally out of bounds to all males except the master of the house, his sons, and perhaps a physician. At the same time, *harim* was also the designation for the women who dwelt in this area; that is, a man's wife or wives, his mother, his sisters, his daughters, and his daughters-in-law. In the palaces of the great men of the country, the Khalifs, Sultans, Emirs, and Viziers, the harem usually consisted of a sizable number of persons—not only the wives of the master of the house but also their numerous female servants, his concubines, the children of all these women and eunuchs to attend and watch over them.

Relatively little is known about the education of girls in Islamic countries before the beginning of modern times in the nineteenth century. It was certainly dependent to a large extent on their social position. It is probable that the majority of them were prepared from early childhood for their future role as housewives; that is, they were familiarized with domestic activities, including needlework, and practiced them from an early age. At any rate, this is what sociologists report about the Bedouins in Central Arabia [134] and small Moroccan towns of the second half of the twentieth century [106], whose markedly conservative way of life has probably changed but little in the course of the centuries.

Girls from patrician families, in which erudition was traditional, were certainly instructed in the fundamentals of the Islamic sciences as well. They were sometimes given the same thorough education as their brothers, who had private teachers, but the girls were entrusted to female teachers only. It must have been exceptional for anyone to give his daughters the same education as his sons, since otherwise it would not have been given special mention in the texts. Nevertheless, Arab biographical literature names a whole series of women who were outstanding in the science of traditions, especially up to the tenth century but in later periods as well.

Until the beginning of the twentieth century, the educational establishment for the majority of children from the lower strata of the urban population was the Koran school, which was almost always reserved for boys. For a small charge, the children learned there to recite the Koran by heart, to read and write, and to manage the basic concepts of arithmetic. If one is to believe the romantic epic of the Persian Nizāmī, which narrates the celebrated love story of Laylā and Majnūn in poetic form, there must also have been some mixed Koran schools, since it was in the Koran school that Laylā and Majnūn fell in love with each other. (Fig. 27)

Daughters of royal families may well have had the same upbringing as Qudiya fakān in *Thousand and One Nights*, who, together with her cousin, learns to ride, "to strike with the sword, and to thrust with the lance." Another princess from this famous collection of tales says of herself: "None shall have me for wife unless he overcomes me with horse and lance in a contest of arms in an open field." Women such as this also appear in the *Shāh-nāmeh*, the Persian national epic poem. Miniatures illustrating other works of Persian literature also depict women on horseback swinging a sword or a club. (Fig. 59) However, such figures were not at all typical of women in Islam. Exceptions in most civilizations, amazons have left their mark as such on literature.

The advice that the Persian Kay Kā'ūs gave his son in the eleventh century clearly indicates that not all princesses were like those in the tales from *Thousand and One Nights* and, indeed, these tales may have only been dreams in literary form. Kay Kā'ūs, a prince of the Ziyārid dynasty, which at that time ruled the southern bank of the Caspian Sea, wrote his *Qābūs-nāmeh* when he was 63 years old as a guide for his son and successor. He has this to say about the upbringing and treatment of a daughter: "Entrust her to chaste and virtuous nurses, and, when she is older, give her to a woman teacher so that she learns to pray and fast and to perform her religious duties, which are prescribed by the law of religion. But do not teach her to write! When she is grown up, try to hand her over to a husband as quickly as possible, since for a daughter it would be better if she did not even live but, once she is there, she should either lie in the grave or be married." What now follows indicates that he was motivated by concern for the girl who, unlike a son, was helpless without the support of a man. He thus advises his son: "As long as she dwells in your house, have compassion for her, since daughters are the captives of their parents," and he tells him to take good care of her. As a dynast entirely dedicated to patriarchal family relations, he also urges his son to find the girl, if she is still a virgin, a good-looking husband who is likewise innocent so that the young woman would feel bound to her spouse and cause him no scandal. His son-in-law should not only be of pure religion, honest, and a good master of the house but also of lower rank and dignity so that the young man might look up to his father-in-law and not expect the opposite. [94, 98 ff.] Thus, in a Persian ruling family of that time, rank and solidarity were important.

In many Islamic countries, the preparation of little girls for marriage included circumcision, in which either the prepuce of the clitoris or the entire organ, and sometimes even parts of the inner labia of the vulva were removed. In modern terms, this is mutilation, and the girl was at least greatly affected in her sexual sensations.

In the traditions, there is usually no express reference to the circumcision of girls but only to that of boys. Thus the circumcision of girls is obligatory only in the Shāfi'ite school; in the Mālikite school it is regarded as customary. The circumcision of boys and girls probably dates from pre-Islamic times, and was simply continued under Islam. Even today, however, it is so firmly established as a popular custom in some countries, such as Egypt and the Sudan, that a law prohibiting circumcision of girls, dating from April, 1959, has not put an end to it, not even in such big cities as Cairo. Even now, the Bedouins of Central Arabia consider that an uncircumcised girl is unworthy of being married. During the Omayyad period, at a drinking party given by Khalif Hishām Ibn Abdal-Malik, the son of a Byzantine woman was abused as the "son of a woman with a clitoris." The man so addressed retorts, however: "Are you even boasting with that which was cut off from the clitoris of your mother?" [34, 80 ff.] Nevertheless, the circumcision of a girl was not celebrated as that of a boy.

Most little girls wore a veil over the face at a very early age—eight or nine years of age and even earlier in noble families. Their feeling of shame developed in such a manner that several European travelers noted with astonishment that an Islamic woman would rather allow a physician to examine her body than unveil her face in front of him.

Marriages were arranged for little girls at an early age, in most cases when they were only ten to twelve years old. One of the reasons for this was certainly the requirement that a young bride had to be a virgin, and, of course, marriage is recommended by Islam. The unhappy figure of the old maid, so often the subject of compassionate laughter or even scorn in Europe, was practically unknown in Islamic countries of the past. Indeed the early marriage of a girl, which allowed her neither an opportunity to mature intellectually nor further education in most cases, was also certainly one of the reasons for the ever increasing degradation of women in the Islamic world. From the early period of Islam it has been repeatedly passed down that a woman or a girl received the proposal of a suitor personally. [164, IV, 412 ff.; 50, 231] On such occasions there were also refusals.

As was also the custom in Europe of not so long ago, marriage was not something decided by two young people who loved each other but was and often still is a matter arranged for the most part by the two families concerned.

Since women, if they appeared at all in public, were always veiled, it was not possible for a man to see his future bride or to become acquainted with her first. Only when he wedded his cousin—and this is still a common occurrence in all Islamic countries—was he already acquainted with his bride before the ceremony. With the close feelings of family solidarity existing among members of the large Oriental family unit, such marriages were always recommended; indeed, a young man even had priority, before any other possible suitors, if he wished to marry his cousin on his father's side. If this was not possible, a man who wanted to marry had to have recourse to the agency of his female relatives or to the services of a professional marriage maker.

The marriage brokers often endeavored to exploit their position and dupe their male clients. Thus in a work of the Arab literature of the eleventh century, it is reported that a man of Bagdad had long sought a beautiful wife. Finally, a matchmaker promised him one who looked like a "bouquet of narcissi." After the wedding, the bridegroom discovered that the vaunted bride was an ugly old woman. The matchmaker, when accused of trickery by the man, became indignant at this reproach and justified the comparison by saying, "Her complexion is yellow, her hair is white, and her legs are of a dark color." [18, XLVI] A similar deceit is reported from Cairo in the 1930's. [105, 33 ff.]

Consequently, it was better for the young man to rely on his mother or other female relatives to make enquiries in the neighborhood about families with daughters of marriageable

age. They arranged a visit, had a look at the young girl, and were perhaps also able to exchange a few words with her. The duration of the visit was a possible indication of whether the visitors had received a favorable impression or not.

The mother of the young girl certainly gave her some advice beforehand, perhaps in words like these: "My little daughter, this is your aunt who has come here to have a look at you. Conceal nothing from her that she would like to know about your appearance and your character, and speak freely to her about the things she will discuss with you!"

One matchmaker, an honest woman, came to the following conclusion: "If one lifts the veil, the suitor is not cheated." [77, 110]

If the young girl pleased the visitor or visitors, they paid a second visit to her family to describe the financial situation of the bridegroom and to describe his appearance. When the matter was in the hands of a professional agent, she usually lauded the bridegroom in extravagant words. Truthfulness was rarely one of her strong points.

The representatives of the bridegroom and bride then carried out negotiations on the subject of the bride money, generally bargaining in the Oriental manner. Once a settlement agreeable to both sides was reached, both recited the opening *Sura* of the Koran and fixed the day on which the marriage contract was to be drawn up.

On this day, the bridegroom brought the agreed dowry to the bride's house and handed it over to her legal representative. Until the early years of the twentieth century, the conclusion of the contract was often only a verbal affair, and here, too, the first *Sura* of the Koran was recited. In most cases, a religious teacher was present and made a short speech. A few refreshments were taken, and it was decided when the *laylat ad-dokhla* should take place, this being the night on which the bride was to be taken to the house of the bridegroom to become not only his wife but also a member of his family. This interval of time could vary—sometimes it was eight to ten days, while in other cases it could be several months. The "engagement period" was used by the bride's family to buy her, with the dowry and with their own money, everything that she needed, clothing, domestic utensils, bed linen, and carpets. Depending on his social status, gifts, such as fruit, sweets, or a scarf were sent by the bridegroom to the bride and she also occasionally sent small presents to him. However, he was not yet permitted to see her. It was only after 1910 that the strict customs could be circumvented to some extent: the bride could send her future husband a photograph of herself as a substitute for a real meeting.

The actual marriage customs varied according to the social stratum to which the bridal pair belonged and also according to the region in which they lived. They did not remain the same for all time either. They were simple in the early days of Islam. The bride was combed, ornamented, and dressed in a particularly attractive gown for her special day. The house of the bridegroom was prepared for the festivities and for the wedding night.

Ā'isha wore a gown of striped red cloth from Bahrein for her marriage to Mohammed; subsequently this gown was borrowed from her by every woman of Medina who wished to marry. This was probably because the gown was not only elegant but was believed by the brides to be especially lucky.

At the marriage of Mohammed's daughter, Fātima, with his cousin Ali, Ā'isha and one of Mohammed's other wives strewed soft sand on the ground, filled two cushions with palm fiber, and prepared figs, dates, and fresh water. In this case, the marriage took place in the house of the bride, but it was customary for the bride to be escorted to the house of the bridegroom. Young girls accompanied her and sang something like this: *Ataynākum, ataynākum fa-hayānā wa-hayā-kum*, "We are coming to you, we are coming to you; greet us then and we greet you." A wedding feast was obligatory by tradition at every Islamic marriage. However, it was held separately for men and women. At Mohammed's wedding to the beautiful Jewess Safiyya, *qays* was served, a dish consisting of dates, cottage cheese, and fat, and it probably included flour from roasted barley as well. Bread and meat were also offered on such occasions. Safiyya received particular praise for offering to her guests a drink which she herself had prepared from soaked dates.

For the wedding night, the *shari'a* recommended the following prayer for the bridegroom: "O God, I beg Thee for the goodness in her and for her good inclinations which Thou hast created and I take refuge in Thee from the wickedness in her and from the wicked inclinations which Thou hast created." It was customary for the husband to spend seven nights with his wife if she were a virgin. If she had been a widow or divorced, this "honeymoon" was shortened to three days.

In later times, and especially at the Courts and among the upper strata of the towns, marriages were elaborately celebrated. One of the most magnificent and extravagant weddings reported by Arab historians was that of the later Khalif al-Ma'mūn, a son of Hārūn ar-Rāshīd, to Būrān, a daughter of the Vizier al-Hasan Ibn Sahl. The Vizier, obviously a man of extreme wealth, entertained the leading figures of the realm, including the top military commanders and the relatives of the Khalif, for 19 days on his country estate near the town of Wasit, arranging all kinds of pleasures for them during this time. The grandmother of the bride arranged for a shower of pearls the size of hazelnuts to pour over the bridegroom. Zubayda, the mother of al-Ma'mūn, presented the young Būrān with a gown embroidered with precious pearls. The Vizier distributed gifts and garments of honor and even organized a kind of lottery. He had little balls of musk and amber—that is, expensive perfumes—thrown among the crowd, each of these balls bearing the name of an estate, a female slave, or a steed. Whoever gained one of these little balls was given what was named on it. The bridal chamber was lit by candles of precious, sweet-smelling amber, each of which is said to have weighed eighty pounds. It is related that this wedding cost fifty million silver dirham, a sum which, from all accounts, does not seem to have been exaggerated at all.

The report of another wedding tells of the gigantic quantities of food consumed on such occasions. When a daughter of the Mamlūk Sultan an-Nāsir Mohammed Ibn Qalāwūn was married in Egypt to the Emir Kausūn, the celebrations lasted seven days; five thousand sheep, one hundred cattle, fifty mares, and innumerable birds were slaughtered for the occasion. Eleven thousand loaves of sugar were used for making confections and sherbets. The Emirs sent 311 hundred-weight of wax candles to illuminate the wedding feast. The bridegroom received gifts worth fifty thousand dinar from the other Emirs. A magnificent fireworks display, held on the night of the wedding, cost eighty thousand dirham, and the artists who performed during the festivities were given the noteworthy sum of ten thousand gold dinar. The princess was presented with a tent on which there were a hundred thousand *mithqāl* of gold, equivalent to 468 kilograms. The Sultan treated eleven daughters in this manner. [4, 154]

In the Cairo of the 1830's weddings of the urban middle class usually began on Monday and lasted until Thursday night which was the wedding night. A particularly pleasant high point in the wedding celebrations was, in most cases, the bathing of the bride. If her parents' house did not have a bath of its own, a public bath was rented for a day or half a day on Wednesday. Often preceded by musicians, the bride was brought to the bath by her female relatives and friends. She was then washed, massaged, combed, and perfumed. Entertainment by female vocalists was frequently provided while this was going on. Food and refreshments were then taken together, before the bride, well wrapped, was discreetly brought back to her parents' house. The "henna night" was the next item on the program. The hands and feet of the bride were dyed with henna, the edges of her eyelids were blackened with *kohl* (sulphur antimonide), and she was dressed and ornamented for the wedding. In many regions it was usual for the bride to appear in seven costly gowns, one after the other. She might also wear a bridal crown, which was similar to a myrtle garland; this was done in Egypt from the fifteenth century on. She was then seated on a kind of throne or high chair, and had to listen, with modestly lowered eyes, while her guests sang, danced, and made music.

On the following day, the Thursday, and more closely wrapped than usual, she was solemnly brought to the bridegroom's house by the light of candles and to the sound of music. Here she was usually welcomed by her mother-in-law and taken to the bridal chamber. In the meantime and accompanied by his friends, the bridegroom had likewise paid a visit to a public or private bath and held a feast. When the bride arrived at the groom's house, yet another meal was served, the sexes again dining separately. [99, I, 175ff.]

The Italian Pietro della Valle describes bridal processions in Turkey at the beginning of the seventeenth century in slightly different words:

I also saw their wedding ceremonies at which the bride was entirely covered, and, if she were only of middle-class rank, went on foot, carrying a sack on her back like a monk; on the other hand, if she were of higher standing, she is led on horseback and covered in a manner resembling the curtains of a bed, the ends of which are carried by the many persons around her ... every bride, whatever her rank, has a fairly high torch carried in front of her, this being decorated with flowers, painted paper, gold foil and other leaf and flower arrangements, even with gold, silver and precious stones, depending on the wealth of the bride. [173, I, 43b]

Wherever weddings were held, they were always one of the principal family celebrations in Islam, and this is still the case. However, if a divorced woman or a widow remarried, the festivities were far less elaborate.

When the bridegroom finally entered the bridal chamber, he was permitted, mostly in return for a gift, to raise the veil of his bride and, if she were not his cousin, see her for the first time. If he subsequently discovered that she was not a virgin as promised, he could immediately repudiate her. Since this was regarded as a great disgrace, brides who were no longer virgins but had been lauded as such used every kind of subterfuge to fool their bridegroom. For instance, they showed a cloth spattered with the blood of a freshly killed dove or, shortly before the arrival of the bridegroom, they made a small cut at the critical spot. Even today, girls prefer to submit to a minor operation rather than admit the truth to a bridegroom holding conventional views on the matter.

For centuries it was the custom in many areas—still followed in rural localities—to show the sign of virginity to the guests. The women greeted this with shrill cries of joy. After the wedding night, the bride and groom took separate baths, and sometimes another festive banquet was provided.

It was now that the life of the young wife in her husband's family began, and she had to adapt herself to their ways and customs. Many parents probably gave their daughters advice of the kind given by an Arab woman to her daughter before her marriage in the pre-Islamic period: "My little daughter, you are now leaving the house from which you originate, the nest from which you came. You are going to a man who is unknown to you, to a husband to whom you are not yet accustomed. Therefore be a maidservant to him so that he will be a manservant to you. Towards him observe ten things that are especially precious to you!" There then follows, in rhyming prose, a list of the qualities of an exemplary wife: she should humbly submit to him, listen to and obey him, she should pay attention to when he wishes to eat and sleep, watch over his property, and take care of his family, she should not oppose him nor betray any of his secrets. "Take care not to be merry when he is worried and not to be sad when he wants to joke!" [77, 83 ff.] were the final words of the mother concerned about the welfare of her daughter.

If the young wife took note of such wise advice, if she was adaptable and her husband was good to her, then her feel-

ings, after a period of married life, were probably similar to those of the women who, according to Arab literature, lauded their husbands in the following manner and thus, at the same time, provided a picture of the ideal husband of that time: "A husband is a support in time of need, a helper in times of prosperity. If I am satisfied, he is good to me, he calms me when I become angry." Another wife praises her husband as follows: "That which worries me worries him, too. He is medicine for that which makes me ill. His kiss is as sweet as honey, his embrace like paradise, I like him, whether he is near or far." The third woman said this: "A husband is like a warm gown in cold weather, he cradles me when I am sleepy. His love is a unique joy for me, afterward he smells sweeter than aloe." And finally the fourth asserts: "A husband is indescribable happiness, pleasure without end, unrivaled by anything else." [78, 124]

But much bitter experience of life was probably reflected in the custom which required a virginal bride, as is known from later periods, to be sad and silent during the wedding festivities, and even to weep. For a young girl, marriage meant a much more drastic change than for a man. She had to leave her own family, become the wife of a man who, in most cases, was totally unknown to her, and fit into a new community, his family. Rural marriage songs from Palestine express this in the following words: "She goes from her father's to her husband's house, she goes from the house of joy to misery, from her own people to strangers." [61, II, 143] Various ethnologists and travelers report that the young wife, who continued to bear the name of her father—and this is still the custom, at least in Arab countries—was more closely attached to her parents than to her husband and his family. It is only with the transformation of the family structure in the Near East of our time that this, too, is changing.

Wise mothers liked to choose as wives for their sons very young girls or slaves who had grown up like daughters in their own house, since they considered them to be more adaptable. The mother-in-law was often glad when a young woman joined the household, since she no longer had to do all the housework by herself and, among the fellahin, to work in the fields as well. Among the fellahin, mothers who had several daughters-in-law in their house were regarded as "ladies" with female servants, since the young women now had to grind the corn, fetch water, do the washing, collect wood, and so on.

On the other hand, it was a matter of great importance for a young wife to produce children of her own as rapidly as possible—especially sons so that she could assume the respected position of a mother. Even the Koran requires that a man respect his mother (4:1), and in the traditions it is stated that the Prophet forbade a man to disobey his mother. Just as a husband had the greatest right to his wife, a mother had the greatest claim to the man she had borne. A well-known Islamic tradition asserts: "Paradise is at the mothers' feet."

A woman's failure to bear children was one of the main reasons for a man to take a second wife, since even in the Koran it is said that those who regarded their children as well as their wives as a joy to behold would partake of Paradise. (25:74f.) According to the views of the Islamic Middle Ages and under the conditions of life then prevailing, children were not simply a source of joy but also a kind of insurance against the misfortunes and poverty of old age; for peasants and Bedouins this still holds true. Thus an astute but childless wife would herself advise her husband to marry this or that woman, mostly one of lower social standing, and then treat the latter's children as her own, while the second wife was sometimes relegated to the status of a maidservant.

The Arabic word for second wife, *darra*, is derived from a stem which also means "harm" or "disadvantage," and this is also how many women have regarded the institution of polygyny. Male "logic" has produced sayings as: "If your wife desires to surpass you, marry a second one to restrain her," or, as in another from Palestine, "Subdue a woman with another woman and do not strike them with the stick!" [61, II, 209] Women, on the other hand, expressed their feelings in sayings as: "The co-wife is bitter, even if she were honey in a jar." (61, II, 186]

Popular humor and popular wisdom are reflected in stories like the one that is related in two versions from different regions: A man had two wives, one old and one young. The old wife, who did not wish him to appear too young, plucked out all his dark hairs (alternatively, the hairs of his beard). The young wife, who naturally wanted the contrary, pulled out his gray hairs. When he washed himself, he discovered, to his horror, that he was completely bald (alternatively, beardless).

Islamic theologians of the present day often assert that Islam, with the institution of polygyny, is kinder to women than Christianity, since the legitimate second or third wife of a man is in a better position than an unlawful mistress. This may have been economically true in earlier times, but it takes no account at all of the psychological situation of wives. As early traditions relate there was even jealousy among the wives of the Prophet. [24, 67, 107] A Moslem woman, who as a child suffered a great deal from the polygynous marriage of her father and who divorced the husband she had married for love when he proposed taking a second wife, says: "The nature and consequences of the suffering of a wife who in the same house shares a husband lawfully with a second and equal partner, differs both in kind and in degree from that of the woman who shares him with a temporary mistress."

[39, 144 ff.] This woman was the Turkish authoress Halidé Edib, and she says that in the first case there are often other persons involved, too—children, other relatives, servants.

The ordinary life of an Islamic woman in the harem varied, of course, according to her social position. The Bedouin and fellah women had, and still have, to perform heavy physical labor. Of the fellahin, it is related that a second wife was not unwelcome for this reason—but only for this reason.

A tradition conveys an impression of the harsh conditions of life of the early female followers of Islam in Medina. Asmā, a daughter of the later Khalif Abū Bakr and an elder sister of Ā'isha, relates the following: "Az-Zubayr married me. But he had no possessions and no slaves, only a camel for carrying water and his horse. I fed and watered his horse and sewed skins to make waterbags. I kneaded dough, but I was not good at baking bread. My neighbors from the Ansār baked bread for me; they were good women. I also always carried home the date-pits (presumably for feeding the animals) from the plot of land which Mohammed had given to Zubayr. This plot of land was two-thirds of a parasang (almost four kilometers) away." She says that Abū Bakr subsequently sent her a manservant, who looked after the horse for her. Her relief is evident from her words: "That was as if he had freed me." [24, 67, 107] It is said of Mohammed's daughter Fātima that grinding corn gave her blisters on her hands—this was one of the hardest tasks performed by women with the primitive domestic utensils then available, and this continued to be so even later.

The wife of a member of the urban middle or upper class in later times had to perform a greater or lesser part of the domestic work, depending on her financial situation, and had to supervise the children and the servants. In an illustrious work of Arab prose of the tenth century, a merchant praises his domestic wife in the following words:

If you had even seen her once—when she toils, with her apron around her—how she rushes and runs—in every corner and everywhere—how she turns and bends—flies from the oven to the pot—and back again immediately—how she blows up the fire—and how she prepares the spices—crushes and powders them—while her pretty face—blackened by smoke—which leaves its mark on her smooth cheeks—The sight would enchant you—if you could see her at work—love for her rises from deep in my heart—since she honestly repays my love—Happiness is only granted to that man—when it gives him a wife of the same mind—a life together with her in harmony and peace. [67, 53 ff.]

The blissful husband stresses here that the harmony in his marriage is so complete because, above all, his wife is his cousin.

Woman crushing corn.

A woman of the middle and upper classes could only leave the house when veiled and with the permission of her husband. Such occasions included visits to relatives or to the cemetery and prayers at the mausoleum of a holy man or, on the major dates of the religious calendar, in the mosque. One of the most popular relaxations for women of the middle class who did not possess a bath of their own at home was a visit to the public baths at the times reserved for women. It was here that the women displayed their finery and spent hours chatting with the neighbors, passing on the latest news of their families, and being manicured, massaged, and so on.

Ultra-strict Moslems like the Hanbali in Bagdad in 934 often voiced their objections to women appearing on the streets at all. Khalif al-Hākim of Egypt considered that he was restoring the original Islamic practice when he forbade women to leave the house and shoemakers to make shoes for them. Midwives and those who washed the bodies of the dead needed written permission to pursue their trade.

What was initially regarded as pious behavior subsequently became a custom of the upper class that was followed with varying degrees of strictness in the different Islamic countries. Thus the French jeweler, Chardin, tells us concerning seventeenth-century Persia that the women there were more closely guarded than anywhere else in the world. Turkish harems in comparison were open houses. Women of the middle class only left the house to go bathing, and then covered from top to toe. Whenever high-ranking ladies actually did show themselves in public then the men had to turn away, although the noblewoman was being carried in a totally closed sedan chair [30, VI, 8], or eunuchs rode in front armed with sticks to drive the people from the streets with loud calls. In contrast the Italian nobleman, Pietro della Valle, relates concerning Constantinople around 1617 that "Turkish fe-

males" came to the basar "in droves" and even tried to flirt with "strangers" there. [173, I, 19a]

The English physician Russell, in describing Aleppo of the eighteenth century, says that the women left their houses fairly frequently, especially on Mondays and Thursdays. They also visited the gardens, where female slaves preceded them with carpets, pipes, food, and coffee. Songs were sung in the shade of the trees. Men were only excluded from the gardens when several harems arranged to rent a park for an entire day so that they could have it to themselves. The sounds of merriment could then be heard from afar. Russell, who lived in Aleppo for twenty years, had this to say of the attitude of women toward the male sex: The women "do not appear very desirous of a liberty which, in many instances, they regard as inconsistent with their notion of female honour and delicacy." [142, I, 257]

In Egypt, as late as 1910, noble women boasted that they never left their husband's house after crossing its threshold as a bride. It is noticeable even today that in a country like Iraq only about a quarter of the people in the streets are women—even in the capital city of Bagdad—and many men still walk a few steps in front of their wives when they go out in public. This is justified by the perceived need to protect and guide women. A young woman of Bagdad of the middle class told the author that her mother, who was 45 years old, still left the house only for an occasional visit to the cemetery or the *sūq*, the market, and then of course wrapped in her black *abāya*.

Thus in many regions the harem became a luxurious prison for women of the upper classes—at least in Western eyes. It was here that they idly passed their time, trying out beauty aids, scenting themselves, smoking water pipes (*nargila*) and later cigarettes, drinking coffee, eating confections, playing

22

A joyous celebration at the Court of the Mogul Emperor Akbar at the birth of a prince. At the top are the court astrologers compiling a horoscope, in the center musicians, a tambourine player, and dancing girls. At the gate of the palace, bread and money are being distributed to the people.

26

To offend the honor of a married woman was considered an insult worthy of harsh punishment. This is a scene from the Kalīla wa-Dimna collection of fables: A falcon is trying to peck out the eyes of his falconer, who had several times attempted—in vain—to win the favor of the wife of the Governor of Balkh. The latter is depicted here endeavoring to drive off the falcon with a stick. The woman is wearing a brightly patterned gown with the typical wide sleeves of the time.

23

An earthenware storage jar from thirteenth-century Iraq with scratched decorations and relief-like figures of women dancing and legendary beasts.

24

These earthenware figures probably come from a Court setting. The girls are holding carafes in the right hand and dishes (tambourines?) in the left; they probably had to assist in the entertainment of male guests. They wear pointed caps and knee-length, belted smocks over long trousers.

25

This faïence figure of a nursing woman is reminiscent of a madonna and reflects East Asian influence.

انك عاينت ما لم تر وشهدت على زور ا مثل وانما ضربت لك

المثل لتعلم انه من عمل مثل مثل ما عمل به البازيار من البهتان
كان جزاه العقوبة في العاجل والاجل ثم ان القاضي كتب ما قال
دمنه وزاد فيه وارسل به الى السحر وانطلق عظما الجند الى منزل

27
Laylā and Majnūn fell in love at the Koran school. Boy and girl pupils are kneeling before the teacher, also on his knees, on brightly colored mats; the copies of the Koran are on the typical lecterns. In the left foreground, a pupil is being given the bastinado while on the right a school servant is grinding ink. As usual, the lesson is being held in a mosque.

28
It may be assumed that only babies of princely families were rocked in such splendid cradles as this one.

*A scene from the Shāh-nāmeh.
Rūdābeh, shortly before the birth of
Rustam, has fainted since the size of her
stomach seems to preclude the possibility
of a birth. An old woman, her mother,
scatters perfumed water over her to
refresh her. In the foreground a eunuch
hands a fortifying meat dish to a maidservant. On the roof, the father of the
child, the white-haired Zāl, asks his
protector, a magical bird, for advice.
The bird describes the Caesarean section by which the child must be born,
and the Mobed, the wise man who
will perform it, is already coming
through the door.*

A scene from a Bedouin camp. In the foreground, men are holding a meeting while to the rear women are performing the tasks which are still necessary for the Bedouin: the erection of tents, the feeding of the animals, milking, washing and, of course, suckling children. Bright carpets cover the floors of the tents.

31

According to the Iranian saga, it was the legendary King Jamshīd who taught his subjects the various crafts. Smiths, dyers, tailors, and weavers are to be seen. The only craft carried out by a woman is spinning. Here, in the Iran of the second half of the fifteenth century, it is the spinning-wheel that is used and no longer the distaff depicted in earlier pictures.

32
From the Shāh-nāmeh. *Princess Tahmīna comes at night to the room of Rustam, the man whom she has long been yearning for. The rich furnishings of an aristocratic bed-chamber of fifteenth-century Iran is shown here. The bed consisted of a mattress on the floor, covered by a brocade blanket.*

A prince surveys a popular celebration from a podium. The ladies of his harem, in white veils and guarded by eunuchs, sit on either side. Music is being played, food is being prepared, and there is boating on the pond.

34
This miniature shows a scene in a Turkish bazaar around 1600. A veiled lady is offering a bracelet for sale, but otherwise business is the affair of men, as it still is today in many areas. The qualities of the merchandise are being extolled, and bargaining is in progress, accompanied by much gesticulation. Market supervisors are depicted with long swords on their shoulders.

35

A lady of the harem is unwell; the physician has been called, and he is now feeling her pulse. He is attended by a colleague. The patient is held by another member of the harem. The master of the house watches the scene from a window opening. In the foreground, medicine is being prepared by one of the inmates.

36
This miniature from a Shāh-nāmeh manuscript depicts a scene at the Iranian Court about 1600: Zāl, wearing a splendid crown as a sign of his royal rank, comes at night, with a servant bearing a torch, to the castle of his beloved, the beautiful Rūdābeh, who is looking out for him from the terrace. The harem guards are asleep. In the foreground, a hare is being roasted on the spit. One of Rūdā-beh's companions on the upper floor has a eunuch fetch her a candelabra to help Zāl enter the castle.

37
Even ordinary objects were shaped in a highly artistic manner, such as this bowl of rock crystal splendidly decorated with gold and precious stones.

Ladies are preparing a picnic against a background of blossoming trees. A maidservant, with full cheeks, is blowing on the fire to make it burn so that the food hanging over it in a large pot can be cooked. Pastry is being kneaded in the foreground, and a eunuch is in attendance. Further back, dancing and talking are going on. The ladies wear brightly colored gowns and attractive embroidered headcloths. Some have their gowns tied back and are revealing highly decorative trousers.

39

A young warrior on a black steed, accompanied by his retinue, fetches his bride. She is seated in a litter on a camel and is wearing the tāj-kulāh, the crown-like headgear of princesses in Iran during the second half of the sixteenth century. She is followed by maidservants, while spectators have concealed themselves behind the hill.

40

It is not only miniatures of Persian epics, such as this scene from a Shāh-nāmeh of about 1600, that show Court ladies taking part in the chase. European travelers of the seventeenth and eighteenth centuries in Iran also tell of this.

41
When deaths occurred, women expressed their grief with loud cries and much gesticulation. The painter of this minia-ture of about 1600 characterizes the sor-row of the women by the posture of their bodies and not by the expression of their faces. In the foreground are Koran readers, and the dead horse of one of the two slain heroes on an elephant.

42

A magnificent Mogul carpet of the late
sixteenth century, depicting imaginary
scenes, for example, two beasts of fable
surrounded by black elephants in the lower
half. Around the body of one of them is
coiled the tail of a winged creature with
four legs. In the upper third is a highly
realistic picture of an Indian residence
with the men's and women's quarters.

43
*This miniature conveys an impression
of a harem during the Mogul period.
A dancer is demonstrating her art in the
garden in front of the house while one of
the women watching is busy with her
hair. A wet nurse is suckling a baby,
and on the upper floor a maidservant is
fanning a woman in childbed. At the
rear of the garden, four maidservants
are preparing a meal.*

44
The Mogul Emperor Akbar—in the center of the picture—is crossing a river with his harem. High-ranking Indian women of this period were not permitted to show themselves in public when they left the harem. They passed through the streets in closed litters on camels or on elephants, while the most exalted of them were carried in a carriage drawn by cows. In his dedication to detail, the artist has not overlooked the artistically carved animal heads on the rowing-boats nor the fish and the ducks in the river.

45
It was the task of the women in the countryside to milk the animals. The fact that the woman milking here is wearing pearl jewelry is probably explained by the desire of the artist for additional decoration.

46
A richly ornamented Mogul lady of the late seventeenth century, surrounded by maidservants, is seated on a carpet in the garden of the harem. The attractive profiles of the women with their black, almond-shaped eyes and curved eyebrows stand out beautifully against the green of their surroundings.

47
During the Rococo period, a room at Schönbrunn Palace in Vienna was decorated with Mogul paintings. In the upper right half of this one, a harem scene: a ruler is shown dictating to a female scribe. The lady's headgear is different from that of the maidservants holding plumes of peacock and ostrich feathers in their hands.

cards or board games, entertained by female singers or dancers, or cultivating the art of narrative. On hot summer days, they probably spent many hours chatting or doing needlework in the shady gardens of their houses, in most of which there was a fountain. However, they were always strictly segregated from all men who were not close relatives. The food, cosmetics, or materials they needed were brought to them by female traders or servants. Russell, the physician already referred to, was surprised that the ladies of the middle- and upper-class harems of Aleppo in the eighteenth century did not read, unlike the women of his own country, who passed their time by reading novels of a more or less sentimental nature. He reports that although they had indeed learned reading and writing in their youth, most of them soon forgot it again "so that reading ought not to be reckoned a common female amusement, and is never a study." [142, I, 249] Since the standards of female education were low, superstition flourished, especially in polygynous households. Recipes for getting a husband, for acquiring supremacy in the household, or for taking the virginity of a new wife so as to make her unhappy were passed on from one generation to another. The targets, in turn, resorted to tricks of their own to upset the plans of their co-wife (or wives). [98; 101]

For centuries, within the family, it was the father who was the undisputed head. Not only his wife (wives) and daughters but also his growing or grown-up sons had to submit to his will and, at times, to his moods. In general, it was the practice for his wife and daughters to wait on him at meals but not to eat anything themselves in his presence. When the husband entered the harem, the women stood up, and many men liked to behave in a particularly taciturn manner in their harems in order to underline their authority. Amina, from the trilogy of the Egyptian novelist Nagīb Mahfūz, may be regarded as a typical example of a woman of the middle classes in the traditional Islamic society of a later period: Every evening she waits up for her husband, who spends his leisure hours with women of doubtful reputation, but she does not ever ask him where he was. When he comes home, she merely lights the stairs for him and helps him change his clothes. She only dares to speak when he addresses her. Yet in her gentleness and humbleness she is a sheet anchor for her children. Not only her daughters but also her sons love and honor her while the father, who is always strict at home, has only the respect of his children. In her obedience and submission to the will of her husband, it is she who holds the family together, and she knows how to influence her husband in those matters that are important for her and her children.

A European traveler wrote about a family of the Islamic Indian military aristocracy at the beginning of the twentieth century. The mother and daughter, who had traveled a great deal in Europe and had moved around freely, talked in a relaxed and easy manner as long as they were alone. When the father of the family appeared, however, they fell silent and said no word as long as he was present. They "became at once true Indian women silent before that superior being —the man." [32, 169]

We will see in the next chapter, however, that particularly in the first centuries of Islam there were women who did not regard this submission as their ideal.

The division into male and female societies was most strictly observed at the Courts of the Khalifs, Sultans, and Emirs. Already at the time of Hārūn ar-Rashīd, large numbers of women lived in harems, and a strict system of regulations was necessary to control communal life. Music and poetry were cultivated in the harems, political decisions taken, intrigues and plots hatched, and Viziers appointed and dismissed. Sensuous scenes certainly took place, too, along the lines associated with the word "harem" in the West. Such harems were found in the Orient long before Islam, of course. Their existence is described in the Iran of the Akhaemenids (700–330 B.C.) and it was essentially the Ancient Orient which provided the prototype for the harems of the Abbāsids and the later dynasties.

A well-ordered hierarchy prevailed in the harem, but it often took the entire governing genius of a ruler to preserve peace there. The friend and secretary of the Mogul Emperor Akbar, who reported in detail about the period of government of his sovereign, lauded him in the following words:

Through order the world becomes a meadow of truth and reality; and that which is but external, receives through it a spiritual meaning. For this reason, the large number of women—a vexatious question even for great statesmen—furnished his Majesty with an opportunity to display his wisdom, and to rise from the low level of worldly dependence to the eminence of perfect freedom. The imperial palace and household are therefore in the best order. [6, 44]

He says that although there were more than five thousand women in the harem, the Emperor had given each her own apartment. He had divided them into various departments and ensured that each performed her duties. The Emperor had appointed "chaste women" as supervisors of each department, and one performed the duties of a scribe. In this manner, everything was in order in the Imperial offices. The women were paid generous monthly stipends, ranging between 1,610 and 1,028 rupees for the senior ones to 51 to 20 for the attendants to 40 to 2 rupees for the lowest ranks of servants. An intelligent and diligent female scribe belonged to the staff of the private audience chamber of the Palace and supervised all the expenditures. When a woman wanted to buy something, she had to contact the bookkeepers of the seraglio, who sent a memorandum to this scribe. The interior of the harem was guarded by serious and active women, the most trusted of whom were stationed before the apartments of Her Majesty. The eunuchs were positioned outside the harem and, at a suitable distance from them, there was a guard of loyal Rajputs.

The harems of the potentates were so closely guarded that as late as the nineteenth century not even the wives of accredited diplomats were allowed to visit them. The women of the local aristocracy had first to apply to the eunuchs when they wished to enter the Imperial harem. Various travelers report from Persia [30, VI, 12 ff.] and India [108, II, 332] of uniformed female battalions who guarded the harems.

In Court harems of the later period, women filled the same offices as those held by men in the parts of the palaces reserved for male courtiers. They included a female general of musketeers, female prayer leaders, treasurers, physicians, supervisors of the linen department, coffee stewardesses, cooks, tailors, and shoemakers.

Regarding the harem of the Mogul Emperor Aurangzēb (d. 1707), Manucci, a Venetian, reports that officials who worked outside the harem but in the Palace were given their instructions by ladies appointed for the purpose on those days when the Emperor did not leave the harem. "All the persons employed in these offices," he says of these ladies, "are carefully selected; they have much wit and judgment, and know all that is passing in the Empire. For the officials outside are required to send written reports into the *maḥal* of all that the king ought to know." Eunuchs were responsible for communications between the two parts of the Palace. Public and secret "news reporters" of the Empire had to summarize the most important news in a kind of newspaper once a week. These reports were usually read to the ruler at about nine o'clock in the evening by ladies of the harem so that he could know what was going on in his realm. In addition, "spies" had to send in weekly reports about other important matters, these mainly concerning the doings of the princes, who were his potential rivals. [108, II, 331] Aurangzēb thus seems to have concerned himself with much of the business of government from within his harem with the assistance of sagacious harem ladies. It may certainly be assumed that he was also counseled by them.

For centuries, the ladies of the princely harems were recruited from subjugated tribes, and included Greeks, Armenians, Georgians, Circassians, and Slavs. When they joined the harem, they were usually given an imposing name with a beautiful meaning. To begin with, Arabic names were preferred in the harems of Turkey, Persia, and India, but Per-

sian names subsequently predominated. Thus empresses and princesses at the Mogul Court in India in the second half of the seventeenth century had such names as Tāj Mahall, "Crown of the Palace"; Nūr Mahall, "Light of the Palace"; Nūr Jahān, "Light of the World"; Nūr un-Nisā Khānom, "Light of Women"; or Dorr-e Dorrān Begom, "Pearl of Pearls." Female slaves of the harem at this period had such names as Gol-andām, "Rose Figure"; Gol-ānār, "Pomegranate Blossom"; Banafseh, "Violet"; or Gol-rang, "Rose Color." [108, II, 333 ff.]

Chardin reports that in Persia it was considered a privilege for noble families to provide a daughter for the royal harem when this was demanded by the ruler. Not only were her close relatives then paid a kind of pension, but her family hoped that she would be able to influence the monarch in their favor and assist their progress at Court.

The Queen Mother was in charge of the royal harem and was usually a very strict mistress. Just as all those whom she supervised had duties according to their rank and were watched, they, too, checked those subordinate to them. The ruler occasionally gave away some of the ladies of his harem, but of course only those who were not of free origin and were not his favorites. They were given an appropriate trousseau, and were a special honor for the recipient, usually a close friend, whose wife they then became. For the other ladies, there was scarcely any chance of ever leaving the harem again, particularly if they had borne the ruler's children. Only the mother of the first-born son could consider herself fortunate; the mothers of subsequent sons, especially in Persia and Turkey during the late Middle Ages, had to live in constant fear for their lives and those of their children. If they were allowed to live, they were practically prisoners, especially when the ruler, on whom they depended, died and another succeeded to the throne.

The Italian Pietro della Valle describes a particular pleasure of the ladies of the royal harem in seventeenth-century Persia. They went hunting in an elevated cabin when men were present and, from this perch, shot with guns. When there were no men present, he relates, "they ride on horseback and display their dexterity both with the sword and with arrows." [173, II, 142b] There are many miniature paintings that show ladies on horseback, hunting and playing polo. (Fig. 68) It will be noticed, as observed by della Valle, too, that sidesaddles were not used, and the women straddled the horse "like a horseman with one foot on this side and the other on that." [173, II, 12b]

Since the standard of education was more advanced than that of middle-class women, at least among the higher-ranking ladies of the princely harems, they also engaged in reading. Manucci relates that the ladies in the harem of the

Indian dancer.

Mogul Emperor Aurangzēb liked to read such illustrious works of Persian literature as Sa'di's *Golistān* and *Bostān*.

The links of the princely harem with the outside world were maintained by eunuchs. The exclusion of high-ranking women from public life necessitated such sexless beings, although the Koran and the traditions prohibited the castration of man and beast. However, castration had been practiced in the Ancient Orient and Byzantium, and here, as in other areas of social life, the established practice proved more powerful than the later prohibition. The devout Moslem left castration to Jews or Christians and purchased his eunuchs from them. The privilege of guarding the inner gate to the harem was mostly given to a guard of black eunuchs, while white eunuchs watched over the outer gate.

With the division into male and female societies, special trades for women became necessary. Mention has already been made of women who laid out dead females and who served as midwives. In addition, an investigation of the situation of women in Egypt at the time of the Mamlūks brought to light the following female professions, which must also have existed in the other Islamic countries: the bath attendant, matchmaker, trader who supplied goods to the harem and often brought the latest gossip as well, a kind of hairdresser who plaited the hair of young girls as part of wedding preparations, and finally professional female mourners, who attended funerals and with their loud cries and lamentations expressed the grief of those present.

The most common trade for women of the lower classes was spinning, which was done at home. Miniatures often depict women either with a spindle under the arm or, in later periods, at the spinning wheel. (Fig. 1) Pietro della Valle has this to say about the fine embroidery of Turkish women in the seventeenth century: "...the women are highly skilled in the working of linen and other materials and also of silks of different colors, also in the embroidering of silver and gold on delicate and transparent cloth so that the same thing appears on one side as on the other; and they know how to make with this gold such a shading that nothing can be more beautiful than this." [173, I, 24b] In *Thousand and One Nights*, there is mention of an unusual trade for a woman: As the daughter of a pigeon-post official in Bagdad, the astute Dalīla raised carrier pigeons and passed this trade on to her daughter, who was just as wily as her mother.

Like many other things forbidden by religious law, one of the oldest professions in the world, prostitution, which was strictly prohibited by the Koran and *Sunna*, was not unknown in Islamic society. Chardin records that in 1666 there were reputed to be fourteen thousand registered prostitutes in Isfahan, the illustrious metropolis of the Safavids. These women were also listed as taxpayers—"non olet" obviously being the rule almost everywhere. They lived together in special caravanseries, and were under the control of a female "superior" who "hired them out." Accompanied by one or two servants, they rode on horseback to those who had ordered them. [30, II, 211 ff.]

Olearius relates that there was a certain place in Qazvin frequented by numerous merchants where, when night had fallen, "many *cahbeha* or immoral women, with their faces concealed, stand in a long line and offer their shameful wares. Behind each of them is an old woman, known as the *dalal*, who carries the bed clothes, namely a cushion and a blanket filled with cotton, on her back and holds an unlit lamp in her hand. When men wish to come to an arrangement with them, the *delal* lights the lamp, and with this the man sees each *cahbeha's* face and orders the one who pleases him most to follow him." [126, 483] Evidently to avoid offending the morality then current, Olearius also says that he had not seen this for himself but had heard it from others.

The everyday life of female slaves varied, depending on the family to which they belonged or the status they held in the harem. The most fortunate were certainly those who were married by the man who bought them or acquired them as booty in war. Of course, he had to set them free first. In *Sura* 4: 3, the Koran recommends marriage with a slave, and in *Sura* 2: 221 it is even affirmed that marriage with a Moslem slave is better than marriage with a beautiful pagan. In the traditions, it is reported in several places that a man who has a slave educated—that is, well educated—then sets her free and marries her shall receive a double reward. [24, 49, 16] On the other hand, there is a *hadith*, presumably originated by race-conscious Arabs, which affirms that whoever sets a slave free and then marries her is like somebody who mounts his own slaughter camel. [179, 141] During the reign of the Omayyads, when race-proud Arabs predominated, marriages of this kind were despised, even though the law approved them. At that time, for instance, a free woman rejected a proposal of marriage from a man because his mother was a slave. [78, 262] The reign of the Abbāsids had a leveling effect in this respect, indeed to such an extent that only three of the Abbāsid Khalifs had mothers who were free Arabs. Slaves could consequently aspire to the most exalted ranks in society, and not a few, in such a position, attempted to exert an influence on politics as well. More of this later.

The bel-esprit Jāhiz (d. 869), who indeed—like many writers—was not a pure-bred Arab himself, finds that most free men prefer slaves to free women and states that the reason for this is that a man can take a good look at a slave and get to know her before he buys her. In the case of a free woman, however, he has to rely on the judgment of other women. But women, in his view, have no eye for female beauty and know nothing of what men want from women and of the qualities in which men and women have to be compatible. He asserts that men are more perspicacious when it is a question of women.

A few decades later, in the *Unique Necklace*, an encyclopedic work of *adab* literature by the Andalusian Ibn Abd Rabbihi, it is said that one has to be surprised at men who take it upon themselves to approach a free woman after they have gotten to know slaves. "A slave is bought with the eyes and is returned when she has faults. But a free woman is like a fetter on the neck of the man to whom she comes." [77, 129] Clearly this text reveals the prevailing opinion of women and reflects their degradation. There is also a verse in this work which states that one should not despise a man because his mother was a Byzantine, Negress, or Persian. Mothers, it is affirmed, are only receptacles in which the seed is placed. Only the fathers are important in respect of origin. [77, 128]

In Islam during the Middle Ages, fantastic prices were paid for beautiful slaves who had a literary and artistic education. In an age in which free Moslem women, like their free Greek sisters in their time, were practically excluded from public life, such slaves celebrated one glorious triumph after another in the salons of the aristocracy. The slave traders used every trick of the trade to match their "merchandise" to the ideals of beauty current at the time, and there was so much of this merchandise from so many parts of the world that slave women could be classified by their suitability for different spheres of life, from domestic work to love and child rearing to the fine arts and the sciences. In the first half of the eleventh century, a Christian physician, in his guide to slave purchasing, describes the ideal female slave as a Berber, who is "exported" at the age of nine years, spends three years each in Medina and Mecca, and then, at fifteen, comes to the Land of the Two Rivers to be educated in the fine arts. When she is then sold at the age of twenty-five, she is a combination of the wit of the woman of Medina with the mildness of the inhabitant of Mecca and the education of the Land of the Two Rivers—a piquant blend of wisdom and femininity that was greatly appreciated at that time.

Slaves of this kind were well aware of their value. In certain circumstances, they could insist that the slave dealer sell them only to men who met with their approval. Indeed, they were even able to lend financial assistance to the men who bought them, since they were allowed to possess assets of their own. Their worth was consequently lauded in many fine words to an interested public in something like the following manner: "You merchants, you men of money! Who will begin the bidding for this slave /the Mistress of the Moon/ the Pearl of High Profit/ her name is Zumurrud, "Emerald," the embroiderer of curtains, /the object of desire/the bliss of him who yearns for love?" [164, II, 210]

Despite their great value and the esteem in which they were held, these slaves were exposed to the moods and whims of their owners until they were set free. Thus the Fātimid Khalif al-Hākim, in 1009, in an attack of religious mania, had all his favorite concubines put in crates, which were then weighed down with stones, nailed up, and cast into the Nile since he had decided to abandon sensual pleasure. In *Thousand and One Nights*, a beautiful slave is made to work in the kitchen since she will not yield to the ugly son of the woman who owns her. The jewelry and silken garments given to her by her former owner, a wealthy man, are stripped from her.

Kitchen work and domestic tasks were the sphere of the less attractive and less well-educated slaves, and these were often the black ones. Negresses were usually less highly regarded than white slaves, even though many men, including some of high rank, prized them as sexual partners. From the eleventh century on, the sons of black mothers were also able to attain high positions.

It was precisely because of the uncertainty of their fate that slaves needed their natural wit and shrewdness to defend themselves—and they were rewarded by the recognition given such gifts in the Arab world of the Middle Ages. "What is given to the slaves depends on the bad qualities of the free women" were the pert and cynical words of a slave to her master when he, on her couch, complained about the bad character of his wife [78, 193], and this obviously at a time when free women were more highly regarded than slaves. The son of a man abused one of his father's slaves with the words "You whore!" to which she sarcastically replied, "If I were that, then I would have borne your father a son like you." [78, 228]

The anecdotes that have been handed down indicate that slaves often had enough self-assurance not to flatter their owners all the time; they often expressed themselves freely in the melodious verses they recited.

We will now take a look at some women who are outstanding by reason of their artistic talents, political ambitions, or life style.

Women
in Islamic History

It has already been noted that the Koran assigns women a social position subordinate to men and that even at an early stage religious tradition required that they subject themselves to the will of men. This culminated in a later period in the saying alleged to be from the Prophet: "If it is proper for a human being to kneel in adoration to another human being, then only for a woman to kneel to a man." [120, VI, 411] However, despite attempts from a very early stage to keep women out of public life, there were always women, who, by reason of a strong personality and/or special gifts, were outstanding members of the society of their time and played a role in the history or cultural life of Islamic countries.

Women even had a direct or indirect part in the emergence of Islam. Among the first is Khadija Bint Khowaylid, Mohammed's first wife. She had been widowed twice before she married Mohammed and had also had children. She increased the considerable fortune that she had inherited by fitting out caravans for Syria and by engaging in trade. At that time in Mecca, this was not unusual for a woman. She appointed Mohammed, who was then 25 years of age and, as an orphan, not very well off, as the leader of one of these caravans. Since he performed this task to her satisfaction and, it may be supposed, made a pleasing impression on her, she—forty years old at the time—proposed marriage to him through the agency of another woman—likewise a procedure that was not unusual in those days. For Mohammed, who had lost his mother at an early age, marriage to the respected and prosperous Khadija represented material security, and the Koran *Sura* 93:6, "Did He not find thee an orphan and give (thee) shelter?" and verse 8 of the same *Sura*, "Did He not find thee poor, and enrich (thee)?" are certainly a reference to this. She bore him seven children, but of these only the four daughters survived. It was she, too, who gave him moral support when he experienced the first revelations which initially had an overwhelming and terrifying effect on him. She prayed secretly with her husband and became the first follower of Islam at a time when the people around Mohammed considered him a liar or a dreamer.

While Khadija was alive, she remained the only wife of the Prophet whom Western critics like to censure for his sensuality, since he subsequently maintained a larger harem than that accorded by the Koran to his followers. Khadija was probably able to insist on this by virtue of her position. Even decades later, Mohammed's child-wife Ā'isha was still jealous of the memory of the "toothless old woman," as she called her in anger, for whom, she said, Allah had given the Prophet a better one as a replacement. But Mohammed chided her with the words: "He has not given me a better one. She believed in me when no one else did. She considered me to be truthful when the people called me a liar. She helped me with her fortune when the people had left me nothing. Allah gave me children from her while he gave me none from other women." [82, VI, 117ff.]

It was only after Khadija died at the age of 65 that Mohammed turned to other women. As already said, however, most if not all of the marriages of the Prophet of Islam were also inspired by his desire to keep the still young community together. Thus his favorite wife, Ā'isha, on whom the discussion will now be centered, was the daughter of one of his first followers, the later Khalif Abū Bakr, for whom he felt a special affection. Ā'isha was proud not only that she was the cause of revelations, as we have already seen, but also because she was the only wife of Mohammed with whom he obviously felt so relaxed that he received revelations in her presence. Despite or perhaps because of her special position, she was particularly jealous and, after Mohammed's death, boasted of her other advantages as well over her "co-wives." Not only was she the only virgin among the wives of the Prophet, but he shared with her the same bowl for washing, prayed in her presence, and was tended by her at his request during the last days of his life. He died in her lap, and was buried under the floor of her living room. At the time, Ā'isha was a young woman of 18 years in full bloom.

Mention should be made here of a happening that took place in Mohammed's harem and was the cause of a revelation because it shows that at times even Mohammed's wives were not subservient. Arab history relates that the later Khalif Omar, after the Moslems had emigrated to Medina, said: "We, the men of the Qoraysh tribe, had supremacy over the women. But after we arrived at Medina, we came to people who were governed by their women; our women then began to acquire the customs of the inhabitants of Medina." He then relates: "My wife was angry with me and began to quarrel with me, but I forbade her to do so. She objected: 'Why do you deny me the right to quarrel with you? The wives of the Prophet also quarrel with him, and today one of them has even left him and has not come back until nightfall.'" [87, VIII, 131] At this, he hurried in consternation to his daughter Hafsa, one of the wives of Mohammed, and urged her to do no wrong to the Prophet since otherwise the fury of Allah might strike her. He also said that she should not be misled by Ā'isha since the latter had a special position. He informed Abū Bakr who immediately put Ā'isha straight. If she wanted goods of this world—and this was what it was about—she should ask him for them and not Mohammed, who could not pay for them. The two men then went to the proud Umm Salama, another wife of Mohammed from the respected tribe of the Makhzūm, but here they met with a cool reception, since Umm Salama said this to them: "What business is it of yours what goes on here? The Envoy of Allah stands over us, and if he had wanted to forbid us anything he would already have done so. Who should we then ask if not him? Does anybody interfere perhaps in your family affairs? We did not ask you to do so." [87, VIII, 129] The two left, having achieved nothing. The other wives of Mohammed thanked her for her courage and said that they had not dared to say anything like that to Omar and Abū Bakr. Mohammed withdrew from his wives for 29 days, and was greatly troubled. However, he succeeded in restoring order in his harem. He received the revelation *Sura* 33:28, which confronts his wives with the alternative of choosing the worldly life with its goods and then being sent away by Mohammed or of deciding in favor of Allah, his Prophet, and the life to come and being rewarded in Paradise. Ā'isha was the first to accept this, then Hafsa, and finally his other wives, one after another. This story shows that Mohammed did not attempt to convince his wives by insisting on male superiority and giving them no choice; instead, aware of his status as the Prophet, he won them over with diplomacy and kindness.

After Mohammed's death in 632, Ā'isha and the other widows lived together as the "Mothers of the Faithful." When, after a reign of two years, Abū Bakr, the first Khalif, found himself on the point of death, he also entrusted himself to the care of Ā'isha, who was obviously his favorite child. When he died, he was buried, like his successor, Khalif Omar, next to Mohammed under the floor of Ā'isha's room. It is said that at his death Ā'isha addressed the faithful in moving words of resounding rhyming prose. It is related in literature that Hafsa did the same for her father, Omar, just as Fātima is said to have delivered the funeral speech for Mohammed. [78, 10 ff.; 40 ff.; 23 ff.]

Ā'isha now became a respected authority on what Mohammed had said or done in certain situations; that is, on his *Sunna*. She was much in demand—women asked her for advice about questions of clothing and cosmetics conforming to religious law, and even respected men consulted her on questions of religion and the way life was to be led, since she, of all his wives who were still alive, had been closest to the Prophet and had obviously been the sharpest observer. Subsequently, more than two thousand traditions were attributed to her, but only a little more than two hundred of these have been included in the collections of Bokhārī and of Moslem which are regarded as canonical.

Besides having a good knowledge of Ancient Arabic poetry and genealogy, Ā'isha is also reported to have pronounced the fundamental rules of Arabic-Islamic ethics. She is said to have affirmed that noble qualities of character were "honesty of speech, reliability, truthfulness and steadfastness in misfortune, the provision of protection for friend and neighbor, and readiness to give aid in the ups and downs of life, to feed the needy, to treat slaves with kindness, and to revere one's parents." [78, 21 ff.]

Ā'isha was also not afraid to tell the third Khalif Othmān what she thought of his personnel policy—he liked to give leading positions to members of his own tribe. Following the murder of Othmān in 656, she once more found herself the center of public attention in sensational circumstances. Responding to the call for vengeance for the murdered Khalif, she joined forces with two early followers of Mohammed, Talha and Obaydallāh, adversaries of the newly elected Khalif Ali. The three of them went with their followers to Iraq, since they hoped to find further support there. A battle took place not far from Basra in 656 which came to be known as the Camel Battle from the camel on which Ā'isha was seated in a litter and from which she urged on the combatants. Although Ā'isha employed all her eloquence and strategic skill, the battle was lost for her and her followers after Ali, perceiving the role that Ā'isha was playing, cut the pasterns of her camel. Talha and Obaydallāh were killed.

Ā'isha's litter was covered with so many arrows that it was compared with a hedgehog, but nothing had happened to her. Ali allowed her to return to Mecca with an appropriate retinue after she declared publicly that there had never been any disputes between the two of them apart from those that occur from time to time between people related by marriage, and Ali confirmed her statement. It is reported that she later deeply regretted this period of her life since much blood was spilled in vain. The childless Ā'isha is even supposed to have said that rather than bear the Prophet ten sons who were as brave as her bravest followers in the battle she would have preferred not to have gone to battle. As late as the early 1940's, a well-known Egyptian author pointed to the Camel Battle as an example of why women should stay at home and not interfere in public affairs. [12]

Ā'isha died in 678, at the age of 64. In the subsequent historiography of Islam, she was depicted as a devout ascetic whose principal wish was to live as a true believer.

Of the other women in the family of the Prophet, special mention should be made of his youngest daughter, Fātima, although she did not play the same role in the early Islamic community as Ā'isha. Early Islamic historiography emphasizes how hard and austere her life was. The bed on which she slept with her husband, Mohammed's cousin, the subsequent Khalif Ali, was the woolly side of a sheepskin, the inner side of which they used during the day for holding the fodder for the camel which brought them water. Their pillow was a cushion of tanned leather, filled with palm fibers. Incidentally, Mohammed forbade his cousin to take a second wife, justifying this by saying that what caused pain to his daughter grieved him as well.

There seems to have been some rivalry between Ā'isha and Fātima. It is said that Fātima was sent to Mohammed by his other wives to protest the preferential position enjoyed by Ā'isha. The Prophet is said to have replied that Fātima, as his daughter, must also like what was pleasing to him. It may be assumed that Fātima was especially close to Mohammed, since she was the only one of his children whose offspring did not die prematurely. He could see his life continued in Hasan and Hosayn, her sons and his grandsons.

As the mother of the Prophet's grandsons, she was of particular importance in later Islamic history, especially for the Shi'ites. Some branches of the Shi'a, for instance the Nusayris, almost deified Fātima, who was given the additional name of "the Shining One," precisely because she was the mother of those who, in the view of the Shi'ites, had the right to supreme power after Ali. Immediately after Mohammed's death, she, together with her husband Ali, had called on the faithful to pay homage to Ali and not to Abū Bakr. Ali swore an oath of allegiance to Abū Bakr only after the death of Fātima at the age of 28, a few months after Mohammed. The gnostic circles of the Shi'a believe that she will play an important role at the end of Time, since, through implacable

vengeance, she will ensure that justice will again prevail. An entire dynasty, the Fātimids, ruling initially in North Africa from 909 and then in Egypt and Syria up to 1171, took their name from the daughter of Mohammed, since their founder reinforced his claim to power with the assertion that he was a descendant of Fātima.

Women have always been prominent in the Islamic religion, especially with regard to Islamic mysticism. Illustrious Islamic mystics, who generally were not well disposed toward women, nevertheless spoke favorably of a pious woman, as illustrated by the following quotation: "An irresponsible woman is worse than a hundred irresponsible men. But a devout woman will receive the same reward as a hundred devout men." [10,64] It was believed that women were exposed to greater temptations than men and possessed a lesser degree of resistance. Another sage said: "When a woman walks on the path of God like a man, she cannot be described as a woman" [16, I, 59]; that is, she loses the negative female characteristics she was thought to be born with.

The first name to acquire fame in Islamic mysticism was that of a woman. Rābi'a al-Adawiyya was a freed slave, born in 714 or 717 in Basra. Through her asceticism and unbounded love for God, in comparison with whom everything of this world was insignificant, she achieved fame and became an example for later mystics. Popular belief associated her life with the kinds of wonders that are also attributed to saintly figures in other religions. It is related that once when she was on a pilgrimage to Mecca, her sumpter mule collapsed and died in the middle of the desert. Other travelers in the caravan offered her their assistance, but she replied that she had not set out on the journey relying on them. When she was alone, she prayed: "O God, is this how the weak, a woman, a stranger, or a sick man are treated? You summon me to Your house and then You allow my mule to die halfway on the journey and leave me in the desert alone." Scarcely had she ended her prayer, so it is said, when the mule moved and stood up. She loaded her baggage on it and continued her journey. [16, I, 61]

An illustrious figure was Fātima of Nishapur (d. 849), who discussed important questions with the most famous mystics of her time and obviously guided her husband in religious and practical matters. In the course of her long discussions with the mystic Bāyazid Bistāmi, she behaved in a relaxed manner and raised her veil, with the result that her husband became jealous. When Bāyazid noticed one day that she had dyed the tips of her fingers with henna and asked her why she did so, she resolutely replied: "If you have discovered that I have dyed my fingers, then you have looked at me with other eyes than those of intellectual friendship. The familiarity between us must now come to an end!" [10, 64]

Even today, Nafisa, greatgranddaughter of Hasan, grandson of the Prophet, is still revered as a saint in Egypt. She was born in Mecca in 762–3, grew up in Medina, and subsequently went with her husband—some say with her brother—to Egypt. Her knowledge of theological matters made her so famous that even her great contemporary, the jurist ash-Shāfi'ī, paid a visit to her to hear her relate traditions. She was famed not only for her thirty pilgrimages but also for her strict asceticism and charity to the poor. When people complained to her about the injustice of the Egyptian governor of that time, she is said to have stood in his path and to have handed him a note in which she accused him of tyranny and called on him to be more just. She died in Cairo in 823–4 and, at the request of the local population, was buried there. A later biographer says that her mausoleum was famed for the fact that prayers said there were heard by God.

Many women combined a devout life with learnedness in religion, for instance, Shuhda Bint al-Ibari, known as Fakhr an-Nisā, "the Pride of Women," who died at more than 90 years of age in Bagdad in 1178. Like Zaynab Bint ash-Sha'rī, who was over a hundred years old when she died in 1218–9, in Nishapur, she heard the most illustrious teachers of her time. Even when they were advanced in years, both women had a large number of pupils, some of whom became respected scholars.

A woman by the name of Fātima Bint Ahmed Ibn Yahyā became prominent in the field of religious law, which she discussed with her father. It is reported that her husband, an *imām*, consulted her when baffled by legal problems he wanted to explain to his pupils. She gave him the appropriate explanations, and he passed them on to his pupils. When they were still unable to understand, they said: "That does not come from you yourself but from (her) behind the curtain." [93, IV, 31 ff.]

There are no monasteries in Islam such as those that played a great part in the religious and cultural life of medieval Europe, but even at a relatively early stage there did exist convents for women who sought the mystical approach to the worship of God or who wanted to lead a devout life. In Egypt of the Mamlūk period, a *shaykhah*, a woman sheikh, led prayers and preached. Female saints were and are known throughout the Islamic world. These saints also have shrines to which women come who seek refuge and comfort in times of distress.

It was probably in India that the cult of female saints flourished most. A whole series of miniatures from the Mogul period depicts women hermits surrounded by young people of both sexes. One of the saints of Mogul India who achieved fame was the eldest daughter of the Emperor Shah Jahān, named Jahān-ārā, whose book about her initiation as

a mystic bears witness to the profoundness of her faith and her mystical understanding. Sidqī, a woman of Turkey who died in 1703, was a poetess and a mystic. Wealthy women were known for their donations to Sūfi sheikhs (mystics) and for the material support given to Dervish orders.

The early historians mention only one woman, Umm Waraqa Bint Abdallāh, who acted as the prayer leader of a mixed community, namely, that of her clan, which was so numerous that it had its own muezzin. Mohammed himself is said to have instructed her to serve as prayer leader. She was also one of the few women who handed down the Koran before it was put in final written form. In addition, she had such a great desire to be known as a martyr that she bade Mohammed to allow her to take part with his forces in the Battle of Badr so that she could tend the wounded. From that time on, Mohammed is said to have called her "the Martyress." [87, VIII, 335]

There is also a report from this early Islamic period of a woman who not only acted as a nurse but also fought in some of the Moslems' battles. Her name was Umm Omāra. With her husband and two sons, she took part in one battle with the intention of tending the wounded and bringing them water. But then she fought boldly with the others, her garments tied around her waist. She lost a hand in one battle, and was also wounded several times. [87, VIII, 301 ff.)

In the first decades of Islam, it was not at all unusual for women like Ā'isha to take part in battles, encouraging the combatants with passionate declamations in rhyming prose from their camel-borne litters. In the battle between Khalif Ali and his adversary, the later Khalif Mo'āwiya, at Siffin in 657, there were several women on Ali's side who gave vocal support to his warriors. Even after this, Mo'āwiya must still have regarded them as exceptional personages, since he ordered them to come to him so that he could converse with them and ask them what had led them to act as they had at that time. All the women asserted that they did not remember the passionate words with which they had encouraged the combatants. But Mo'āwiya remembered them, and he quoted the words they had used. When Mo'āwiya asked Zarqā the reason for her behavior, she laconically replied: "O Commander of the Faithful, it has already happened quite differently. Whoever ponders on it, sees more and what happens happens." When the Khalif bade her to ask for something for herself, she sagaciously replied that she had sworn never to request anything from a prince against whom she had fought, but he was generous anyway. In this way and thanks to his generosity, she received a prosperous fief. [78, 50 ff.]

In another battle in the first century of Islam, the Moslem women used a trick to help their men. They turned their veils into battle banners and moved up behind the men with "standards" flying. The enemy, assuming that reinforcements were arriving for the Moslems, decided they would be no match for them and so retreated.

Female trickery in a good cause, but more often in a bad one, is a popular theme in the literatures of Islamic countries. Old women, in particular, have the reputation of possessing great cunning, but for a person who has no power and no resources at all at her disposal, this can actually be a matter of life or death. In Morocco, there is even a saying that "What the devil does in a year an old woman does in an hour" [181, 68], and at one point in *Thousand and One Nights* it is said that "Bagdad is full of women who trick men." [164, IV, 731] Whoever accuses women of trickery can even refer to the Joseph *Sura* of the Koran where it is said of the wife of Potiphar, who tears Joseph's shirt from his back, "It is some of your guile, verily your guile is mighty." (12:28)

The first century of Islam was characterized not only by women who were bold and courageous but also by proud beauties who played such an important role in the social life of their time that romances were woven around them in the literary tradition.

Sukayna was a granddaughter of Khalif Ali, the daughter of his son Hosayn, who was killed at Kerbela in battle and is still revered by the Shi'ites as a martyr. Sukayna was not part of the pious opposition to the worldly rule of the Omayyads that gathered in her time in Mecca and Medina, the holy cities of Islam. Rather, she reflected the high-spirited society which, untroubled by political wrangles—Damascus, the residence of the Khalifs, was a long way away—wanted to enjoy its wealth and indulge in luxury. Music and poetry flourished in the Hijāz—a subject that will be examined later.

The attitude of these circles toward Islam is evident in a remark attributed to Sukayna. Asked why she was always so merry but her sister Fātima always so solemn, she replied that she had been named after her pre-Islamic greatgrandmother but her sister after her Islamic grandmother. Sukayna was famous not only for her beauty, humor, and practical jokes but also for her keenness and wit. She once assembled poets around her, had them declaim their latest works, and then judged and rewarded them according to the way the poets described their beloved or their relationship in the poems. She was known for her elegance, too. She wore her magnificent hair in a special style that was named after her when it became fashionable. However, when men also began to imitate her, the pious Khalif Omar Ibn Abd al-Azīz had them whipped and their heads shorn.

Sukayna must also have been bold and courageous. When she had a tumor removed below her eye—naturally without an anesthetic—she endured the operation without moving and without a sigh of pain. She was left with a scar that was considered especially attractive. She was married at least four times, but the sources differ as to the sequence and names of her husbands. At least, they, too, came from respected families. Special attention is devoted by the sources to her marriage with Zayd Ibn Amr, a grandson of Khalif Othmān. She married him on condition that he would never repudiate her on his initiative, nor touch another woman, nor refuse her anything she wished—she forced her moods on him—, allow her to live where she wanted, and not contradict her in anything; otherwise he would have to repudiate her at her wish. The two often quarreled. When, because he was angry with her, he went to one of his estates where he had numerous female slaves at his disposal and remained there for seven months, she went to the Governor of Medina and lodged a complaint. He had Zayd brought to Medina and ordered one of his subordinates to judge between them. Sukayna provoked the judge to such an extent that he threatened her in the following words: "If you were not a woman, I would have you whipped." A violent altercation broke out between the two, and when one of those present urged her to be reasonable she abused him as well. It is said that the judge became nervous because his wife was sitting in a niche and could hear everything uttered by Sukayna in her rage. Zayd, who does not seem to have had much courage, "kept as close as possible to the raised seat of the judge as if, from fear, he wanted to creep into it." Sukayna called to him: "Have a good look at me! From now on you will no longer see my face." The Governor of Medina, who had waited in the same building for the end of the meeting and then received a report of it, "laughed till his sides split," so it is said. [5b, XVI, 155ff.]

Sukayna's rival in beauty and elegance was the capricious Ā'isha Bint Talha, through her mother a granddaughter of the first Khalif Abū Bakr. For a time, they were both married to the same husband, Mus'ab Ibn az-Zubayr, who was as handsome, chivalrous, and generous as he was hard and unyielding. Of Ā'isha it is reported that she never veiled her face. Her husband Mus'ab did not approve of this at all, and he urged her to observe the customs. But she countered this by saying: "God, the Almighty, has honored me with beauty. I want the people to see this and understand what rank I enjoy before them. I will not veil myself. Nobody can reproach me with a fault." [5b, XI, 176]

She, too, was married a number of times, and it is told that she liked to annoy her husbands by lauding in the most fulsome tones the virtues of a deceased husband in comparison with the one she was married to at the time. Mus'ab is said to have admired her for her beauty, her carelessness, her attractive figure—her large proportions at the rear are especially lauded—her will power, and her virtuousness. It is also reported, however, that he was only able to make her obedient after verbal abuse and blows. One day, he spread precious pearls over her lap as she slept. This spoiled person was awakened by this, and only grumbled, "I would have preferred to sleep." [5b, XI, 181] His secretary once promised Mus'ab to help force her to give in. Mus'ab encouraged him by saying: "Do as you please, for she is the best of all earthly things I have." One night, in her presence, the secretary had two black slaves dig a grave in her house and told her that Mus'ab had ordered him to bury her alive in it. She was so alarmed by this that he was able to make her promise to be more obliging to her husband in future. [5b, XI, 181 ff.]

Ā'isha Bint Talha's next husband bribed her maidservant so that he really could spend the wedding night with his new wife. When this husband died, she rejected all subsequent suitors and never married again.

Incidentally, she was so highly respected that the Governor of Mecca agreed to delay the hour of prayer so that she could complete the circumambulation of the Ka'ba, while on a pilgrimage. She could not, or would not, prevent his dismissal, which resulted from this episode. Her beauty was lauded in many verses. It is also reported, however, that she was the equal of learned men from the ruling house of the Omayyads in her knowledge of Ancient Arabic history and its battles, Arabic poetry, and astronomy.

It is apparent that in the early days of Islam women from noble families, especially when they had property of their own, not only had the same de facto rights as their husbands but were occasionally able to demonstrate their superiority as well. It is related that one day Umm Salama, who had been married to two respected men from the family of the ruling Omayyads, happened to notice the young Abū l-Abbās as-Saffāh, who was later to become the first Abbāsid Khalif. His handsome appearance attracted her, and she sent a maidservant to him with a proposal of marriage. At the same time, she sent him money for the dowry. On their wedding night, she wore so many jewels that he could not touch her. And even when she removed them and changed her clothes, he was unable to demonstrate his prowess as a husband so that she had to console him by telling him that this also happened to other men on occasions. He then swore that he would never take a second wife nor a concubine. She bore him two children, and until he became Khalif, he decided nothing before obtaining her advice and approval.

It is said that one day one of the authors at his Court expressed his regret that as-Saffāh had restricted himself to only one woman. "O Commander of the Faithful," he said, "if you saw a tall, white-skinned maiden or a brown-skinned with dark lips or a yellow one with round hips, yea, those that have come to Kufa or Basra and are sweet-tongued, slight in stature, with a small waist and with curly locks around their temples, with dark eyes, firm breasts, dressed in beautiful garments and wearing fine jewels, you would see something wonderful." The Khalif liked the sound of this and bade him repeat his words. When his wife Umm Salama subsequently saw him sitting there lost in thought, she soon discovered what had been said to him. Seething with anger, she sent some men to the man of letters—Khālid Ibn Safwān was his name—with instructions to give him a good beating. Khālid allowed the men to enter in the belief that the Khalif wanted to reward him for his good advice, but he was bitterly disillusioned. Several days passed before he was in a fit state again to leave the house. When he then came, still groaning with pain, to the Khalif, who had sent for him, he noticed a slight movement in the curtain before a door and guessed that Umm Salama was behind it. The Khalif wanted to hear his words once more, but Khālid said to him that the Arabs derive the word *darra*, meaning "co-wife," from a root that also means "damage, misfortune." "None of those who had more than one wife was happy ... three wives are like three stones on which a pot is simmering, and four wives are the worst thing that can happen to a man, they make him gray, old, and sick." The Khalif constantly interrupted him, saying: "You certainly didn't say that." Nevertheless, Khālid also told the Khalif that virgins were like young men, only without testicles, that he had married a wise lady from a noble family and should not look around for other women. At this, peals of laughter came from behind the curtain, followed by words of approval. Khālid did indeed receive a rich reward eventually, but it was from the wife of the Khalif. [112, VI, 110–18]

Arwā (Umm Mūsā), wife of Khalif al-Mansūr, successor to as-Saffāh on the throne, traced her ancestry back to the Southern Arabian kings of the Himyarits. She also demanded written agreement from her husband that he would never take either a second wife or a concubine while she was alive. The Khalif subsequently regretted this declaration and wished to have it annulled. But his wife appealed to the supreme judge of Egypt, who was brought to Iraq solely for this purpose. His verdict was in favor of Arwā, since she was able to produce the marriage contract with the appropriate clause. When she died, in the tenth year of his reign, al-Mansūr established a large harem.

To his son by Arwā, the later Khalif al-Mahdī, who had a special weakness for women, al-Mansūr gave the fatherly advice that he not involve them in his private affairs, but this obviously went unheeded. Al-Mahdi was very much influenced by his concubine and later wife Khayzurān, "Bamboo Stem," mother of his two sons, Mūsā and Hārūn, and a daughter for whom al-Mahdi had such great affection that, clothed as a youth, she was allowed to accompany him on his travels. When she died, he publicly acknowledged the expressions of sympathy by his subjects.

During the reign of al-Mahdi, Khayzurān, although she had to share her spouse with co-wives and concubines, became so addicted to the intoxicating drug of power that she did not wish to abandon it when her son Mūsā al-Hādi ascended the throne in 785. In the first four months of his Khalifat, people still gathered around her and sought her advice, and veritable "processions pilgrimaged to her door," in the words of the historian Tabari. [162, VIII, 205 f.] This was too much for the young Khalif, who obviously attached more importance to getting his own way than his father had done. He, who had yielded to her every wish until then, used a pretext to refuse a request in harsh words; he also resisted her urgent pleas. He even said to her: "Women are not permitted by destiny to interfere in affairs of government. You have to pray, to praise Allah, to withdraw from the world, and to devote yourself to the service of Allah. Then you have to obey, as is proper for women." He threatened her in the following words: "Beware, if you do not heed my words ... If I hear that one of my chief people or servants is at your door, I will strike off his head and take his property. What are those processions which go to your door every day? Have you then no spindle to claim you or a copy of the Koran to call you to obedience and no house that shelters you? Be careful not to come to me to bore or reproach me!" [112, VI, 269 ff.] After this, the hatred between them became so great that each tried to have the other murdered. After Mūsā's premature death, which was not unconnected with Khayzurān, she made sure that her beloved son, Hārūn, would succeed to the throne.

Khayzurān was one of the richest women of her time, and her annual income, at the peak of her power, amounted to 160 million silver dirham. It is said that in her palace she had eighteen thousand gowns of embroidered brocade. When, on one occasion, she demanded even more from Mūsā al-Hādi, he put a complete warehouse at her disposal. This love of pomp and luxury was a great stimulus for the textile industry, of course, but she also invested her money in other undertakings. For instance, she had a canal built to the Iraqi town of Anbar. She had a secretary of her own for her business transactions.

After Khayzurān's death in 789—she could have hardly been fifty years of age—another woman soon assumed a similar position of power in the Khalif's harem and in the country:

Zubayda, cousin and wife of Khalif Hārūn ar-Rashid, known to us principally from *Thousand and One Nights*. In actual fact, her Islamic name was Amat al-Azīz. But since she was such a pretty and chubby child, her grandfather, Kalif al-Mansūr, called her Zubayda, "Butterflake" or "Marigold," when she danced on his knee. In 781–2, during the Khalifat of al-Mahdi, she became the wife of Hārūn ar-Rashid and fascinated him to such a degree that he almost gave up his claim to the throne in order to devote himself to her. Although he later had very many beautiful and artistically gifted concubines, she obviously continued to enjoy a favored position not only because of her royal origin but for her personality as well.

Zubayda was famous for her generosity to poets. She had a hundred female slaves in her palace who all recited the Koran in sets of ten verses, so that it sounded like the buzzing of a swarm of bees. At a time of drought, she had an aqueduct twelve miles long built from a spring in the Hijāz to Mecca, across valleys and hills. The man entrusted with the work objected that it would be very expensive, but she ordered him: "Build it, even when every stroke of the mattock costs a dinar!" And it is said that she spent 1.7 million dinar on this project. She also had houses, cisterns, and wells built in the Hijāz and along the frontier routes, and was active as a benefactress. [81, I, 337; 112, VIII, 297]

Islamic historiography, which likes to credit famous people with being the first to introduce this or that, affirms that Zubayda was the first to use vessels of gold and silver encrusted with jewels, the first to wear brocade gowns worth fifty thousand dinar each, and the first to recruit a palace guard of young men and girls to carry letters and bring messages. Finally, she is also said to have been the first to use candles of amber and to have worn sandals embroidered with jewels. She was thus considered responsible for the increasing pomp and splendor at the Khalif's Court.

Zubayda also tried to influence the succession to the throne. She wanted her beloved son Mohammed al-Amin, who was not very competent, however, to be Hārūn's successor, and not al-Ma'mūn, his son by a Persian concubine. When Hārūn then decided to leave all the Arab areas of the Empire and the throne to al-Amin and to give al-Ma'mūn the Persian areas under the sovereignty of his brother, Zubayda still reproached him with being unjust, since he had not ensured the support of the generals and major figures of the Empire for Amin. Hārūn then replied: "What business of yours (a woman) is the judgment of our actions and the experience of men?" [112, VI, 325 ff.] When discord subsequently arose between the two brothers in the course of which al-Amin was executed in 813, Zubayda went into mourning and wore gowns of haircloth. Like Ā'isha, the

The dinar of the Sultana Shajarat ad-Dorr bears the place and date of minting (Cairo 648h), the name of the Khalif al-Musta'sim bi-llāh and the surname and title of the Sultana.

favorite wife of Mohammed, she was urged to wreak vengeance, but she replied: "What interest have we women in this demand for a blood feud or in vaunting ourselves as heroes?" She sent al-Ma'mūn a poem in which she expressed her sorrow at the death of her son and her admiration for Ma'mūn, the new Khalif. He was so moved by this that he paid her his respect and also granted her a substantial *apanage*. Zubayda died in Bagdad in 831.

For centuries, Islam's attitude toward the idea of a woman on the throne was negative. It is true that the Koran mentions the legendary Queen of Saba without any deprecating comments but from about the eighth century on, *hadiths* such as these are found: "When men obey women, ruin is certain"; [82, V, 45] or, "A people which entrusts its affairs to a woman will have no success." [24, 92, 18] Nevertheless, in the course of Islamic history, there have always been women who influenced their leader husbands or sons on political questions. But rarely indeed and then only for a short time did women themselves ascend to a throne. For the most part, these women were children of their time, just as ruthless, cruel, scheming, and extravagant as their male counterparts. If they had not been so, they would probably have been unable to assert themselves.

In Egypt, there was the slave-sultana with the euphonious name of Shajarat ad-Dorr, "Pearl Tree." She was initially the slave and subsequently the wife of the last Ayyūbid ruler al-Malik as-Sālih, after she had borne him a son who died at an early age. Her husband died shortly after the Crusaders of Louis IX landed at Damietta. His son and successor Tūrānshāh was murdered immediately afterward. In this situation, she officially assumed the title of Sultan on May 2, 1250 and remained sovereign regent of Egypt until July 30 of the same year. A contemporary Arab historian described her as a "strong personality of great nobility ... and an exemplary way of life," who had been "much loved" by the Sultan. [150, 43] A Syrian historian of the same period wrote of her: "She was a Turk, the most cunning woman of her age, unmatched in beauty among women and in determination

among men." [150, 44] After her subjects had sworn the oath of allegiance to her, she carried on the business of government, signed the Sultan's decrees, and, as usual for an Islamic ruler, was mentioned in the Friday prayers as the sovereign. For the first time in an Islamic country, coins were minted bearing the title of a sultana. Under Tūrānshāh, a crushing defeat had been inflicted on the Crusaders, and a few days after the Sultana came to power, Damietta was returned to the Moslems. But then, when the oath of allegiance to the Sultana was required from the Syrian viceroy, a dispute broke out in the course of which the Mamlūk Emirs decided that they could not leave the reins of State in the hands of a woman and transferred power to Aybak, Supreme Commander of the armed forces. Shajarat ad-Dorr became his wife afterward. Arab historians generally present this dismissal as a tactical renunciation of the throne by the Sultana in favor of her future husband. However, the struggle between Syria and Egypt, which had allegedly been caused by the presence of a woman on the throne, increased in intensity after this step. It is not known exactly when Shajarat ad-Dorr married Aybak, but her Oriental contemporaries continue to describe her as the real regent who did what she wanted with the realm and issued orders which were obeyed. Of her relationship with her husband, a historian comments: "She dominated him, and he had nothing to say." [150, 79] There is also evidence that she continued to sign Sultan's decrees and was addressed as Sultana. Finally, when she heard that Aybak intended to take a daughter of the Prince of Mosul as a co-wife, she had her husband murdered. Since she had taken no steps with respect to his successor, rioting broke out in the course of which the murderers were crucified. Shajarat ad-Dorr's half-naked body was found in the moat of the citadel.

At almost the same time as Shajarat ad-Dorr, who later became the subject of legends in the popular Baybars novel, Sultana Raziyya ruled as sovereign in Delhi; her regency lasted three years, six months, and six days, from 1236 to 1240. Raziyya also came from a Turkish slave dynasty.

A Persian historian, who had met her in person and who always showered praise on the rulers of the dynasty anyway, writes of her: "Sultān Raziyyat was a great sovereign, and sagacious, just, beneficent, the patron of the learned, a dispenser of justice, the cherisher of her subjects, and of warlike talent, and was endowed with all the admirable attributes and qualifications necessary for kings; but, as she did not attain the destiny, in her creation, of being computed among men, of what advantage were all these excellent qualifications unto her?" [116, 637f.] Her father recognized her abilities and named her as his successor, although he had several sons. This caused dissatisfaction, however, among his subjects. The view was taken that since the ruler had sons he should have appointed one of these to succeed him. "Be pleased to remove this difficulty from our minds," they said, "as this deed does not seem advisable to your humble servants." [116, 638f.] But the Sultan was of the opinion that, unlike his daughter, none of his sons was capable of ruling his realm. When she ultimately ascended the throne, riots broke out, but she was able to suppress them. She won over most of her adversaries and gave them official positions. But then the Royal Master of the Horse, an Abyssinian, became the subject of her special favor, and this provoked the envy of the other Court officials and Emirs. Finally, Sultana Raziyya put aside women's clothing—a remarkably early form of female emancipation in Islam—and dressed as a man. She wore a turban and appeared thus in public, naturally without a veil, probably because she believed that this would enhance her authority and she would obtain firmer control of her empire. In 1239, rebellions again broke out among her liege-lords and Emirs, and this led to her arrest. The governor, to whom she had been entrusted for safekeeping, married her and sent troops to Delhi to recapture her throne for her. But Raziyya's brother, who had taken over her position, sent troops against her and her husband. Her forces deserted her and she and her husband were killed in 1240.

In a biographical lexicon by an Arab scholar, the twelfth volume is devoted to women, and here is mentioned a princess by the name of Tandū of the dynasty of the Jalā'irids, who was the ruler of Southern Iraq and Khuzistan. This woman of exceptional beauty was married, so he relates, to the Prince Shāhwalad Ibn Shāhzādeh as her second husband. Wanting to take power herself, she conspired against him, and he was murdered. His son by another wife, Mahmūd, succeeded him, but Tandū carried on intrigues against the latter, too, and had him killed. She then reigned by herself from 1416–7 to 1419. She was named in the Friday prayers, and coins were minted bearing her name. [144, 16] In actual fact, however, this energetic lady claimed to be ruling for her son Uwais II, who was eleven years old at the time.

Power-hungry mothers took over the business of state for their young or weak and incompetent sons on more than one occasion in the world of Islam, despite a public opinion that was becoming increasingly hostile toward women, as reflected in the following remark alleged to have been made by the Prophet: "I know nothing of lower rank in knowledge and religion which overpowers intelligent people more than you (women)!" [54, 25]

There was, for instance, the mother, a slave, of the Abbāsid Khalif al-Moqtadir. When her son came to power in 908 at the age of 13, he was still so much a child and dependent on her that the government was de facto in her hands. This did not change very much either when the Khalif became older, but he also took advice from other ladies of his harem, which sheltered no less than four thousand women. Incidentally, in 918–9, his mother appointed her confidante, the castle bailiff Thaml, "Drunkenness"—who was also a slave, judging by her name—as the principal arbitrator of the Criminal Court, which met once a week. This resulted in general outrage, but the lady was able to exercise her office satisfactorily after recruiting male jurists to help her. The 25-year reign of al-Moqtadir, or rather that of his mother and his harem, was marked, it must be admitted, by riots and an increasing degree of disintegration within his empire.

The beautiful Basque Sobh, "Aurora," mother of the Spanish Omayyad Khalif Hishām Ibn al-Hakam, in Cordova, used her influence, even during the lifetime of her husband, to obtain a leading position both at Court and in the Empire for the ruthlessly ambitious upstart al-Mansūr (the Almansor of Christian chroniclers). He was able to exploit the good will of the lady, who was later accused of having been his mistress, in combination with his own political abilities to achieve a position of absolute power. While this was going on, the young Khalifs were allowed to grow up in total seclusion and concentrate on their theological studies.

In the eleventh century, Sayyida, a Būyid princess of West Iran, and the Qarakhānid Princess Terken Khātūn of Bukhara, wife of the Seljūq Malikshāh, ruled in the name of their young sons. The latter even proposed marriage to her brother-in-law in order to guide political and military developments in the direction she wanted.

That the mothers of the Ottoman Sultans, at least in the period of the gradual decline of Turkish rule, possessed special political influence was a fact that was certainly taken into account by their adversaries as well as their political partners. The *Wālide Sultān*—the equivalent of "Queen Mother"—was usually a former slave, who had borne a successor to the ruling Sultan. She usually enjoyed the respect of her son, and was in charge of his harem, making the final decision in every matter concerning the ladies of the harem. It has already been noted in the previous chapter that mothers enjoyed a special position of respect in Islam. In a polygynous society, a man can have several wives, but only one mother. And the *Wālide Sultān* was thus the First Lady of Turkey. One or two weeks after her son ascended the throne, she was fetched in a ceremonial procession and accompanied from the old to the new seraglio where her son resided. A special etiquette was necessary for those who came into contact with her. It was only possible to speak to her after a request for an audience had first been submitted. Once permission was granted to appear before her, the applicant was allowed to speak and sit down only after being told by her to do so.

When the Sultan was under age, and also when he was too weak or too addicted to the pleasures of his harem, real power was in the hands of the *Wālide Sultān* who with energy and a greater or lesser degree of ability, directed the affairs of state, assisted by loyal Viziers. Thus Nūr Bānū (d. 1587), a Venetian of the Baffo family, under Murād III, Safiyya (d. 1609) under Mehmet III, Māh Peiker Kösem (d. 1651) under Murād IV and Ibrāhīm I, and Tarkhān Khadijeh (d. 1683) under Mehmet IV played an active part in the policies pursued by their sons. Their opinion counted when it was a question of appointing or dismissing Viziers or other dignitaries of the Empire and anyone with ambitions to advance at the Court endeavored to obtain their good will by gifts. Tarkhān, for instance, concealed by a curtain, took part in and influenced the meetings of the *Diwān* (council).

Incidentally, under Ibrāhīm I, a struggle for power took place between the old and the new *Wālide Sultān*, between Kösem and Tarkhān, each of whom recruited followers and endeavored to assert her policy. This ended by Kösem's being cruelly strangled with the cord of a curtain by the eunuchs of her rival.

By reason of her large income, the *Wālide Sultān* also possessed great economic influence. She had her own ships with which she carried on trade and possessed wealthy estates whose tenants had to render military service. Her financial resources were so great that she could afford to erect mosques and other buildings as well as live in luxury.

Clever and energetic favorites of the Sultans also influenced their policies. The best-known of these was Khorrem, "Merry," a slim slave girl (d. 1558), who, by reason of her origin, was known to the scholars of the Renaissance as Roxolane, the Russian, and was mentioned by this name in European descriptions of Ottoman history. Under Sulaymān I, the lawmaker, she achieved such power that he not only kept her in luxury and magnificence but also, to please

Mogul princess on the throne.

her, married his other slaves to officials and officers of his Court. She was also an expert in the art of intrigue, and did not hesitate to have Viziers executed if they stood in the way of her plans. Through pious endowments and public buildings—she built a mosque, a hospital, and a school—she was remembered by later generations.

It should also be mentioned that Sultan's sisters and daughters, who were married to Court officials, just like most of the wealthy women of the first centuries of Islam, usually had the principal say in their marriages. Whether it was really true, as reported by various European travelers, that their husbands on the wedding night had to climb on the marital bed at the foot and gradually work their way up under the blanket—just as the concubines did with regard to the Sultan—can no longer be confirmed with any certainty. However, a sixteenth-century Turkish Vizier, who boxed his wife's ears—she was a member of the Sultan's family—immediately lost his wife and his position.

Of the women who influenced regents, one who must be especially noted is the Mogul Empress Nūr Jahān, wife of the Emperor Jahāngīr. She was born in Kandahar in 1577, and, four years after the death of her first husband, married Jahāngīr when she was 34 and he 42 years of age. At the time they met, at the Spring Festival of 1611, she was lady-in-waiting of the widow of Emperor Akbar. He was immediately attracted to Nūr Jahān, and married her two months later. She soon became the real ruler since Jahāngīr's health had been undermined by asthma and addiction to alcohol. Her father and brother assisted the Empress, who was astute, educated, charming, and politically ambitious. It is reported by her husband's biographer that Jahāngīr repeatedly stated that he had handed over power to his wife and that he was content with a flask of wine and a pound of meat. Jahāngīr's memoirs reflect his pride in his wife, who possessed the spirit of a man and of whom it is reported, for example, that during a hunt she shot four tigers from her litter on top of an elephant despite the animal's nervousness from the danger around it. His gratitude for her ability and for the affection with which she tended his ruined health—better than any physician in his opinion—and gradually eliminated his dependence on alcohol is also apparent here. The Englishman Thomas Roe, who stayed at the Mogul Court from 1615 to 1619 and subsequently described his time there in his diary, spoke of the Emperor Jahāngīr "whose course is directed by a woeman, and is now, as it were, shutt up by her soe, that all justice or care of any thing or public affayrs either sleepes or depends on her, who is more unaccesable than any goddesse or mistery of heathen impietye." [139, 337] Of Nūr Jahān, he says that she "fullfills the observation that in all actions of consequence in a court, especially in faction, a woman is not only alwayes an ingredient, but commonly a principall drug and of most vertue." [139, 325] It should be recalled here that the reign of Elizabeth I of England had drawn to an end little more than a decade previously. When Nūr Jahān was at the zenith of power, coins were minted bearing her name. She was a leader in fashion, and her gowns, veils, and brocades, and also her sandalwood-colored carpets, were generally imitated by those around her.

Shah Jahān, a son-in-law of her brother, came to power in 1627. Nūr Jahān, who had not supported his succession but that of her own son-in-law—then withdrew from politics. She received an appropriate pension and until her death in 1645 devoted her time to erecting splendid tombs for her husband and father and spent her money on worthy causes.

48

The mosque was not only the place for ritual prayer and divine service but also for studies with illustrious teachers. However, it did not happen every day that a lady came to the mosque for this purpose, as depicted here. The teacher squatting in front of her is explaining an example of Arabic grammar. In the mosque are people at various stages of prayer, two theologians are debating in front of the prayer niche, and next to the carved wooden pulpit is a member of the faithful deep in contemplation. Before the entrance, a man is performing the obligatory ritual washing, and a black servant is handing him a cloth. At the door, a dervish is requesting alms.

49
*Gesticulating in lively fashion, a sheikh
and a lady are engaged in discussion.*

50
*The wife of a goldsmith helping her hus-
band to escape from a prison tower. In the
background, the battlements of a town, on
the left a landscape with blossoming shrubs
and trees and a watercourse with birds.
Female cunning for good as well as evil
is a favorite theme of the literature of the
Islamic countries.*

A Turkish miniature from the end of the sixteenth century. Before the heavily veiled Mohammed, three women are kneeling who were of great importance to Islam. From right to left, they are Fātima, Ā'isha, and Umm Salama. All three, like Mohammed, are depicted with a nimbus of flames, and wear a veil completely concealing the face. The maidservants, however, are not veiled.

For the Mongols, there was nothing
unusual about a woman on the throne.
This lady is talking with vigorous gestures
to a bearded man, who has apparently just
completed a tiring journey since a maidservant is preparing a footbath for him.

53
In the first half of the fourteenth century, there were princesses in Iran who
played a part in politics. A crowned
lady is depicted here with a courtier
kneeling in front of her and two servants in attendance in the background.
The ruler wears a brightly patterned
gown with the wide sleeves customary
in Iran at that time.

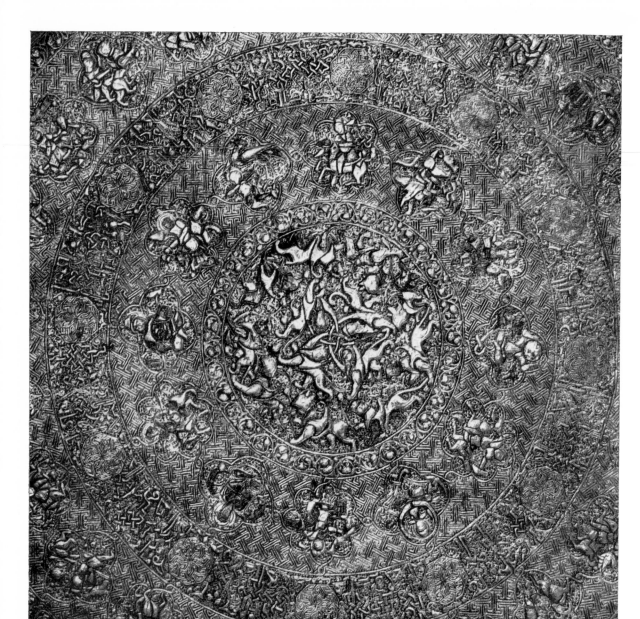

A harp player entertaining a lady of high rank. She wears a precious diadem, secured by long ribbons, long and heavy earrings, and an anklet. The two of them are clothed in the brightly patterned gowns fashionable during the Seljūq period at the end of the twelfth century.

54

This brass basin with fine silver inlay was presented by an Atabeg of Mosul to a princess in the first half of the thirteenth century. The figurative and geometrical decoration can be seen more clearly in this detail view. In the center are nine griffins around four sphinxes. Around them, between mounted figures, are depicted the planets in quatrefoiled patterns, the sun (or the full moon), the waxing moon, Jupiter as a judge, and Venus as a lute player.

56
*This Iranian princess of about 1540
is wearing the* tāj-kulāh, *a matching
embroidered collar, long ear pendants,
and strings of pearls around her face
and neck.*

Leaning against a tree in blossom and wearing the typical head covering of the early fifteenth century in Iran, this noble lady holds a manuscript in her left hand while a kneeling servant offers a bowl of wine to her.

58
Tīmūr Leng's wives and daughters with their Court ladies ride out from Samarkand to meet him. On their heads, the princesses wear plumes of heron feathers over decorated white headcloths.

59
Women on horseback and fighting a male adversary appear, as here, in Firdousī's Shāh-nāmeh *and in popular literature, such as* Thousand and One Nights, *but they were certainly not typical of Islam. Both combatants carry quivers full of arrows and swords. Their steeds have splendid saddlecloths. Warriors watch them from behind craggy rocks or the battlements of a lofty castle.*

60

This lacquer-painted lid of a mirror-box shows Court scenes from the Iran of the seventeenth century. Some ladies are entertaining a prince; others are playing instruments or serving wine. Beasts of all kinds frolic in an imaginary landscape.

62

The wisdom of an old woman of the people is a popular subject of Iranian miniature painting. She complains to Sultan Sanjar that one of his soldiers has robbed her. He answers that he is too busy to concern himself with such trivialities. She replies: "What use is it to you to go to war when you cannot even keep your soldiers in order?"

63
A magnificent example of artistic metal-work. The silver inlays of this brass candlestick of thirteenth-century Egypt depict Court scenes with musicians, wine drinkers, and a pair playing a board game. In the medal in the middle is a ruler surrounded by courtiers, with two female musicians and a dancing girl in front of him.

64
The upper of these two decorative ivory strips from the Fātimid period shows hunting scenes, while the lower one depicts musicians with various instruments and a dancing girl entertaining wine-drinking courtiers.

"She plays the lute with such artistry that even the hardest rocks crack with joy." [*164, II, 600*]

66
A troop of tumblers entertaining male
spectators, including a high-ranking per-
sonage astride his horse. To a musical
accompaniment, women perform acrobatics
on a suspended beam, one of them even on
stilts. Another performs a sword dance.
In the background are splendid palaces of an
Indian city of the Mogul period in the
eighteenth century with great gates, towers,
and minarets. Behind a river with boats
upon it, other settlements can be seen between the hills.

67
I eighteenth-century India, too, the
ladies of the harem were obliged to
entertain their lord and master in a
variety of ways. We see here the inner
courtyard of a harem at night, illuminated by wind-lanterns, with its numerous pavilions closed only by curtains.
In the foreground is the ruler, playing
a board game—probably chess—with
his partner. Two ladies are playing
instruments, two others are preparing
refreshments. On the left, two maidservants with palm fans are conversing.

Polo was a popular amusement of Court society. Miniatures like this one from India c. 1800 show that women also took part in it.

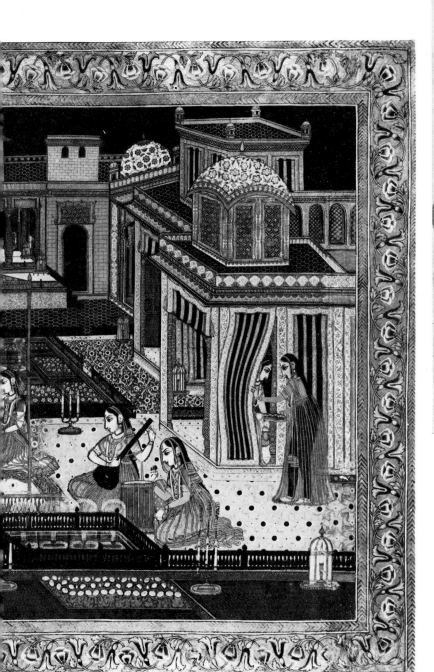

In the fine gold and silver inlay of
this pen case, a tambourine player and
a dancing girl can be identified on the outside at the front and pictures of the planets
on the inside of the lid. In the third
position from the left, Venus is depicted
as a lute player.

There were women who were famous
for their calligraphic expertise.
This elegant Persian, in the process of
writing a letter, is wearing strings of
pearls around her face and neck, and
has dashingly wrapped over her head a
brightly colored cloth topped with a
peacock feather. She has thrown her
veil of delicate white material over her
shoulder, and her corkscrew locks hang
down over both ears.

71
A ruler and his courtiers amusing them-selves in a palace garden. A dancing girl moves gracefully to the sound of lute and tambourine.

Women in Islamic Culture

Women played a considerable role in the art of Islam, especially in poetry and music. They do not appear to have been active in the field of miniature painting. In an Arab source of the ninth century, it is reported that a daughter of the Abbāsid Khalif al-Mahdī painted a glass with a verse in golden letters [89, 187], but this was at a time when it was the fashion to decorate gowns, cloth, and headbands with golden verse or lettering. Perfume of a dark color was even used to write letters on the face, for instance the name of the beloved. The same source reports that women liked to amuse themselves with embroidery of the same kind. Female calligraphists from Spain are particularly well known; learned and artistic women were sometimes lauded for beautiful handwriting.

In Arabic *adab* literature, there is frequent mention of a popular and witty Court game, in which women, especially slaves, liked to take part, namely, to answer verse with verse in intricate improvisation. Arabic verse has a complicated system of poetic meter, formed from a variation of long and short syllables according to certain rules and the poem must have a continuous rhyme. Consequently, the game was more difficult than might first appear to an outsider, who might easily regard the verses as off-the-cuff rhymes. In poetry games of this kind, the person giving the answer had to use the same meter and rhyme as the challenger.

In the pre-Islamic and early Islamic period, free Arab women wrote mostly elegies in praise of brothers, father, or husband slain in battle. Al-Khansā, who expressed her profound sorrow at the death of her two brothers killed in tribal feuds of the pre-Islamic period, was famous for her poetic laments of this kind. Islam, however, exercised no influence on the poetry of this woman, and she was so dedicated to the pre-Islamic tradition that both the second Khalif Omar and Ā'isha, Mohammed's favorite wife, are said to have criticized her for centering her laments on two men who had been killed in pagan times. She is said to have replied to Omar that this was precisely the reason her grief was so profound, since the two were now suffering in the fires of Hell. Whether that was true or not, her imagery and the wealth of forms in her poetry was an inspiration to later poets.

The Arab poetess Laylā al-Akhyaliyya, of the seventh century was famous for her funeral odes. The custom of the time was for poets to compete against each other in sarcasm and invective, and she exchanged such verses with Nābigha, another famous poet of the time. Poetic diatribes of this kind, in which blunt abuse—even in the sexual area—was not spared, were at times directed by Arab women of this period against their husbands [78, 149ff.], hardly a sign of modest submissiveness as required by Islamic tradition.

The women of Islamic Spain, where a variety of ethnic and cultural elements had successfully synthesized, enjoyed a greater measure of freedom than women in the East of the Islamic empire. It was here that the art of Arabic poetry flourished among women as well as men. In a monograph dealing with cultural history, an Arab author of the first half of the seventeenth century, in introductory remarks to a long section on Spanish women who wrote poetry, says: "... and so I will name a number of Spanish women who are very skillful in the art of words, so that it will be clear that this talent is almost a natural instinct among the Spaniards, even among the women and boys." [109, II, 536]

Only three of the most famous Spanish poetesses will be mentioned here. There is first of all Wallāda, daughter of a Khalif, who died unmarried in 1087–8 or 1091–2. She became famous for the frank love poems which she exchanged with her more illustrious fellow poet Ibn Zaydūn. One of her contemporaries, who was personally acquainted with Wallāda, extolled her qualities to her biographer, namely, presence of mind, purity of language, passionate feelings, sagacity of speech. Another Arab author lauded her in a colorful language:

Her poetry and elegance were of the most perfect form, sophisticated presence of mind paired with passionately beautiful expression.

She was beautiful to look upon and of a noble nature. It was pleasing to go to her and whoever left her felt himself refreshed and renewed. Her circle at Cordova was a rendezvous for the noble minds of the region, her court a race course for the proud stallions of poetry and prose. The learned were blinded by the radiance of her face, poets perished to partake of her sweetness. Although easy to approach and surrounded by many, she was of high rank, of noble heritage and virtuous nature. But a source of gossip were her unconcern and poems of sensuous openness. [109, II, 565]

Verses that she embroidered on her sleeves—a fashion of the time—are also evidence of her pride and candor. The right sleeve carried the words:

I am by God fit for great things
And go my way armed with pride.

and the left:

My lover I offer the curve of my cheek
And my kiss to whoever desires it.
[109, II, 563]

Nevertheless, according to the same author, she was famed for her morals and virtue. In this respect, however, attitudes then prevalent seem to have been much more liberal in Spain than in the Islamic East. We know that in addition to Ibn Zaydūn other men, too, desired her and that she exchanged love poems with them as well. Ibn Zaydūn celebrated a night he spent with her in the following words: "... plucking the camomile blossoms of her lips and harvesting the pomegranates of her breasts." [75, 22] After they spent a night together, she took leave of one of her lovers thus:

Thou brother of the Moon
Radiating brightness and sublime like him,
That I may see you again,
May God the Lord grant! ...
The nights now seem long to me.
And I complain night after night,
That only those were so short,
Which I once spent with you.
[109, II, 564; 147, I, 290]

"To gaze at her and listen to her was such a complete pleasure that she stole hearts and restored to old men their youth" [109, II, 566] is how an Arab author extols her beauty and spirit, her way with words, and her charm.

Naz'hūn came from Granada. She lived in the eleventh century, and was famed for her kindness, her beauty, her talent for improvising poems, her knowledge of the art of poetry, and her memorable and apt turn of speech. She, too, was candid in her love poems. Thus she immortalized the joys of a night of love in which one could have seen "the morning sun lying in the arms of the moon" or "rather the white antelope of the tribe of Khazima in the embrace of a lion." [109, II, 637]

The most illustrious poetess of Islamic Spain was Hafsa Bint al-Hājj, who was born after 1135, died in 1190–1, and was famous for her long love affair with the poet Abū Ja'far Ibn Sa'id. This love was the point of departure for nearly all her poems that have survived. Yet she was not so flippant as her predecessor, Wallāda. She once gave voice to jealousy relating to her beloved in the following words:

Jealousy fills me with pain,
Not at my looks, at you and me alone,
Also at the time and place where you may be,
And if I closed you in my eyes,
Until the Day of Judgment, it were not enough.
[55, 13th stanza]

Hafsa lived in a stricter time than Wallāda, as the Berber dynasties of the Almoravids and later the Almohads were puritanical in their views. Nevertheless, it can be inferred from her verses that she was free to visit her admirers. One of her poems begins: "Whether I visit you or you visit me, my heart always inclines to that which it desires." [109, II, 544] When she once visited the house of Ibn Sa'id without prior notice, she gave the maidservant who opened the door a note bearing a poem in which she lauded her beauty—poems honoring oneself date back to pre-Islamic Arabia—and this began: "A visitor with the (slim) neck of a gazelle has come ..." and ended, "Do you think she may enter with your permission or do you believe it is better that she departs?" [109, II, 545]

Her love for Ibn Sa'id was endangered when the newly appointed Almohad Governor of the city and later Khalif Abū Sa'id Othmān, fell in love with her. For a long time, she endeavored to keep harmony between the love of the poet with a respected aristocratic background and that of the representative of the State. The Governor, who was about seven years her junior, appears at first only to have admired her as a beautiful and witty woman. It was not long before he sent her with a deputation to his father, the Khalif, whose favor she quickly won with a poem. Subsequently, however, her long-standing admirer Ibn Sa'id reproached her as follows: "Why do you love this black man (the Almohad was the son of a Negress)? I can buy you ten Negroes at the slave market who are more handsome than he!" [109, II, 546] This must have reached the ears of Abū Sa'id. Ibn Sa'id was later accused and not unjustly—of being involved in a plot; he was thrown into prison and executed in 1163. Hafsa mourned him in her poems, which bear witness to her profound feelings. She wore black clothes as a sign of grief, although, as she complains in a poem, she was rebuked for this. One of her poems to him reads:

He outshone me with the brightness of a star,
But now I see the blackness of night.
I mourn his virtues full of sorrow,
Far from the grace and joy which he brought.
[55, 18th stanza]

It was not long after the death of her beloved poet that she abandoned the writing of verse. She ended her life as a teacher of Almohad princesses at the Court of Marrakesh and in this activity won such esteem that a later biographer described her as the greatest woman educator of her time.

What is said about Hafsa and Wallāda, the poetesses of Arab Spain, namely, their ability to express original feelings in a natural form despite their close links with the traditions of Arabic poetry and their skill in the use of traditional poetic diction, is similarly true of two Turkish poetesses, Mihrī Khātūn and Zaynab, who lived in the second half of the fifteenth century. They both came from families where education was a tradition. In other respects, little is known about their lives. To achieve a reputation in Arabic, Persian, or Turkish poetry, poets first had to learn by heart hundreds of verses written by others, since they had to be expert in the poetic tradition of their native tongue, its images, metaphors, and other poetic devices. Since this was not normally part of the education of a young girl—with the exception, of course, of educated slaves in the Golden Age of the Khalifat—one of Mihrī's biographers feels obliged to say something in favor of women by quoting an Arabic verse: "From femininity no shame to the sun's name is there, Nor aught of honour to the moon from masculinity." [56, II, 129, n. 1] (The Arabic word for "sun" is feminine, and the word for "moon" is masculine in gender.) Mihrī herself protested against the discrimination experienced by women:

Since they cry that woman lacketh wit alway,
Needs must they excuse, whatever word she say.
Better for one female, if she worthy be,
Than a thousand males, if all unworthy they.
[56, II, 130]

Feelings of love inspired both Mihrī and Zaynab. Yet their relationships in Ottoman Turkey of that time were never other than platonic. A biographer lauds Mihrī, who never married, for having remained a virgin until her death. Zaynab gave up writing poems when she married, obviously at the insistence of her husband.

Finally, mention must also be made of Golbadan Begom, a sister of the Mogul Emperor Humāyūn, who, in her *Hu-*

māyūn-nāmeh, wrote an enthralling report about the reign of her brother.

At least in the early centuries of Islam, women were particularly active in one branch of the arts—music. The attitude of Islamic religious scholars toward music was not at all positive. They regarded the beating of tambourines as permissible only at weddings, since such festivities should not take place in silence. It is related that Mohammed put his hands over his ears at the sound of a shepherd's pipe and, on hearing a woman singing, is said to have commented that the devil had blown in her nostrils.

One *hadith* expressly forbids the training, sale, and purchase of female slaves as singers. But here, as in other spheres, devout Moslems were unable to make the pleasure-loving aristocracy and upper classes adhere to this tradition.

In the first century of Islam, singing was an art, inspired by Persian and Byzantine influence, which was cultivated especially in the merry society of the Hijāz, in the cities of Mecca and Medina. It was not long, however, before the Hijāz met serious competition at the Court of the Omayyads in Damascus and, later, from the Abbāsids in Bagdad. From the music-loving aristocracy comes a song in praise of singing; to be found in Abū l-Faraj's *Book of Songs*, it was surely used as a weapon against the disapproving attitude of the religious scholars.

Jamila of Medina, the most famous singer in the seventh century, is said to have decided one day to give up singing. She had a natural gift, and had developed her talent after hearing a neighbor sing. She had also established a school of her own, and was a recognized authority on the art of singing. On the day she decided to stop, she invited men and women to come to her house, where she informed them that she had had a bad dream and feared for her soul. She asked those present to comment on her decision, and opinions were divided. "An old man full of wisdom, experience, and knowledge of the law" then raised his voice. He encouraged her not to give up at a time when others, such as the Iraqi, were challenging the people of Medina in an art form they had inherited from them. He then began to praise singing, although, from what he said, it can be inferred that the ruling classes cultivated it not only for pleasure, but also as a kind of instrument of power for the maintenance of the status quo socially:

Singing is one of the greatest of pleasures and is more pleasant for the soul than any of the things which it desires. It stimulates the heart, strengthens understanding, brings joy to the soul, and provides wide scope for free opinion. Difficult tasks are made easier by it. Armies become victorious through it. Despots are so captivated by it that they despise themselves when they hear it . . . It heals the sick and those whose heart, understanding, and perception have withered away. It makes the rich richer and the poor more contented and satisfied when they hear it so that they no longer demand possessions. He who retains it is a man of learning, and he who renounces it is ignorant. There is nothing more exalted and nothing more beautiful than song. Why is it considered right to abandon it, and why is use not made of it in Divine service? [5 b, VIII, 224 ff.]

Jamila and all the others present were won over by this argument.

Men and women singers put music to the works of illustrious Arabic poets, but in most cases the singers were themselves poets and composers as well as performers. With very few exceptions, the women who cultivated music were slaves, whose talents were recognized as children and who were trained by the great artists of their time. Depending on their abilities and of course on their physical charms, too, they were traded at appropriate prices, and some of them ascended the social ladder with such success that they became the wives of Khalifs. However, the fate of most singers probably took them to the wine taverns of the towns where, remaining nameless, they led an existence that did not differ much from that of prostitutes.

From the early Abbāsīd period, we know of only one singer of free origin, Olayya, the beautiful and gifted half-sister of Hārūn ar-Rashīd, who had inherited her talent from her mother, a singing girl—they were known as *qayna*—at the Abbāsīd Court. With her poems, songs, and merry charm, Olayya was always able to win over the Khalif, even for example when he once grumbled at her because she had made a slave the subject of her love songs. "There was nothing which gave her greater pleasure than reciting poems at the appropriate moment," says Abū l-Faraj. [5 b, X, 163] With this talent for the then popular art of impromptu composition of poems and songs, she was largely responsible for the happy atmosphere in the Khalif's harem. When she died around 825–6, it was the Khalif al-Ma'mūn who recited the prayer for the dead for her.

Most of the famous primadonnas were slaves, but they played an important role at the Courts. There was no celebration by the Khalif or his senior officials that was not embellished by their art. However, since a great deal of money had been invested in their education, more than singing was expected of them. They were expected to use their artistic ability, education, wit, humor, and knowledge of spicy anecdotes and bons mots to amuse and distract the great people of the Court, who were already glutted with a wide range of pleasures. They also had to be able to play such games as chess and trictrac. Some famous singers were also expert at

preparing delicate dishes. They were consequently responsible for practically all kinds of sophisticated pleasures since, of course, they were frequently the concubines of their owner as well.

The later Khalif al-Mu'tamid refused to eat any food not prepared by the singer Shāriya. Arīb, probably the best-known singer at the Court of the Abbāsīds in the middle of the ninth century, once wrote the following lines to the Governor of Mosul, who, at her request for a share of his table, sent her bread, meat, and confectionery: "In the name of Allah, the Merciful, the Compassionate! O you stupid barbarian! Did you think that I belong to the Turks or wild soldiers that you have sent me bread, meat, and confectionery? May Allah protect me from you!" To put him right, she then sent him some of the delicacies of her kitchen on a plate covered with a gold-brocaded cloth, these being pies of bread dough filled with fried partridge breast, vegetables, and palm blossom. [159, 77]

Famous entertainers, including singers, liked to compare their ability with that of others. Much to the enjoyment of the spoiled guests present, and often under the stimulus of wine, "competitions" were held in the houses of patrons. Fadl, better known for her poetry than her songs, had a real literary salon. Poets and men of letters met at her house—she was still the Khalif's slave at the time—not only because she was the "most poetically gifted woman of her time" [5 a, XVIII, 185] but also because they hoped to win her protection at Court.

A passage in the *Book of Songs* deals with Arīb and Shāriya, the two most famous singers of the period when, for a few decades, Samarra was the capital of the Khalifat. "The inhabitants of Samarra were divided into two parties: one group was for Shāriya and the other for Arīb, as a result, the members of each group did not mix with adherents of the other." [159, 84] The two rivals, who were "deadly enemies," thus transmitted their feelings to the entire metropolis.

Men and women singers usually accompanied themselves on the lute, but we know from miniatures and the *adab* literature that there were women who also played the tambourine, harp, oboe, and flute, and also the *kānūn*, a string instrument resembling the harp.

Fewer in number than the singing girls were slaves educated in various branches of formal knowledge. The most famous of these is the slave girl Tawaddud, "Showing Love," from *Thousand and One Nights*, who boasted that she was familiar with all the known sciences from grammar to poetry and music, religious law, theology, mathematics, astronomy, philosophy, and even medicine and who carried on discussions with scholars in the presence of Hārūn ar-Rashīd to demonstrate her knowledge. She not only proved herself better than those who were supposed to examine her but also defeated the trictrac player and entertained everybody with her playing of the lute and her singing.

The principal purpose in educating such slaves was to cater to the spoiled tastes of sophisticated courtiers. The greatest ambition of the slaves, once they were educated, was to win the favor of the Khalif and to find a place in his harem. One highly educated slave, whom Hārūn ar-Rashīd had had tested by the famous philologist al-Asma'ī, rewarded the scholar with a purse of one thousand dinar when, on his recommendation, she was selected for the immediate entourage of the Khalif. "Your daughter would like to share her good fortune with you" [2, 149] was the message she sent to him, and her tact also shows that in this new position on the social ladder she felt herself to be a stage above the man of learning to whom she expressed her thanks.

"*In love there is sweetness and bitterness*"

Only he who feels real love,
Knows the joy and sorrow of life.
For in love there is sweetness and bitterness,
And only he who has tasted tells you of them.

al-Kumayt (d. 743) [89, 67]

The Lebanese writer Laylā Ba'labakkī was prosecuted by the police at the beginning of the 1960's when, in a very delicately written story called "Spaceship of Tenderness to the Moon," she has a newly married woman speak of her tender mental and physical feelings toward her husband. And yet it was Lebanon in particular that had long enjoyed the reputation of being liberal in the erotic sphere. It was Lebanon, in the 1950's, that saw publication of a rather frank book about the sex life of Arabs in the past [119] and a

collection of love poems by Arab women of earlier centuries. In the latter work, the editor wanted to show that Arab women of the past spoke about their love for men just as openly as men did about their feelings toward women. [143] However, in Islamic countries, not only in past decades but right up to the present, a distinction is clearly drawn between the rights of men and women to express opinions on sexual subjects. It is consequently not surprising that the publisher of the last-named book feels the need to argue strongly that a woman has just as much right to sexual expression and fulfillment as a man.

Indeed, *adab* works of classic and postclassic Arab literature speak openly of the sensual pleasure which, at least in the early centuries of Islam, both men and women expressed quite freely and frankly. There is a great deal of literature in Arabic on the subject of profane love, ranging from philosophical disputes on the nature of love, which are mostly influenced by Neoplatonism, to the pros and cons of certain states and manifestations of love, the whole spiced with anecdotes and verses intended to prove or reinforce with examples what is first described theoretically.

In addition, there is a vast sexological literature filled with recipes for mixtures to enhance men's potency and for cosmetics women can use to arouse men sexually. There are also works that classify women physiologically and psychologically as to suitability for the sex act. These works of medieval Arab medicine, whose authors were mostly renowned natural scientists, were also stimulated by translations from the Greek.

All this literature, even that in which—in our eyes—totally frivolous verses and anecdotes are followed by yet more frivolous verses and anecdotes, begins with the introductory formula of all Arabic literature of the Middle Ages and of many of today's Moslem books, letters, transcriptions of lectures, and contracts; that is, the *basmala:* in the name of Allah, the Merciful, the Compassionate. For example, a small sexological treatise by the Egyptian as-Suyūtī, a respectable learned man of the fifteenth century, begins: "In the name of Allah, the Merciful, the Compassionate. Praise be to Allah who decorated the upper part of virgins with breasts and made the legs of women as platform for the privy parts of men, who raised up the spear-like penis of the man with which he thrusts into the vagina of the woman and not (like a real spear) into the breast (of an enemy)." [161, 1]

It would certainly be wrong to judge such literature by today's standards of either morality or writing. Love poetry is known to have been written by pre-Islamic Bedouin poets of Arabia, but it was not an independent genre, appearing in what is known as the *nasib*, the erotic introduction to what was then and even later the most widespread form of Arabic poetry, the *qasida*. The actual purpose of the *qasida* was to praise a patron or a tribe or even oneself or to abuse an enemy or a hostile tribe. However, the *qasida* also contained detailed descriptions of the environment of the Bedouins, including the animals which these nomads used for riding. The *nasib* certainly shows that pre-Islamic poets were not always content to express merely platonic feelings. The ideal woman they lauded was very different from the average Bedouin woman, whose appearance was marked by the harsh life the nomads led. The Arab poets of this and also later periods celebrated a buxom and white-skinned type of beauty. More of this later, however.

In the period of the Omayyads, an independent love poetry appeared for the first time, an example of which is that of Omar Ibn Abī Rabi'a, the Meccan Don Juan from the tribe of the Qoraysh. In his numerous poems, he celebrated his amorous adventures with women from respected families, and there is no reason to doubt the truthfulness of his poems. It has already been noted that the aristocratic woman of Mecca at that time was self-assured and independent, as instanced by Ā'isha Bint Talha and Sukayna in an earlier chapter. It is also probably true, as we can infer from Omar's poems, that some of these adventures were initiated by the women themselves, that they arranged rendezvous with the poet.

At about the same time, however, a love poetry of quite a different kind emerged, which, to begin with, was mainly cultivated in Medina. It is known as *Odhrite*, after the tribe in which this kind of love first and most frequently appeared. Heinrich Heine's verse from "Romanzero" recalls this: *Und mein Stamm sind jene Asra, welche sterben, wenn sie lieben,* "And my tribe are those Asra who die when they love." The religious basis of *Odhrite* love is the alleged saying of Mohammed that is as famous as it is contested: "He who loves, hides his love, waits patiently and dies, dies as a martyr." [86, 194] This means that he shall go directly to Paradise.

The most important representative of *Odhrite* love of this period is the Bedouin poet Jamil (c. 660–701), who loved his childhood sweetheart Buthayna from the same tribe, as she loved him. But her father married her to another man. Jamil described the purity of his feelings and of the grief he had to bear on her account. In his poems, Buthayna became the "cruel one," who dominated him entirely. They both pined because of their unfulfilled love for each other and died of broken hearts.

From about the ninth century on, *Odhrite* love became the exalted ideal of Court society in Iraq, although its actual moral views were clearly quite different. It was at this time that moving love stories were told about tragic lovers, perhaps because people had had enough of the constantly increasing fickleness of erotic relationships. Whatever the reason, entire books were written about lovers who died of unfulfilled love for each other.

Kuthayyir (d. 732), a poet famous for his pure love for his cousin Azza, is reported to have once said to the Omayyad Khalif Abd al-Malik Ibn Marwān:

One day I met Jamil, who asked me, "Will you go with me to Buthayna?" I agreed and went with him. When we drew near to the place where she was, he bade me, "Go to her and tell her where I am." I did so. She then approached with some women of her tribe. When the women saw Jamil, they left them alone, and I went away also. The two of them, however, remained standing there, from nightfall until the gray of dawn. When they decided to take leave of each other, she bade him, "Come closer to me, Jamil!" He then approached her, and she whispered something secretly in his ear.

At this, he fainted and fell senseless to the ground, and it was only the heat of the Sun (much later) that woke him up again. [89, 60 ff.]

The most famous lovers of this kind were Laylā and Majnūn, who are probably better known throughout Islam than Romeo and Juliet in Europe.

In some cases, genuine social reasons may have affected such relationships, since fairly often *Odhrite* couples were the result of a father's refusal to give his daughter to the man who loved her and asked for her hand because he did not consider the suitor's social status to be good enough. She was then married to a more prosperous candidate, the lovers pined for each other, and eventually both died of broken hearts.

Poems and traditions appeared which affirmed that the upper part of a woman down to her navel was for the man she loved and only the part below was the property of her husband. [86, 96 f.] Reports like the following have survived: The philologist al-Asma'i (d. 828) once asked a Bedouin: "What does love mean to you?" The man replied: "To look at each other time and again, and when one can repeatedly kiss each other this is already Paradise." To this al-Asma'i commented: "For us (townsmen) that is not love." The Bedouin then asked: "What then is love for you?" to which al-Asma'i replied: "You spread out her legs and go into her." "Oh," said the Bedouin, "you are not a lover, you just want a child." [89, 77].

The Court society of Iraq in the eighth century produced the classic voice of Court love in the person of Abbās Ibn al-Ahnaf, one of the circle of poets gathered around the Khalif Hārūn ar-Rashid. Fauz, a clearly fictitious name, was the subject he celebrated in his poems. Many suspect that in reality she was Olayya, the lovely sister of Hārūn ar-Rashid, to whom reference has already been made.

It may be assumed that some of Abbās' poems that have survived were commissioned by high-ranking ladies at the Court. The love celebrated here did not remain unfulfilled as with the *Odhrites*, but the brief hours of happiness are followed by long sorrow and hopeless laments and ultimately acceptance of a relentless fate. Practically nothing is learned about the intellectual and mental qualities of the lady, which might have given an indication of the ideal woman of that time. Neverthelesss, this genre of Arab love poetry was a forerunner of the poetry of the troubadours of Provence.

From the ninth century on, books appeared on the theory of love, which initially corresponded to the ideal concepts of Court circles concerning a person of good breeding. One of the maxims in the *Book of the Flower* by the jurist Ibn Dāwūd (d. 909), a codification of what we have described as Court love, reads: "He who wishes to be well-bred and educated must be chaste" and "It is not a sign of well-bred behavior when the beloved is treated in a contemptuous way by describing her."

In this literature, love is defined as unity of soul and character between two people which causes a lover to consider that the beloved is also beautiful in appearance even when that is not at all the case in the eyes of others or which causes him to look continually at the object of his affections and then to feel sensual desire as well. This is also why the lover wishes to be united with the beloved in a kiss since the breath of Man comes directly from his nature and is thus in immediate contact with his soul. An embrace also enhances the spiritual nearness of lover and beloved. Seeking sensual pleasure for its own sake, an Islamic theologian of the fourteenth century affirms in a treatise on love, is to be condemned, since it is only followed by even greater pain or is an obstruction to finer pleasures, such as those that await the Faithful in Paradise. [86, 170] These, too, of course, are only a continuation on the highest level of those experienced on earth.

It is sometimes said that love makes one blind and deaf, but those who praise it affirm that it has ennobling qualities. "It gives the coward courage, makes the avaricious generous, conveys understanding to the ignorant, and lends eloquence to the tongues of the inhibited. The power of kings bows before it, the arbitrariness of the bold is shaken by it, it leads to decency." [86, 190] On being told that his son had fallen in love, a prominent man replied: "Thanks be to Allah, now he will become courteous and friendly, pleasant in his attitude and elegant in his movements, agreeable in his expression and serious in his messages, his nature will become freer for he will devote himself to the beautiful and avoid that which is ugly." [*Ibid.*] Wise people, it is said in the same source, consider that love is for the soul as a good meal is for the body; if one does not enjoy it, it is harmful but when one eats too much of it, it will kill you. [86, 189]

An Arab anthology of early love stories from the fifteenth century contains the philosophical remark: "If women are snares of Satan, then they are also guides which lead to knowledge, since through love for them an intelligent man will acquire knowledge of their Creator ..." [11, 57]

While jurists, theologians, and philosophers argued about the nature of earthly love, *adab* authors regretted, even at the beginning of the tenth century, the increasing decline in moral standards, although they admittedly took an idealized view of the early period. Thus in his book about good morals, Ibn al-Washshā of Bagdad writes: "In the past when a man loved a woman, then he did not desert her until death, his heart concerned itself with no other, and he did not endeavor to find consolation elsewhere ... and the woman behaved in like manner. When one of them died before

the other, the latter killed himself or lived on in a spirit of love for the other, remained true, and honored the memory of his partner." [89, 77] As to the happy-go-lucky poet who wrote:

I see a maiden and fall for her,
Then catch sight of another and love her,
I fall in love with eighty every day,
And to none can my heart true stay.

Ibn al-Washshā wishes that Allah will show him the hatefulness of his words and declares: "Inconstancy is not a quality of educated people, and constant change is not the affair of the well-bred." [89, 79]

Even sharper is the commentary in an *adab* work of about 984 on a lascivious anecdote:

In the past, when a man loved a girl, he exchanged letters with her for the course of a year. After this, he was happy enough to chew the mastic which she (first) had in her mouth, and then, when they met each other, they talked to each other and recited verses. Today, however, when a man loves a girl, he has nothing else in mind but how to lift her legs as if he wanted to make Abū Horayra (a famous Early Islamic source of hadiths *from the Prophet) a witness to his coitus with her.* [163, 55]

But before these things are dealt with in more detail, a brief résumé is necessary of the attitude of the Koran and *Sunna* to sexuality. The Koran exhorts Islamic men in metaphorical manner thus: "Your women are to you (as) cultivated land; come then to your cultivated land as ye wish, but send forward something for yourselves, and act piously towards Allah, and know that ye are going to meet Him. Give (thou) good tidings to the believers!" (2:223) Thus the sexual relations between man and woman in marriage are treated here as something natural which had also to be viewed with reference to Allah and the Day of Judgment. On another page, the Believers—obviously men and women who are not married to each other—are urged to observe chastity. They are told here to "cast down their eyes" and to "guard their private parts." (24:30) The first exhortation was a popular subject of the literature on worldly love.

With regard to the Prophet of Islam, early Arab historians —who certainly took account of their own interests, too— report that he took particular pleasure in three things in life: pleasant smells, women, and good food. [87, I, 2, 112] When it is affirmed in the same source that the archangel Gabriel, a messenger of Allah, had given Mohammed, through a certain dish, the potency of forty men [*Ibid.*, 112], this merely shows that the Moslems of that time expected above average sexuality from a man who was supposed to be an example to them in every respect—a concept of a founder of a religion that is totally different from the image of Jesus in Christianity.

The Moslem idea of Paradise also takes account of male wishful thinking; every Moslem man is promised the potency of eighty men there. [*Ibid.*] A later source promises him every day a hundred buxom virgins whose virginity is continually renewed. [86, 270] They will be free from all the discomforts that plague earthly women, such as menstruation, and will also know no jealousy. Nor will they cause injury to their men, reproach them, or adorn themselves for any other.

The interests of women are considered here only in the answer that Mohammed is said to have given a woman, who asked what man she would belong to in Paradise when she had been married to several in succession on earth. He said that she would be able to choose and could take the one whose character had pleased her most. [86, 257] At any event, it is emphasized that there would be no bachelors in Paradise, and indeed a well-known saying affirms: "There are no monks in Islam"; that is, asceticism of any kind, including sexual, is not wanted. The great Islamic theologian al-Ghazāli (d. 1111) considers sexual abstinence permissible only for those without sexual desires. [54, 43 f.]

Arabic has a comprehensive vocabulary for dealing with sex and, as for other aspects of life, has different designations for many nuances. The Arabic word *nikāh*, which even in the Koran is used exclusively to mean "marriage," originally meant coitus, and in classic Arabic a woman who was married to a man was said to have been "under" him. This can, of course, be interpreted figuratively.

To begin with, there was no trace of prudery in the Arabic language, and the freethinker Jāhiz of the ninth century protests at the pious hypocrites among his contemporaries who preached it: "Many of the people who display their piousness and ascetic way of life are disgusted and turn away when words such as vulva, penis or coitus are mentioned, but most of those who behave thus are men whose hypocrisy is greater than their knowledge, noble-mindedness, refinement, and dignity." [48, 434]

That sexuality and eroticism were not considered exclusively male attributes in the enjoyment of life can be proved in various ways. Jāhiz, who advocated a broad view of life, regards women as superior to men in matters of love: "Women are above men in many things. It is they who are wooed, wished for, loved, and desired, and it is they for whom sacrifices are made and who are protected." [48, 414]

The recommendation that consideration should be given to the woman in physical love is clearly made in a saying attributed to al-Hasan, grandson of the Prophet and a much-married man: "Flirt with the women, and do not behave like a wild animal where the male suddenly descends upon the female. Flirting is to desire what thunder and lightning are for rain. The kiss is the herald of the game of love." [133, 159]

What is probably the only book by an Arab on sensual love known to nonspecialists, *The Blossoming Garden* by the Tunisian an-Nafzāwi, of about 1400, recommends that the man should prepare the woman for love and afterward should "not rise too quickly" [121, 81]; in other words, he should respect her feelings. But the Egyptian Suyūti, a man of many interests, to whose book reference has already been made, only gives instructions to the woman as to how she should behave toward the man.

Almost everything that we know of the frank remarks of women of that time concerning their feelings toward their male partners comes from reports by men, since, as we have already seen, it was only very much later that Arab women began to write love poetry, and this was in the West of the Islamic empire which was somewhat morally unrestrained anyway. Consequently, it can be assumed that some of the frivolous stories concerning the erotic behavior of women that are found in *adab* literature were related as "male jokes" in the evening conversations at Court or among the aristocracy. It is true that women were usually present at such entertainments, not free-born women, of course, and certainly not wives, but the educated entertainers, the singing girls. And it is quite certain that not everything handed down here was solely male wishful thinking.

The literature that has survived credits not only pre-Islamic Arab women with frankness in sexual matters—it is said that it was a woman who taught the people of Mecca various forms of the love act hitherto unknown [78, 215]— but also women of the Arab aristocracy of the seventh century. Overhearing what was obviously passionate love play between Ā'isha Bint Talha and her husband, a woman of Mecca once reprimanded the capricious Ā'isha with the words: "You, a free woman, behave in such a manner!" She replied: "We long for this kind of man with everything which excites them and of which we are capable." [5b, XI, 186]

The second Khalif Omar Ibn al-Khattāb is said once to have heard a woman lamenting on the roof of her house:

This night was long and black for me,
And, without my beloved to play with, I slept not,
This bed would have shaken from our love,
But for fear of Allah, the only God.
[86, 229]

At this, the Khalif, who could appreciate her feelings, is said to have enquired how long her husband had been away at war and to have had him fetched back.

The following tale is related of the poet Omar Ibn Abī r-Rabi'a, the Don Juan of Mecca, in the *Book of Songs*: Hind, daughter of al-Hārith of the tribe of the Murra, invited him to her house one day so that she and her companions could talk to him. She said to him: "Oh, oh, Omar, listen to this. If you could have seen me a few days ago. I was with my family, and I put my head under my gown and looked at my nakedness. It was just as if it filled a hand and was very desirable. At this I called out: 'Omar! Omar!'" Omar replied: "I would have called out: 'At your service! At your service!'" [5b, I, 176] It was not unusual in poems for a woman to extol the charms of her vagina nor for a man to sing the praises of his penis.

However, as already indicated, an amorous adventure by a married woman was regarded as unchaste, and could result in grave consequences for one or both partners. The poet al-Waddāh is said to have paid a secret visit to the wife of the Omayyad Khalif Walid I. A servant told the Khalif that the visitor had hidden in a chest shortly before the Khalif appeared on the scene. The Khalif asked his wife for the chest as a gift and had a deep hole dug in the floor of his palace. Before he had the chest lowered into it, he said to it: "We have heard something. If it is true, then we have wrapped you in a shroud and will bury you and the memory of you and will remove the traces of you until the end of time. But if it was only gossip, then we are burying only wood and how worthless that is!" The narrator of the *Book of Songs* then closes with the words: "After that and up to the present time, no trace was ever seen of him." [5b, VI, 225]

In the centuries that followed only female slaves as a rule were still permitted to express openly their feelings for a man. A slave of a Khalif is said to have sent a poem to a female slave in which he said that he had dreamed he was lying hand in hand with her on a couch. It is said that she answered:

What you saw was good and what you beheld,
Despite the envious, once you will have.
I wish that you would embrace me,
My swelling breasts resplendent under you.
I see you between my bracelet and my ankle-band,
Enclosing my breasts and my body.
[80, 219]

The narrator relates that the Khalif had them married to each other when he heard about them. From the reports of European travelers of a very much later date, however, from Turkey, for example, we know that such affairs often ended tragically with both lovers being thrown into the Bosporus.

The singing girls were actually trained so see their beauty and talents as a commodity and were known for their skill in marketir ₃ it. They were seldom honest when they told a

man of their feelings for him. Jāhiz, the bel-esprit of the ninth century, has this to say about how a *qayna* (singing girl) attracted men:

When an admirer looks at her, she glances discreetly at him, infatuates him with her smile, says words of love to him in the poems that she sings, is eager to return his approaches, drinks merrily, and demonstrates her desire that he should stay for a long time, her yearning for his speedy return, and her sadness at his departure. And if she notices then that her charm has trapped him and that he is ensnared, she even goes beyond that which she began with and makes him believe that her affection for him is even greater than that which he feels for her. She writes him letters in which she laments her passion and swears to him that the inkpot is filled with her tears and the paper wet with her spittle, that she worries about him day and night in her heart and in her mind, that she does not wish to have any other . . . that she does not have the intention of turning away from him and that she wants him for himself alone and not because of his money. She then places the letter in a sheet of parchment folded six times, seals it with saffron, and ties it with a piece of string. [48, 427]

At times, she trifled simultaneously in this manner with several admirers.

As a libertine, however, Jāhiz does not take a negative view of these cunning arts of seduction: "However, this should not be a criticism of her but, on the contrary, great praise. Is it not said in a tradition that 'The best of women are those who understand charm and seduction'?" [48, 429ff.] And, too, he certainly recognizes the reasons for the behavior of the singing girls:

How should the singing slave be safe from temptation, or how should it be possible for her to remain chaste since she acquires passion from her environment in the same way as she learns languages and customs and lives, from her birth to the hour of her death, in a milieu which discourages her from thinking of God, since it consists only of delectable entertainment and all kinds of diversions and vulgarities in the midst of depraved and shameless people from whom no serious word is to be heard, in whom one can have no confidence and who have neither religion nor honor. [48, 433]

On the other hand, Ibn al-Washshā, in his book on the good morals in Bagdad at the beginning of the tenth century, includes a chapter headed, "Damnation of the Singing Girls," which begins thus: "One must know that no virtuous and educated man, no person of good morals, can be afflicted by a greater tribulation than a passion for the singing girls, since their affection is treacherous, their love false, and their passion rapidly fades." [89, 92] He then describes, like

Jāhiz, how they "angle" men of money and good family in order to take advantage of them. He does not, however, share Jāhiz' understanding of the reasons for their behavior.

The illustrious Arīb, to whom reference has already been made, may be taken as an example of the singers' loose morals, even among those who had attained a high position. She openly admitted that she had slept with eight Khalifs but had felt no affection for any of them apart from al-Mo'tazz, who reminded her of a man she had once loved. It is therefore not surprising that she found ways to slip away at night from the Khalif's harem, which was presumably strongly guarded, to meet her current lover and then to return just as discreetly. The reports vary on the reaction of the Khalif who, if not before, realized what was going on when it became apparent that she was pregnant. [159, 149]

It once happened that a number of admirers paid a visit to Arīb. When they wanted to leave, she begged them to stay a little longer since she wanted to serve them a dessert which one of her pupils, Bid'a, also a well-known singer, had prepared with her own hands from fresh almonds and which would be accompanied with a song. The narrator continues:

I said: "On one condition." She asked: "And what is that, by Allah?" I replied: "Something which I have wanted to ask you for a long time, but I am ashamed to ask it in your presence." She answered: "You have my permission, and I will give you the answer before you ask the question since I already know it!" At this, I was astonished and challenged her: "Then say it!" She went on: "You wanted to ask me about the conditions which I demand (from a good lover)." I replied: "Yes, that is what I wanted to ask." She then answered: "A hard penis and a pleasant smell and if an unusually good appearance and great handsomeness, then my lust increases but when not, the two first-mentioned things are something which I would not like to do without." [5a, XVIII, 185]

On another occasion and probably when she was older, one admirer asked another in her presence: "What about her desirability now?" The other laughed, and she noticed it and wanted to know what they had spoken about. When they declined to tell her, she threatened to send all her singing girls away. They then told her, and she dryly commented: "So what? The desirability is quite in order, but the instrument is inactive." [*Ibid.*]

Many anecdotes in *adab* literature are evidence of the frivolity of the singing girls. One story tells of a young man, who was obviously a little out of touch with the world and not very prosperous and who pursued a *qayna* with flattering words and high-flown letters, saying that he couldn't sleep at night, had no appetite and other "endless, meaningless twaddle," as the narrator puts it. One day, he sent a letter

to the girl, writing that if she did not permit him to visit her, she should at least come to him in his dreams. She then sent a message to him—"she was a woman of Bagdad and wanted only the world and its money," says the narrator—that he should send two dinar to her, then she would come herself and from this he would have more than from her appearance in a dream. [18, 72 ff.]

Here, again, it would be wrong to make generalizations, since there were also singing girls who were famed for their faithfulness, for example, Mahbūba's to Khalif al-Muta-wakkil or Farīda's to Khalif al-Wāthiq. It is even said that Bid'a, Arīb's pupil mentioned above, died a virgin. [159, 144]

To save herself from an insistent lover, a slave could only resort to her sharp tongue, a quality that was much respected anyway, as is apparent from many anecdotes, including that concerning the poet Abū Nuwās of Bagdad (d. c. 803), who was famous not only for his frivolous verses, mainly on the subject of pet boys but also for his excellent drinking and hunting songs. When he was once visiting a friend, a white-skinned girl appeared, wearing a green gown. Abū Nuwās rubbed his eyes when he saw her and said: "I dreamt I was riding on a white mare with a green blanket, and she moved right merrily under me." The girl replied: "If you want to make your dream come true, order a white radish for the night." [177, 141] The following anecdote is more pungent. The well-known singer Ibrāhīm al-Mausili (d. 804) is said to have once asked a singing girl in a verse to have sex with him, arguing that he was requesting something for which she did not even have to bare her back. She replied: "No, but I get a fat stomach from it." [133, 70]

The free-born woman, on the other hand, could rely on her family to protect her from male impertinence. This is demonstrated by an anecdote, which, at the same time, il-lustrates the Early Islamic concept of a virtuous woman. It was told by a servant of Hajjāj Ibn Yūsuf, Governor of Iraq from 694 until his death in 714. Hajjāj had a nephew, who was the Emir in the Iraqi town of Wasit. A woman lived there who was more beautiful than any other at that time. He made propositions to her and sent her gifts, but she re-fused to yield to him and demanded that he ask her family for her hand. However, he did not wish to do this. So he told her that he would visit her one Friday night. She reported this to her mother, who did not believe it, but then told the girl's four brothers about it anyway. The brothers took up a position in the house opposite. When the nephew of Hajjāj arrived, he handed over his mount to his servant and ordered him to come back with it when he heard the muezzin calling the Believers to come to prayer at daybreak. He then entered the girl's house and found her lying on a bed. He lay down beside her and took hold of her, saying: "How much longer

are you going to play cat and mouse?" She cried out that he should leave her alone. At this, her brothers rushed into the house, slew him with their swords, and wrapped the body in a leather blanket, the kind that was used for executions, and threw it into a lane in the town. The inhabitants of this lane subsequently discovered the body and took it to Hajjāj. He had his nephew's servant brought to him and ordered him to tell what had happened; otherwise he would be made a head shorter. He then ordered the appearance of the woman and her family, who confirmed what the servant had said and admitted the murder. Hajjāj praised the woman for what she had done and wished that there were more women like her. He had his nephew fed to the dogs and the servant cut in two. [123, 182 ff.] The end of the story shows that it was intended to have an educational effect and that such an attitude on the part of a woman was considered exemplary, even though it was certainly not the rule.

In his treatise on earthly love of the fourteenth century, the theologian Ibn Qayyim al-Jauziyya leaves no doubt about the woman's having exactly the same right to sexual satisfaction in marriage as that demanded from her by her husband. He quotes disputes about how often this must take place and how long a married woman can go without intercourse with her husband. Various authors even assert that women have a stronger libido than men. Ibn Qayyim considers the physical union, sanctioned by marriage, of two persons who love each other as the highest stage of fulfillment of their feelings for each other and that this is enhanced by their humble love of God.

Others took a different view. The Ziyārid ruler Kay Kā'ūs of the eleventh century draws a clear distinction between marriage and eroticism. "A wife," he says, "must be chosen from a good family, and you must know whose daughter she is. For a wife is intended to be a housewife, not to serve for sensual pleasure. For sensual lust, a slave can be purchased at the bazaar without much effort or expense. But a wife must be fully mature and intelligent, a woman who has been trained by her mother and father to take charge of the household." [94, 93] Indeed, in the Europe of the past, marriages in noble or royal families were arranged for dynastic or political reasons, and not much attention was paid to the possible feelings of the two partners.

Kay Kā'ūs considers it self-evident that a husband should have sexual intercourse with his wife, since one of the reasons for marriage is the procreation of children, but he should not do so too often, even when he loves his wife, so that she does not derive pleasure from it and make unreasonable demands. In this way, he says, the husband also preserves his freedom. [94, 94]

A tradition from the very early period affirms: "Whoever of you marries the most women is the best Moslem." [87, I, 2, 95] The grandson of the Prophet, al-Hasan Ibn Ali, is said to have been married to two hundred women in the course of his lifetime, and the Persian poet Sa'di (d. 1292) affirmed, it is related: "Take a new wife every year, friend, since a used calendar is really not much use." [166, 224]

In the chapter on Islamic law, as was already observed, it was easy for a husband to cast out his wife. A particularly crass example is told of al-Moghira Ibn Sho'ba, who had twice served as Governor of Kufa in the seventh century and was known both for his dubious morals and for his opportunism. One day, he saw his wife remove a fragment of food from her teeth. At this, he said to her: "You are cast out, for if that remained from today's meal it is a sign of your gluttony, but if it was from yesterday's evening meal, your breath must smell." She replied: "No, may Allah soon replace you by another, it was from the toothpick." As if to justify her, the narrator closes by remarking that she remarried after this and bore the later Governor al-Hajjāj Ibn Yūsuf. [50, 136]

It was certainly such an attitude toward women that led to the saying, allegedly from the Prophet: "Women are only playthings, and a plaything should be pleasing to the one who plays with it." [133, 117] This saying is not found in the canonical collections of traditions.

It is to be assumed that most of the women in polygynous marriages, like the slaves in large harems, were physically frustrated. The following is told of the harem of Khalif Hārūn ar-Rashīd—but it could be equally true of any other large harem: Hārūn ar-Rashīd had two hundred female slaves and visited each of them in turn in the course of two hundred nights. One night, as he went up to the harem palace, he heard a slave singing thus: This house is full of desirable women, but a single penis is just as incapable of satisfying two hundred harem ladies as a weak plaster-carrier of filling two hundred cracks. He had her brought to him and made her repeat her verse, at which he said: "Then we will visit you more often." But she provocatively replied: "But I do not want that if it happens as Abū Hokayma said in a poem: 'She came with her sack to fill it with corn, then she stood up and the sack was empty.'" He answered: "No, we do not wish to leave the sack empty," stood up and had sex with her. He then said to her: "Beware lest you have made me a weak plaster-carrier!" to which she said: "I could not have eaten this bread with such a fierce hunger without making you that." [133, 157f.]

However, the ladies of the harem were also faced with competition from another quarter since, from the period of the Abbāsids, a custom became established that had been brought into Islam from the Byzantine-Persian area. Tired of the multitude of women at their disposal, many men turned to pederasty, finding it more seductive than love for women. Perhaps the less prosperous were also driven to this by the exclusion of women from public life. A pious man remarked: "I fear more for a servant of God from a beardless young man than from seventy virgins." [123, 202]

Some men found pleasure in both sexes. The Ziyārid Kay Kā'ūs advised his son in the eleventh century to enjoy both sexes and thus avoid being satiated.

Zubayda, wife of the Khalif Hārūn ar-Rashīd, is said to have resorted to a particularly interesting trick. To cure her son, the later Khalif al-Amīn, of his predilection for eunuchs, she selected pretty young girls of slim stature, had their hair cut like that of boys, dressed them in jackets with tight belts, and had them appear thus before the young Amīn. These slaves were called boy-girls, and they became the fashion in the spoiled and luxury-loving society of Bagdad for at least a hundred years. Tavern girls subsequently appeared in the same fashion.

An Arab source of the eleventh century quotes a letter condemning passive pederasty. It was written by the Iraqi writer Abu l'Aynā (d. 896) to a contemporary: "It is strange that you allow people to use you sexually instead of your taking your pleasure ... Why do you pay the dowry for a bride, anyway, when you need men and have no love for women. Your women are with your neighbors and your men with

Laylā and Majnūn have fainted with love.

117

your youths ... O pity the bride whose gown is not removed. ..." [133, 161]

It is consequently not surprising that in these circumstances some women looked for alternative means of satisfaction or—not a difficult thing in the harems, of course—sought fulfillment in lesbian relationships. Nevertheless, an Arab historian with an appreciation of the dramatic reports of Abbāsid Khalif Mūsā al-Hādī that he presented to his courtiers the perfumed heads, decorated with diadems, of two beautiful young women from his harem, who had been decapitated after being caught in flagrante delicto. [162, VIII, 221] Yet this says less about the high morals of the Commander of the Faithful than, in all probability, about his sense of property in regard to the ladies of his harem. Conversely, pederasty was indeed condemned by Orthodox Moslems, but it was not considered to be detrimental to honor in high society.

At a later time, there were women who deliberately chose to become lesbians for intellectual reasons. Thus, a sexological treatise of the twelfth century by a Jewish convert to Islam reports:

There are also women who are more intelligent than the others. They possess many of the ways of men so that they resemble them even in their movements, the manner in which they talk, and their voice. Such women would like to be the active partner, and they would like to be superior to the man who makes this possible for them. Such a woman does not shame herself, either, if she seduces him whom she desires. If she has no inclination, he cannot force her to make love. This makes it difficult for her to submit to the wishes of men and brings her to lesbian love. Most of the women with these characteristics are to be found among the educated and elegant women, the scribes, Koran readers, and female scholars. [66, 16]

Certain feminists of the present day would not find this an alien view.

The *adab* literature also contains chapters on jealousy between men and women—men are regarded as more jealous, since women are accustomed to sharing their husbands with co-wives and concubines. Female guile or maliciousness is a favorite subject, including tricks by which wives deceive their husbands with lovers or try to eliminate their co-wives—an indication that women could also be jealous.

It also includes discussions as to whether a virgin is preferable to a deflowered woman or whether it is better to take a young or an old wife. The first alternative is generally favored in both cases, but there is also evidence in support of the alternatives. Finally, there are quite a few chapters on female fidelity or infidelity. In his book on good behavior, Ibn

al-Washshā of Bagdad takes the view that in general women are unfaithful, but for didactic reasons, he also tells stories of faithful women. For example, the third Khalif Othmān Ibn Affān heard from one of his companions that he had married a woman from the tribe of the Kalb and, in a letter, asked him about her genealogy and appearance. His friend told him the name of her father, a distinguished man, and wrote that she was white-skinned and tall. Othmān then established contact with the woman's father and asked him for one of his daughters. His request was granted.

When she came to Othmān, it is related in this description of the wedding night, *he was sitting on a cushion, and threw one to her so that she could sit down opposite him. He then removed his turban, and it could be seen that he was bald. He said to her: "Daughter of Farāfisa, my baldness should not alarm you, behind it is that which you like." She replied: "I am a woman for whom a distinguished man of mature age and in a ruling position is the best of husbands." He then asked her: "Will you come to me or shall I come to you?" She answered: "From the aversion of heaven I have nothing worse to withstand than the distance which is now between you and me." She then stood up, went over to him, and sat down next to him. He gently stroked her hair and prayed for God's blessing. After this, he bade her: "Remove your veil." This she did. Then he said: "Take off your shirt." This she did, too. Next he demanded: "Undo your girdle!" but she answered: "You must do that." He then did so, and she became his dearest wife.*

When at a later date Othmān's murderers entered his room, she threw herself in front of her husband to protect him, as a result of which two of her fingers were severed by a sword. After the death of Othmān, which she could not prevent, Khalif Mo'āwiya sent for her to ask for her hand. At this, she extracted her front teeth so that no other man would desire her, and it was as she wished. [89, 83 f.]

In Persian poetry, the words of earthly love are mostly exaggerated in mystical fashion. For Hāfiz and his predecessors, for example, earthly love is "a symbol of the all-embracing yearning for God." [25, 48] It "consequently remains something which is transitional; the character of unfulfilled, unfulfillable yearning is necessarily associated with it. Final fulfillment comes only with death or the complete submission of the individual personality." [25, 49] But this goes beyond the scope of our subject.

While Arabic *adab* literature of the Middle Ages was noted for its anecdotes, a literary genre that has remained alien to Arabic literature achieved an exalted standard in Persian literature. This was the epic. In Persian love poetry, which is mostly full of mystical images anyway, it is often unclear whether the beloved who is celebrated in the words of earthly love is a man or a woman, since in Persian there is no grammatical distinction for gender. However, love of women is glorified in some Persian romantic epics, and it is precisely these epics which have supplied a great deal of inspiration for the painting of miniatures in Islam.

The love story of Khosrou and Shīrīn, or Ferhād and Shīrīn, was the subject of more than two dozen works of Persian literature and even for the screenplay of a film. Numerous Turkish authors have also concerned themselves with the subject. Even at the beginning of the 1930's in Turkey, relatively large editions of the popular story of Ferhād and Shīrīn were published time and again, and guests in coffee houses were entertained with a magic lantern version of this romantic story. In 1942, the Azerbaijan poet Samed Burgin wrote a romantic epic entitled *Khosrou and Shīrīn*, whereas Nazim Hikmet, a Turkish writer, took up the subject in his drama, *A Legend of Love*, in 1948.

Traces of the Khosrou and Shīrīn story are to be found in works by early Arab historians and geographers. Consequently, this subject must have been a traditional tale that survived from the pre-Islamic period and never lost its popularity. Firdousī, author of the Persian national epic, the *Shāh-nāmeh*, was the first to put it in poetic form. Its most splendid version as a romantic epic, the model for all that followed, was the work of Nizāmī, who was born in Qum in 1141 and spent most of his life in Azerbaijan. He wrote the work in 1180 as the second of his five epics, which are known by the name of *Khamseh* (Quintette).

Nizāmī makes it quite clear that in Shīrīn, who is probably the most moving female figure of New Persian literature, he has immortalized his beloved wife Āfāq, who was a slave of Turkish origin presented to him by the ruler of Derbend and who died at an early age. We can certainly agree with the Soviet Iranist Bertels, who considers that all the passages of the epic in which Shīrīn refuses to become the mistress of Khosrou because she wants to belong to him only as his lawful wedded wife were inspired by the behavior of Āfāq.

The plot of the story is briefly as follows: The painter Shāpūr describes the Armenian (Christian) princess Shīrīn to his friend and drinking companion Khosrou Parvīz, the young and handsome but irresponsible son of King Hormoz, in such glowing terms that Khosrou begins to love her, finds no peace, and cannot sleep. He begs Shāpūr to bring Shīrīn to him. The painter sets out for Armenia and, with a picture of Khosrou, succeeds in awaking love in Shīrīn, too. Urged on by Shāpūr, she rides to Khosrou's residence at Madā'in (Ctesiphon) the very next day on the fantastically speedy horse of her aunt, Queen Mihīn Bānū. During the journey, as she is about to bathe in a cool spring, she catches sight of Khosrou who is now riding to Armenia himself. They fall in love, but without recognizing each other. They miss each other twice and meet only after Khosrou, who has in the meantime succeeded his father on the throne but has been driven away by his people, seeks refuge in Armenia. But Mihīn Bānū warns Shīrīn of the tricks of men, and so she resists Khosrou's attempt to talk her into freely enjoying life. She advises him to practice self-control as the foundation of all power and to reconquer his kingdom first of all. Khosrou rides away in anger. The Emperor of Byzantium gives him his daughter Meryam as his wife and helps him reconquer his kingdom. Following the death of her aunt, Shīrīn ascends the throne of Armenia, and the country flourishes under her just rule. But when she hears of Khosrou's marriage, she fears that her confused feelings will not permit her to be a good ruler any longer. She hands over the business of government to a minister and rides to her castle in the mountains near Ctesiphon. Through Shāpūr, Khosrou begs her to come to his castle for at least one night, but she angrily refuses. Also through Shāpūr, she makes the acquaintance of the architect Ferhād, who is to build a milk pipeline from the distant meadows where the cows are, through the mountains, and up to her castle. When Ferhād sees Shīrīn, it is love at first sight as far as he is concerned. Khosrou, who wishes to get him out of the way, charges him with the task, which is apparently impossible, of driving a road through a mountain that has never been crossed before. He promises to give up Shīrīn if Ferhād succeeds in building the road. Since the architect, stimulated by the power of his love, makes good progress, Khosrou resorts to a trick; he sends news that Shīrīn is dead, and so Ferhād, desperate with grief, throws himself to his death from the rocks.

After the death of Meryam, Khosrou consoles himself with another woman, but after a short period of happiness his feelings for Shīrīn return. Since he finally realizes that he can bring her home only as his lawful wife, he has her brought to his castle as his bride, and the wedding ceremony takes place. When, even on this night, Khosrou tries to approach her in a drunken state, she repulses him, and it is only the next morning that she gives herself to him. She subsequently counsels him to be just in his government.

Years later, Khosrou's son from his marriage with Meryam has him murdered as he lies on his couch. The king experiences a great thirst as death comes to him. But, rather than disturb Shīrīn who has spent so many sleepless nights on his account, he dies without waking her. Shīrīn's love has thus changed the egoist. Shīrīn mourns Khosrou for a long time. She only pretends to agree to his son's wooing of her and destroys all the things that remind her of her beloved husband. In the burial chamber where Khosrou lies on his bier, she plunges a dagger in her breast.

Another epic from the *Khamseh* of Nizāmī is "Laylā and Majnūn," which was also imitated by Persian and Turkish poets. In this Arab story of the unfulfilled love of the Bedouin Qays for Laylā, whose hand he was refused, Qays becomes Majnūn, the "crazy one" (from love), who seeks refuge with the animals of the desert and eventually dies for love. Even in this century, the story was told by Bedouins of the Syrian desert, but various Arabic versions of it were known as early as the tenth century and were subsequently recorded in the *Book of Songs*. In the Arabic version, however, Laylā is almost always a passive figure, who is loved and feels love, too, but without being allowed to express it. The following lines are attributed to her in the Arabic version:

Whatever happened to Majnūn,
I felt the same as he,
But love for him was an open thing,
While I pined silently.
[143, 24]

Nizāmī's love for Āfāq is obviously reflected in the figure of Laylā, too. Yet Majnūn is the principal figure in the tale, fated to feel love that is never to be requited. "A love which is not everlasting remains the plaything of sensual enjoyment and fades like youth." [122, 48] However, another moving factor is expressed here, the social coercion to which Laylā, as a woman, is exposed. She must subordinate herself to her father's will who marries her to a man she does not love. The only thing she can do is to refuse to give herself to her husband in order to be true to Majnūn. She says of Majnūn:

He does not need to fear anybody, he can go where he wishes, can shout, say and put in verse whatever he feels. But I? I am a prisoner here. I have nobody to whom my heart can talk, whom it can trust. Only shame would be my fate ... A woman may conquer a hero and enslave him so that he lies prostrate at her feet, but she still remains a woman and cannot act in the same way as he can. ...
[122, 226 ff.]

To find out how her beloved is faring in his solitude in the desert, she gives a letter to a rider to take to Qays. It is all about her love:

I am with you with all my love and, tell me, who are you with? Like your happiness, I am separated from you, but I am your companion, even when I am far away from you ... Do you understand me, my dear? I have given everything to share your pain with you, everything except one thing: I have not come to you in person because this one thing is not possible for me. But what does it matter? It is true that our bodies are separated, but my soul does not leave yours for one moment. I know how you are suffering and how your heart is breaking. [122, 232 ff.]

She endeavors to console him for the death of his father: "Do not let your heart be so heavy, and do not think that you have nobody. Am I then nobody? Does it not help you that I am there? And belong to you—only you?" [122, 236]

Majnūn answers her and describes her as his unattainable mistress and his heavenly grove. He laments that he has lost himself on her account. Thus Laylā's love appears much more emotional and personal to us than his. Laylā dies—his unrequited love has already killed her husband. As she dies, she reveals her feelings for Majnūn to her mother and asks her to tell him that she loved him and remained true to him until the last. Her mother is to dress her as a bride. Majnūn's grief for Laylā is so great that he ultimately dies at her grave.

Another frequently imitated epic is *Yūsuf and Zulaykhā* by the Persian Jāmī (1414–1492). This is the poetic presentation of the "best of stories," as it is called in the Koran at the beginning of the 12th *Sura*, the Joseph *Sura*, a story known to us from the Old Testament. Mohammed borrowed it from Jewish tradition. In Jāmī's version, it is a tale of the devotion of a woman, Zulaykhā, to Yūsuf, of whom the poet says that "the most beautiful of the beautiful faded into nothing before him as the stars disappear in the glory of the Sun." [51, 21] Zulaykhā, the daughter of a king, sees Yūsuf one night in a dream, and his handsomeness fills her with profound, consuming love. In further dreams, he reveals himself as a man of flesh and blood for whom she should keep her purity, and he indicates that he is the Vizier of Egypt. Her royal father, in whom she confides, asks the Grand Vizier of Egypt to take her as his wife, but when she arrives in Egypt with a splendid retinue and magnificent dowry, she realizes that her future husband is not the man she saw in her dream, and is plunged from the heights of happiness into the depths of despair. A dream advises her that she can only achieve her real aim through the Vizier—"Be quite comforted regarding his behavior for he will leave your silver lock untouched." [51, 53]

As the wife of the Vizier of Egypt, treasures abound for her, but her yearning remains unfulfilled. The poet then relates the story of Yūsuf the Canaanite, more or less as we know it, of the love of his father, of the jealousy of his brothers, who throw him in an old well from which he is eventually rescued and brought to Egypt with a caravan. He is so handsome that even the king wishes to buy him, but Zulaykhā begs her husband to acquire him as a substitute for a real son, and so it happens. She clothes Yūsuf in silk and gold and tries to win his love. Her agony increases the more he rejects her, since he considers himself a true and grateful slave and the friend of the Vizier. She resorts to all kinds of tricks, as a consequence of which Yūsuf is finally cast into the dungeons. Zulaykhā is tortured with remorse, since her beloved is now further away from her than before. It is only when Yūsuf is

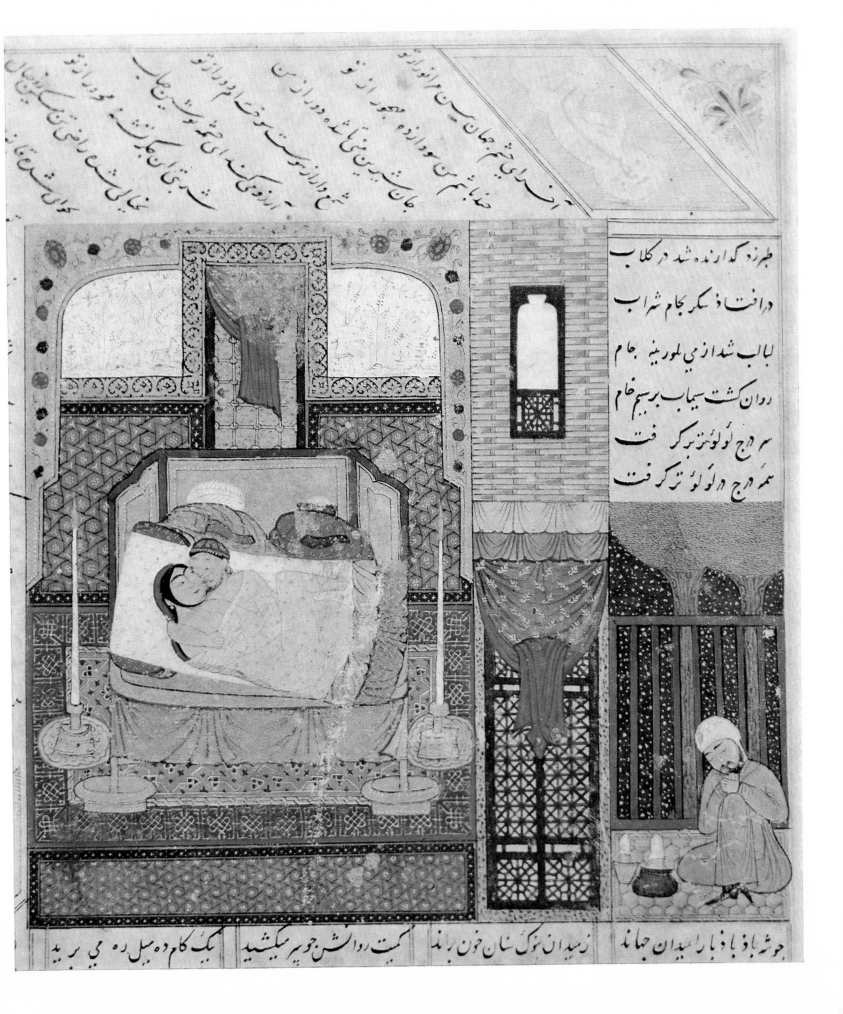

Preceding page:
72
*A royal pair in bed. They have placed
their clothes at the side, and the artist has
left them only their head coverings as a
sign of their rank. Tall tapered candles
are burning on either side of the bed, and
the room is ornamented with colored tiles,
murals, and a carpet. The curtains at the
barred window and at the ornately carved
door are tucked up to allow the cool night
air to come in. A servant is asleep on the
floor outside the door.*

73
*A tender love scene from one of the most
talented Iranian miniaturists of the second
half of the sixteenth century. The young
man offers the girl a bowl of wine, but,
with a gesture of refusal, she turns her
head away.*

74
*With his arm around his
beloved, the young man passes
her a cup of wine with one
hand and some fruit with the other.*

75
In the love story of Warqa and Gul-shāh from the Seljūq period, Warqa, the woman, fights for her happiness. In this scene, she comes to the assistance of her lover, thrusting a spear into the body of his rival.

76
A love scene from the Shāh-nāmeh. *Zāl has fallen in love with the beautiful Rūdābeh from hearsay and she with him. At night, when the harem guards are asleep, he climbs up a rope ladder into the palace where she and a maidservant are awaiting him on the roof terrace. In this night, they swear everlasting love.*

77

From her litter on a camel, a beautiful lady has watched two admirers fighting for her hand. The duel has ended disastrously for one of them.

78

From a Persian epic. The princess kneeling before the ruler tenderly embraces his thigh while he tickles her chin. Three maidservants are waiting at the door with refreshments.

79
*The old servant has fallen asleep
while the young pair amuse themselves in
love play.*

80
*This Persian beauty of the first half of
the seventeenth century has playfully
placed the great turban of her admirer
on her own head while he, on his knees,
encircles her waist. His friend puts
"the finger of astonishment" in his
mouth at this sight.*

81
With a goblet of wine in his hand,
a young man watches his beloved dancing.

82
This picture of a pair of lovers from seven-
teenth-century Iran reveals frank pleasure
at the realistic depiction of the beauty of
the naked female body.

The preliminaries for the wedding night of a royal pair. The bride seems to be a little nervous. Musicians are playing, a servant is bringing refreshments, girls are talking, and a black eunuch is keeping watch.

84
*Despite the passionate embrace,
the countenance of this pair is radiant
with peace and beauty.*

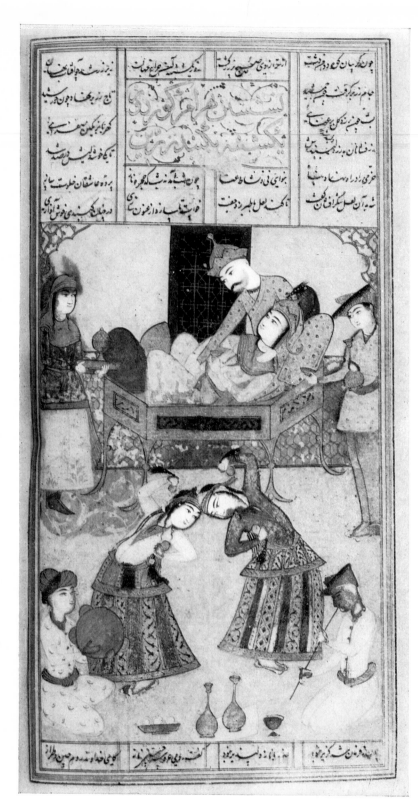

85
*Intimacy for two alone was certainly
not always the rule in the harems of great
personages.*

86

Also in his epic Haft Peykar (Seven Pictures), *the Persian poet Nizāmī celebrates a woman's wisdom founded on love. He gave a new accent to the old saga of Bahrām Gūr and his favorite slave Āzādeh who had already appeared in the* Shāh-nā-meh. *In Firdousī's version, Bahrām Gūr has Āzādeh killed because she only remarks smilingly, "Practice makes perfect," instead of expressing due admiration for the fine shot he has made. In Nizāmī's epic, she takes refuge from the angry ruler. Much later, to his surprise, he sees a woman carrying a full-grown cow up sixty steps. She calmly explains that "practice makes perfect," since she had carried it thus from the time it was a calf. He then recognizes her, regrets his earlier anger, and is reconciled with her.*

87

On a terrace in front of a pavilion, a Mogul lady reclines affectionately against her lover, who, gazing at the glass of wine in one hand, strokes her with the other.

88

Shah Jahān had a "miracle of white marble" built as a tomb for his beloved wife Mumtāz Mahall in Agra. The picture shows the gate, built in brickwork.

89
The beautiful princess Shīrīn sits among her companions in a garden full of flowers and looks at the picture of Khosrou with whom she falls in love. In the background, on the right, the painter Shāpūr, who placed the picture for her to find, steals away.

90

In an imaginary landscape, Khosrou sees his future wife Shīrīn for the first time but does not recognize her. He puts his finger in his mouth as a sign of admiration. The boyishly slim Shīrīn has left her clothes, crown, quiver, and bow by a tree, and, after bathing in a cool spring, is rearranging her hair. Her horse stands saddled in front of her since, when she notices the young prince, she trembles with shame, puts on her clothes, and rides off as fast as she can.

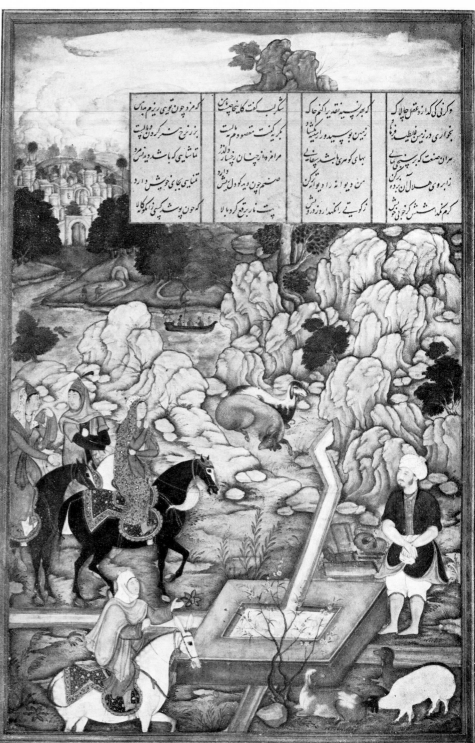

91
His love for Shīrīn makes the sculptor
Ferhād so strong that after her visit to him
at the rock Bīsutūn, he effortlessly carries
her and her horse on his shoulders and
takes her back across hill and vale to the
castle.

92
Shīrīn, in a delicate lace shawl, and her
ladies-in-waiting visit Ferhād who has cut
a canal for her through an imaginary rock
landscape and built a pipeline to take the
milk from a herd of cows in a distant
meadow to her castle.

93

Khosrou and Shīrīn are united at last. In a splendid palace ornamented with colored tiles and inscriptions, Khosrou embraces his bride and offers her a beaker of wine.

94

As a wedded pair, Khosrou and Shīrīn hold a discussion with the sage Buzurg-umīd, "Great Hope", who teaches them about the religion of the Arabs and the Prophet and strengthens Princess Shīrīn in her determination for justice.

This Persian carpet from the sixteenth century shows huntsmen, legendary beasts, and, in the center, Laylā, who is visiting Majnūn, whose yearning has reduced him to a skeleton, in the desert.

96
Majnūn tries everything to get to Laylā. He persuades an old beggar woman to take him on a rope instead of the man she leads around under the pretext that he has become mad. Thus Majnūn comes to Laylā's tribe. A dog barks at him, and boys throw stones. In the background is the Bedouin camp with its brightly colored tents. Women are preparing a meal; an old woman is milking. Herdsmen are watching over their animals, and one of them is playing a flute.

97
*Laylā is dead. Overcome by grief, Majnūn
dies at her grave. The beasts of the desert,
which had once consoled him in his solitude, gather around him. In the background is again a Bedouin camp with herdsmen and their animals, a woman milking,
and another at the spinning-wheel.*

98
*In the top left corner of the picture, a man
is dreaming. For their true love with all
its tribulations, Laylā and Majnūn enter
Paradise as martyrs, and are at last
united there. The miniature shows them as
a royal pair on a throne. Angels and virgins of Paradise gaze at them.*

99
*Zulaykhā meets Yūsuf for the first time
after being consumed by passion for him
for years. She is seated in a camel howdah
and is surrounded by her ladies. From the
windows and parapets of the royal palace
in front of which the meeting takes place,
other ladies take an interest in the proceed-
ings. The artist has turned the scene into
a popular festival. On the right in the*

*foreground is a troop of musicians with
acrobats in animal masks; among them,
a few boys, who look like small adults in
their turbans, mix with the crowd.
In keeping with the Islamic ideal of
beauty, Yūsuf is depicted as a beardless
youth.*

کرای گلرخ روی من نظاره کن   بچشم لطف سوی من نظر کن

اگر خورشید روی من ببیند   چو ماه از خجلتم خجسه چیند

100
*To win Yūsuf's affec-
tions, Zulaykhā has had
a magnificent pavilion
built and decorated with
pictures of their love as
she imagines it.
But Yūsuf runs away.*

able to interpret the king's dream of the seven fat and the seven lean kine that he is released. The king makes him his Grand Vizier. Zulaykhā's husband dies, and, pining for her lost beloved, Yūsuf, she rapidly becomes old. Impoverished and alone, she lives in a hut of reeds. Still filled with love for Yūsuf, she meets him one day on the road, but he refuses to listen to her. At this, she destroys the statue of her heathen god and embraces the religion of the true God. When she goes to Yūsuf a second time, he has her brought before him and she reveals who she is. He has to weep at the harshness of her fate, and, at her request, he prays to God to restore her youth and beauty. She then stands before him as a beautiful virgin and once more declares her love for him. The angel Gabriel commands him to marry her. Their love is fulfilled in passionate embrace on their wedding night:

> *Tenderly inclining to her, his kiss met hers,*
> *Enchanted, intoxicated with the fire of love.*
> *That lasted, long, as if the world were forgotten. . . .*
> *But the kiss was only the foretaste of love,*
> *Like salt, tantalizing the tongue before the meal,*
> *That the desire to feast more quickly comes.*
> *Thus the kisses aroused Yūsuf's passion, too,*
> *Until he clasped the body of the beloved in his arms*

> *And below the navel found the virgin's jewel,*
> *As untouched as when she left the mother's womb,*
> *He thereupon made haste and freed the arrow of love,*
> *To seek the pearly treasure in the hidden shrine.*
> [160, 206f.]

Years of happiness now follow in which children and grandchildren are born to them until Yūsuf, weary of this world, begs God to take him. His prayer is heard. Zulaykhā is afflicted by bitter grief until death comes to her at his grave. She is laid to rest at Yūsuf's side.

In Islamic mysticism, Laylā and Majnūn symbolize the love of man for God which is unattainable on earth. Zulaykhā, the woman who loses herself in her complete dedication to love, just as Majnūn "abandons" his personality for love, becomes the image of the soul searching unceasingly for God. In his introductory chapter, the poet Jāmī, a member of the Naqshbendī order, considers sensual love as only a step on the way to true love:

> *Even when you are trusted in a hundred kisses—*
> *Love only makes you free from you yourself.*
> *Feel love, even sensual love:*
> *It opens the way to true love.*
> [51, 18]

"My eyes shall gaze for ever
only at your beauty"

[164, I, 179]

The cypress in the grove is not as tall as you.
The Pleiades cannot match the glory of your countenance.

[43, 159]

These lines describe Rūdābeh in the *Shāh-nāmeh*, the Persian national epic of Firdousi.

Medieval Arabic, Persian, and Turkish poetry delights in elaborate and, as it were, high-flown comparisons when it celebrates beautiful people.

The Syrian poet al-Mutanabbī (915–965) calls the faces of beautiful women "full moons that rose in veils and necklaces." [13, 18] To appreciate this, one must know how pleasantly cool moonlit nights are in the Orient after the hot sun of the day. The sun is also used, although more rarely, as a comparison for a beautiful human countenance. But it is not simply a question of comparisons; terms from nature, such as flowers, trees, precious stones, scents, or celestial bodies, also serve as metaphors. A beautiful woman not only resembles the cypress, she is also "a swaying cypress," her lips are like coral or rubies, her eyes narcissi, her hair amber or musk, her face, framed by dark hair, is the moon or the sun between dark clouds, and her words are liquid honey. The same colorful metaphors are used to describe a handsome man. Images and metaphors are also supplied by the speech of combat: moonlike faces "shooting arrows whose feathers" are "eye-lashes, piercing hearts before the flesh." [13, 18] It may sometimes be difficult for us, with our sober standards, to follow the elaborate speech of this poetry or to appreciate it, especially in translation. However, even in Arabic, Persian, and Turkish, these images became rigid and were sometimes no more than clichés. Their full effect, especially in Persian poetry like that of Nizāmī, was achieved only by subtle association with other metaphors, elaborate plays on words, and comparisons.

The virgins, who, according to the Koran, make the sojourn in Paradise pleasant, are dark-eyed. Their name, *hūris*, is derived from an Arabic word which describes eyes with a particularly marked contrast between black and white. For centuries in Islamic countries, blue eyes were regarded as an ominous omen, presumably because enemies from the North —like the Crusaders—were frequently blue-eyed. "Blue-eyed devil" was a word of abuse in Iran, even at the begin-

ning of this century. Blonde slaves had their hair, eyebrows, and eye-lashes dyed black to conform to the prevailing ideal of beauty.

Thus eyes had to be dark and almond-shaped, resembling the Arabic letter *sād*, under thick, arched, black eyebrows, which met above the root of the nose. It was considered particularly attractive when a birth-mark embellished the cheek of a young girl or youth. Pearly white teeth, a small mouth, and a straight nose were regarded just as charming, as was the contrast between small breasts, slim waist, and heavy hips crowning ample thighs. An Arab text of the fourteenth century describes the beautiful body of a singing girl in the following words:

Then she raised her garments to her neck and she looked like a silver reed, illuminated with golden water, trembling over something like a sandhill, she had breasts like roses on which two pomegranates or two small ivory cups swell up, filling the hand of him who touches them, and a slim waist, below which a swaying posterior quivered, . . . a round navel, so beautiful that my fantasy cannot describe it, below it a crouching hare or the brow of a treacherous lion, generous thighs and full calves, guarded by the ankle-rings, and narrow feet. [85, 134]

It has been noted several times that men not only appreciated the physical beauty of a woman but also liked to hear her speak well. "When she speaks, it is as pleasant as when a shepherd hears a raindrop fall after long years of drought" is the description given of a singing girl from Bagdad of the eleventh century. And: "She decorates herself with words, as pleasant as an ecstasy or flowers from the gardens of Paradise, sweeter than cool water." [18, 54]

While poets celebrated human beauty in colorful words, others did not hesitate to define the ideal of female beauty in a "scientific" manner, for instance:

The experts agree that the following should be lauded with regard to the face and body of a woman: four black things: the hair of the head, eye-lashes, eyebrows, and the black in the eyes; four white things: the skin, the white of the eyes, the teeth, and the eyeballs; four red things: the tongue, the lips, the cheeks, and the buttocks; four round things: the face, the head, the ankles, which should not protrude, and the posterior; four long things: the neck, the figure, the eyebrows, and the hair; four fragrant places: the nose, the mouth, the armpits, and the vulva; four broad places: a high forehead, large eyes, a full upper part of the body, a smooth face; a single narrow place: the vulva; four little places: the mouth, the hands, the feet, and the breasts. [8, 4 ff.]

But even this Arab text, the Book of Marriage of a Syrian physician of Aleppo from the eleventh century, in which the woman is primarily regarded as a sexual object for the man, does not describe only the physical features appreciated in a woman. She also has to be "kind" and have "a pleasant laugh since that is the first thing with which a wife wins the love of her husband. ... She should speak softly and her voice should be melodious." [8, 6 ff.] It may perhaps be assumed that this was a description of what would now be called "charm."

It might be asked whether women in Islamic countries during the Middle Ages, who went out only when veiled in most cases, were at all familiar with the exciting game of fashion. In addition to the miniature paintings, there is considerable evidence that they did indeed know about fashion and, if they had the necessary financial resources, liked to follow fashionable trends.

In the early period of Islam, simplicity was still the general rule in the conditions of material life in the Arabian Peninsula. Particularly as a result of Persian influence, however, the upper classes soon acquired a marked predilection for splendor and luxury. The conquest of foreign countries with their riches created the material conditions for this.

The Islamic traditions of the eighth century reflect the confrontations that must have taken place between the devout, who advocated a simpler way of life, and those who sought luxury. There are traditions which say that Mohammed forbade men to wear garments of silk or brocade, also the—bright—colors of yellow and red, that men and women were not permitted to wear trains of excessive length and wide sleeves, and certain headgear—obviously of an exceptionally extravagant kind—was banned for women.

Nevertheless, such rules could not prevail in the long run. Arab and Persian historians and geographers, like European travelers of a later date, often tell of a level of material magnificence of the upper classes in the countries of Islam that almost seems like a fairy tale to us. Clothing played a principal role. Men in leading positions, as well as women, attached importance to luxurious garments, usually in glorious colors, and this was how fashions were created.

An Arab historian says of the Abbāsid Khalif al-Mutawakkil of Bagdad (ruled 847–861) that he preferred clothes of a silky fabric which was subsequently named after him—*mutawakkilī*. It is reported that all the members of his household imitated this fashion, which then spread to the rest of the population. This material soon became expensive. The workshops which produced it were expanded so that the demand for this fashionable cloth could be satisfied. [152, 75]

The Mogul Emperor Akbar not only took a special interest in the development of the textile industry in his country but also changed the names of certain garments and thus created "new and pleasing terms" for them. As his friend and minister Abu l-Fazl writes in his report on the Imperial Household, Akbar also had a special system for listing his personal wardrobe, from which it can be guessed how large it must have been. His clothes were classified according to the day, month, and year of acquisition and also according to price, weight, and color. The hues that are mentioned are not simply red, blue, green, or yellow. They include terms such as ruby-red, gold, orange, brass, cotton-blossom, sandalwood, honey, almond, lilac-brown, and so on. [6, 91 ff.]

The custom of bestowing garments of honor is also a clear indication of the value attached to exquisite articles of clothing. Already widespread in the Ancient Orient, it was also practiced under the Omayyads. As with the conferring of orders during the Middle Ages in Europe, here, too, could be found distinctions of rank and reputation and specific ceremonies. If one of the high dignitaries or officials had not yet been awarded this distinction, he endeavored to acquire it by more or less acceptable means since he wanted to demonstrate to his subordinates the esteem in which he was held by his exalted superiors.

Differences in clothing for certain professional groups, such as scholars or legal experts, appeared during the early Abbāsid period. Certain colors became associated with certain families, for example, black as the color of the Abbāsids and green as the color of the Alids in the second half of the fourteenth century. Jews and Christians were usually required to wear clothing different from that of the Moslems. Thus an edict of the Khalif of 849 prescribed that members of other faiths should wear honey-colored headgear and belts but, understandably enough, those affected often preferred to ignore such regulations. As early as the beginning of the second half of the eighth century, a Council of Sages decreed that Christian women had to wear blue coats, Jewish women yellow ones, and Samaritan women red ones.

It would be a mistake to consider that this was a forerunner of the ill-famed Jewish star of the Hitlerite period. The intention clearly was that people of other faiths should be distinguished from Moslems, but, in view of the tolerance displayed by Moslems toward Jews and Christians for the whole of the Middle Ages, this is rather to be seen in the same light as the distinctive clothing for the various professions.

Trousers, a garment exclusively for men for centuries in Europe, where the expression "to wear the trousers" is synonymous with being in charge, were for a long time part of the basic kit of a woman's wardrobe in Islamic countries. The Arabs probably adopted them from the Persians, and it may be assumed that they were worn earlier by women than by men. At any rate, in the Islamic traditions, it is expressly recommended that women should wear this garment, the justification being that trousers were the best covering. However, women's trousers in the countries of Islam during the Middle Ages were never tight and figure-hugging—other clothes were worn on top, of course—as has long been the international fashion in our time. A *hadith* states that "Allah has mercy on women who wear trousers." The traditions mostly define a seemly length as down to the ankles. In the course of the centuries, material, width, and color were determined by fashion and sometimes by social and local factors as well. Thus silk trousers were a Persian speciality, whereas white linen was preferred for quite a long time in Egypt. It is said that at times red leather trousers were worn by the prostitutes of Cairo.

Trousers were gathered at the waist by a special belt, the *tikka*, which was very elaborate, although generally hidden by the other clothes. Inscriptions, usually erotic poetry, were a favorite motif for decoration of these belts which, like at times women's garters in Europe, also served as signs of love. On the occasion of her wedding, the daughter of the Tūlūnid ruler Khomārawayh Ibn Ahmad Ibn Tūlūn of Egypt in the ninth century, is said to have received a thousand *tikkas* ornamented with precious stones—but certainly not for love.

A shirt was worn over the trousers. This was probably introduced by the Romans, who had seen it in Germania and Gaul, in the pre-Islamic period. To begin with, cotton was probably worn, but later more transparent materials were preferred. Thus it is reported of the beautiful slave of an Omayyad: "She wore a shirt of material as delicate as dust, under which the white of her body, the roundness of her navel, and the design of her sash was to be seen." [77, 69] It was only after the decline of the textile industry that the material for such shirts was imported from Europe. Thus at night the king's daughter in *Thousand and One Nights* wears "a fine Venetian shirt with two golden hems and decorated with the finest embroideries." [164, II, 373]

It was also generally the case that in the course of the centuries women's clothing in the countries of Islam differed less from men's clothing than in Europe during the Middle Ages.

At any rate, this is what European travelers such as Chardin, Olearius, and Tavernier report, and Islamic miniature painting indicates that it was already so at an earlier date.

In one of the first Arab sources containing information on clothing, the Book of Customs by Ibn al-Washshā (c. 900), to which reference has already been made, the chapter on the clothes of the elegant lady lists only what distinguishes her from a fashionable man. He mentions smoke-colored wraps and various kinds of coats, mostly designated by their origin or their material, also wide sleeves, white trousers with a train, veils from Nishapur, black head scarves dyed with spikenard, and collars with clove chains. Since Ibn al-Washshā assumes that these garments are known to his readers, he does not describe them. He only sets out to give guidelines on what was seemly, in his time, for a lady or man who wished to be respectable.

The color of clothing in Ibn al-Washshā's time gave an indication of moral standards; it might also be a pointer to marital status or certain social features. Thus the lady of the world during this period did not wear dyed cloth but only materials in their natural colors. Men wore white, which was recommended by the traditions, but white (with the exception of trousers) was worn only by divorced women, blue and black only by widows and professional mourners. As regards the *tikkas*, the belts or sashes for the trousers, both men and women could wear poplin, but brocade and braided silk tassels were reserved for men.

Wide shirt sleeves were also in fashion during the Mamlūk period in Egypt, but they often met with the disapproval of the rulers. Thus Emir Kumushboghā, viceroy of the country during the absence of the Sultan, prohibited in 1390 shirt sleeves which were wider than twelve ells, a nonetheless very considerable size. Since the women were not willing to observe this edict, he sent his slaves a little later through the markets and streets with instructions to shorten excessively wide and long sleeves with their knives. When the Sultan returned, the ladies followed their favorite fashion again. The shirts, which had to be long according to religious law, were often only of knee length, at least in the fourteenth century. A wrap, the *mi'zār*, was worn over the shirt.

There is evidence that Egyptian women of this time also wore trousers from the fact that the slave-sultana Shajarat ad-Dorr, who was murdered and thrown in a trench by the girls of her harem, was dressed only in shirt and trousers when found. Over their shirt and trousers, they wore a dress-like gown with short, wide sleeves, plus a wide, white coat held together by a belt. Part of the coat covered the hair, and a cloth wound into a turban was worn on the head (this was often richly embroidered and ornamented with precious stones).

The wearing of turbans by women frequently met with the disapproval of religious scholars, but repeated utterances on this subject show that this fashion was followed time and again by women. Indeed, judging by the miniatures, it seems that female headgear was more influenced by fashion than other garments. It was often an indication of social status. Olayya, the beautiful half-sister of the Abbāsid Khalif Hārūn ar-Rashīd, is said to have created the fashion of wearing headbands, the aim being to conceal a birthmark she had. These headbands were often ornamented with jewels and also with verses or quotations from the Koran embroidered in silver or gold thread. Thus the following lines are said to have been embroidered on the headband of one of Hārūn ar-Rashīd's slaves:

Tyrant, you were cruel to me in love,
May Allah judge that which was between us!
[68, 22 f.]

For centuries belts and shirts were also decorated with sayings like this. Outer garments of the upper classes were ornamented in like manner at the neck and on the sleeves, both above the elbow and at the wrist. When worn by rulers, this strip of lettering, known as *tirāz*, was not, of course, an erotic jingle as above, but usually proclaimed his name, titles, and often felicitations or blessings.

On account of their occasional extravagance, female head coverings in Islamic countries seem to have attracted official criticism more often than any other article of clothing. It is reported that the Mamlūk Sultan Qayitbey forbade the women of Cairo in 1471 to wear certain kinds of silken headgear or caps decorated with a kind of coxcomb. He decreed that the paper foundations for these caps had to be one-third of an ell long and carry the seal of the Sultan on both sides. His chief of police was instructed to patrol the markets and to beat and pillory all women found wearing the kind of headgear he had banned. Understandably, this made the women apprehensive, and they preferred to go out bareheaded.

The women did not leave the house without their veils, of which there were various types: a black one of a kind of netting which covered the entire face or had holes for the eyes and the *borqo'*, a white or black veil which covered the face up to the eyes.

The Egyptian historian al-Maqrīzī (d. 1442), who as a police official must have known what he was talking about, reports that the wealthy women of his time were wildly extravagant about clothes. According to him, the wife of an Emir spent ten thousand gold dinar on an elegant pair of trousers, and a wife of the Sultan Baybars paid thirty thousand dinar for a dress she had made for her son's circumcision. To convey an idea of the crass social contradictions which prevailed in Egypt at that time—and continued for the whole of the Middle Ages in Islamic countries—it may be mentioned that a water carrier in the early Mamlūk period earned 1 to 1.5 dinar per month, a minor official 2 to 3 dinar, and a royal Mamlūk who held a fief between 83 and 125 dinar. [15, 297, 284] In the first half of the fourteenth century, 1 *ratl* (449. 28 g) of mutton cost 0.03 dinar. [15, 295]

Trousers, a long shirt, a dress-like topcoat, and, outside the house, a veil for the face were also the basic items of a woman's wardrobe in the East of the Islamic realm, which, from 1258 on, was under Mongol and then Persian rule. In the Mongol period, princesses and ladies of the Court indulged in an exceptionally extravagant piece of headgear, the *bōqtāq*, as shown in Fig. 103. It may be assumed that ladies with this bush of feathers on their heads could walk only in a stilted fashion.

In the first half of the fifteenth century, the ladies of Tabriz and Herat wore a kind of topcoat, which reached down to the ground, was often left open at the front, and had narrow sleeves extending over the hands. The belt had been adopted from male fashion before, and was worn loosely over the hips. Now preferred as covering for the head were softly hanging cloths, which exposed the front of the head and hung down over the shoulders and back. (Fig. 109) In general, fashion in the fifteenth century made women look more graceful. As the century wore on, clothes became increasingly varied and luxurious.

Once the Safavids became established in Persia and brought a united Persian Empire under their central control, the country experienced an economic and cultural upswing. A rich material civilization emerged in which high fashion of exceptional magnificence was the hallmark of the upper classes. Qazvin and later Isfahan, the residence-cities of the rulers, were fashion leaders for the whole of the East of Islam.

Fashions in female headgear changed so rapidly that it is difficult to list them in detail. In about 1530, there were brightly patterned cloths with a bush of feathers over the forehead. (Fig. 58) Very splendid indeed was the *tāj-kulāh*—literally the "crown hat"—worn by Persian princesses circa 1550. To begin with, it consisted of a narrow crown worn over a flat cap. Fig. 56 shows what it looked like in the middle of the sixteenth century. An attractive fur-trimmed cap is to be seen in Fig. 65, a miniature of the mid seventeenth century. Other miniatures show cloth head coverings attached to a triangular headband.

In comparison to the rapid change in fashion in headgear, hair styles do not seem to have changed very much at all. Braids are to be seen in illustrations from the thirteenth century—on men as well as women. (Fig. 75) The French

Young woman making her toilet.

jeweler Chardin, who was in Persia on several occasions in the 1660's and 1670's and whose record of his travels is one of the most comprehensive and detailed that we possess, says that the hair styles of the women at that time were not elaborate. The hair was combed back and plaited in several strands.

The beauty of the hair style is that the plaits are thick and reach to the ground. Silken plaits are also attached to them to make them longer. The ends of the plaits are decorated with pearls and a bouquet of precious stones or with gold and silver jewelry. Under the veil, the head is covered only by the tip of a delicate, triangularly cut headband of different colors, which is held over the forehead by a ribbon about one inch wide. The ribbon is embroidered or ornamented with precious stones, depending on the rank of the wearer. Only married women wear it. Girls wear small caps instead of the headcloth or the tiara. [30, IV, 12]

E. W. Lane also reports that in Egypt in about 1830 the hair styles of the women consisted of 11 to 25 plaits, which hung down over the back, were made longer by braiding in black silk ribbons, and were ornamented with gold jewelry. [99, III, 211 f.]

The head coverings of the women differed not only according to the marital status of their wearers but also according to the professional status of their husbands. This information comes from the Dutchman Cornelius Le Brun, who was in Persia from 1702 to 1704. He says that military men, for instance, dressed quite differently from jurists, and this also applied to their wives. In addition, there was not only a great difference between the clothing of married women and young girls but also between old and young women. Since Le Brun considered the clothes of the Persian ladies of this time to be very attractive, his other remarks are also worth hearing:

They also have a white, gold-embroidered veil hanging down over their shoulders, necklaces of precious stones and pearls, and golden chains which hang down to the belt and carry a little jar of perfume. Their outer garment is of brocade with flowers of gold or silver. But sometimes they wear one which is just of one color. Beneath this stola, they wear a jacket extending below the waist. Their shirts are of taffeta or of fine silk, embroidered with gold. They also wear trousers and skirts, fabricated by craftsmen, and boots, which rise four fingers above the ankle and are made from embroidered materials, velvet, or very richly decorated cloth. Their slippers are of green or red leather and have high heels in the same color. They are doubled and decorated with little flowers. Their belt, two or three inches wide, is ornamented with precious

stones and pearls. At stomach level, they wear sashes which extend above the belt. In winter, they put on over this clothing a padded jacket of cotton cloth which reaches the width of a foot below the belt and, when it is very cold, a robe of gold or silver brocade, lined with sable or other furs. When they leave the house, they are wrapped from head to foot in a large white veil, covering everything except their eyes. This veil is usually made from a single piece of cloth. They also wear bracelets of precious stones, and their fingers are ornamented with rings. The women of lower status clothe themselves as well as they can. The wives of the nobility or of military commanders wear netting of silk or something similar over their clothing, and this has a very pretty effect. [100, 217]

Scarcely any of the other travel accounts makes mention of these differences in clothing which resulted from social position.

The Englishman James Morier, who visited Persia between 1810 and 1816, reported of the Shah's First Lady that her clothing was embroidered with such a profusion of jewels that she could hardly move under the weight. Her trousers in particular carried so many pearls that they looked like a mosaic, while the legs of the exalted lady seemed like pillars. The English ambassador's wife, who told him this, was sent clothes as a gift from the Court on the day following her visit.

Of these, the most remarkable were brocade trousers which were so stiff that they could stand by themselves. [118, 61 f.]

From about the middle of the nineteenth century, the European influence on policy and economics, which had really been felt since the beginning of Qājār rule in Persia, also affected fashion. The ladies wore crinoline-like skirts with hip-length jackets, but when they left the house they preferred to wear trousers. A dark cloak enclosed them down to the knees, and a white veil covered their faces.

A very impressive picture of the clothing of a Turkish lady of 1717 is conveyed by Lady Wortley Montague. This very emancipated member of the English aristocracy was probably the first European woman to dare to travel Turkey. In comparison with male travelers, apart from physicians, she had the advantage of being able to enter the harems. With feminine awareness and much sympathy, she sensed the atmosphere of the women's world of the Turkish upper classes of that time, and in her letters she describes it with great enthusiasm and with the desire to awaken the understanding of the reader. She describes herself in Turkish clothing to her English correspondent:

The first peice of my dresse is a pair of drawers, very full, that reach to my shoes and conceal the legs more modestly than your

Petticoats. They are of a thin rose colour damask brocaded with silver flowers, my shoes of white kid Leather embroider'd with Gold. Over this hangs my Smock of a fine white silk Gause edg'd with Embrodiery. This smock has wide sleeves hanging halfe way down the Arm and is clos'd at the Neck with a diamond button, but the shape and colour of the bosom very well to be distinguish'd through it. The Antery is a wastcoat made close to the shape, of white and Gold Damask, with very long sleeves falling back and fring'd with deep Gold fringe, and should have Diamond or pearl Buttons. My Caftan of the same stuff with my Drawers is a robe exactly fited to my shape and reaching to my feet, with very long strait falling sleeves. Over this is the Girdle of about 4 fingers broad, which all that can afford have entirely of Diamonds or other precious stones. Those that will not be at that expence have it of exquisite Embroidery on Satin, but it must be fasten'd before with a clasp of Di'monds. The Curdée is a loose Robe they throw off or put on according to the Weather, being of a rich Brocade (mine is green and Gold) either lin'd with Ermine or Sables; the sleeves reach very little below the Shoulders. The Headress is compos'd of a Cap call'd Talpock, which is in winter of fine velvet embroider'd with pearls or Di'monds and in summer of a light shineing silver stuff. This is fix'd on one side of the Head, hanging a little way down with a Gold Tassel and bound on either with a circle of Di'monds (as I have seen several) or a rich embroider'd Handkercheif. On the other side of the Head the Hair is laid flat, and here the Ladys are at Liberty to shew their fancys, some putting Flowers, others a plume of Heron's feathers, and, in short, what they please, but the most general fashion is a large Bouquet of Jewels made like natural flowers, that is, the buds of Pearl, the roses of different colour'd Rubys, the Jess'mines of Di'monds, Jonquils of Topazes, etc., so well set and enammell'd tis hard to imagine any thing of that kind so beautifull. The Hair hangs at its full length behind, divided into tresses braided with pearl or riband, which is allways in great Quantity. [117, 326 ff.]

The countries of the Arabian Peninsula, at that time provinces of the Ottoman Empire, which had long been experiencing a decline in its power, presumably followed the lead of the capital in matters of fashion. However, even the Italian nobleman Pietro della Valle, who traveled the Near East a century before Lady Montague, reports that the women of Bagdad—once the splendid metropolis of the Khalifat—clothe themselves like the Turks but "still in the old manner ... since the new fashions, such as those that appear at the Turkish Court, reach them so late." [173, I, 210a/b] This is not surprising, considering the channels of information and communication of the time.

Everything that has been said about clothing **and** fashion in the Islamic countries refers to the ruling classes, who considered it their privilege to live in luxury. The great mass of the people never possessed the financial resources needed for this. In *Thousand and One Nights*, there is a description of how a woman disguises herself as an itinerant vendor; she puts on a patched robe, wraps a honey-colored veil around her head, takes a stick in her hand, and picks up a basket containing the merchandise. [164, III, 226]

Pietro della Valle describes the clothing of Bedouin women for which the term "fashion," even now, is inappropriate, although the more prosperous ones had a kind of "Sunday-best" wardrobe, consisting of a "violet-brown or Turkish-blue shirt reaching down to the feet." It had such wide sleeves that babies who had to be suckled could be put to the breast through the sleeve. When it was cold, he reports, Bedouin women pulled over the shirt "a coarse sleeveless upper garment, known as an *aba*, which is not so fine nor so wide as when they want to show themselves but narrow, such as all the women wear." They wrapped their heads in black linen and concealed their faces with a black or blue veil. [173, I, 207a] Della Valle observes that the fellah women did not wear veils.

All that now remains is to take a brief look at fashion in India of the Mogul period. Under the first Mogul rulers of the sixteenth century who had come to the country as alien conquerors and had scarcely anything in common with the subjugated Hindus, clothing—like the entire culture and civilization of these rulers—was marked by features predominant at the time in Persia and Turkestan. This is evident from the miniature in Fig. 115.

From the end of the sixteenth and the beginning of the seventeenth century, the constantly growing influence of the Indian environment on Mogul culture became increasingly apparent in fashion, too. The lady in the miniature in Fig. 119 demonstrates this. Emperor Aurangzēb (1659-1707) took exception to the erotically charming and transparent garments. Thus it was that a long jacket of gold brocade with flower embroidery came into fashion, at least for the winter months; it was worn on top of the other clothing. The Venetian Niccolao Manucci, who spent several years at the Mogul Court as physician-in-chief to Shah Ālam, the eldest son of Aurangzēb, reports that ladies' dresses did not usually weigh more than one ounce, that they slept in them, and that they wore them only once before giving them to their maidservants. "During the cold weather ..., they wear the same clothes, covering themselves on the top of the other things, however, with a woollen *cabaye* (*qabā*, a long open gown), of fine Kashmīr make. Above their other clothes they put on fine shawls, so thin that they can be passed through a small finger-ring." [108, II, 341]

Here, too, at this time, the head coverings of the ladies were symbols of rank: "Some of these princesses wear tur-

Preceding page:
101
*One side of this jug from the Seljūq period
shows two men and a woman in conversation. All three wear gowns with a large
and bright pattern. The lady is wearing
long earrings and a diadem, and her long
black hair hangs down her back.*

102
The wearing of turbans by women was reprobated by Orthodox Moslems, but it was seen time and again. This Egyptian lute player of the eleventh century is also wearing trousers which reveal her navel.

103
This lady is wearing the imaginative headgear of the Mongol ladies of about 1300, the bōqtāq, *and is sitting on a throne with her husband. Her kimono-like gown with its V-neck lined with brightly colored material scarcely differs from the robes of the male courtiers around her or that of her husband, who is tenderly stroking her on the chin.*

104
This star-shaped tile, probably part of a wall decoration, depicts the ideal of female beauty at the middle of the thirteenth century: long, high eyebrows curved over Eastern Asiatic eyes and a straight nose. On her head on top of her hair, which is loosely combed back, is a high cap. On either side of her face are two strands of hair combed forward over her ears. The lady is wearing a gown with a large pattern.

105
This ivory jewel box belonged to a Moorish princess of the tenth century. It is decorated with finely carved leaf tendrils and with lettering which spells out the name of her father.

106
Flasks such as this one of almost modern design from tenth-century Egypt were used for holding perfume or kohl *(eye make-up).*

107
In the Bagdad of the first half of the thirteenth century, women also wore shawls enclosing them from head to foot when they left the house. However, these were not black, as they now are, but were in bright colors with large patterns. The scene shows men and women during a sermon in a mosque.

108

This princess models the Court fashion of Qazvin at the end of the sixteenth century. She wears a calf-length, short-sleeved, open topcoat over a long-sleeved, patterned trouser-dress with very wide legs. On her head she wears a vividly patterned three-cornered cloth, on the right of which is attached a long ribbon which loosely hangs down over her ear and goes over her breast and back to the corner of the cloth at the back. She has dyed her finger tips with henna.

109
A scene from Nizāmī's epic of Khosrou and Shīrīn in which Shāpūr is introducing the architect Ferhād to Shīrīn. This gives the artist the opportunity to convey an idea of the Persian Court at Tabriz at the beginning of the fifteenth century. Princess Shīrīn is wearing a gown with the typical extra-long and narrow sleeves of this period; underneath it is a dress without belt, which buttoned well down below the waist and revealed the upper edge of her shirt. Her hair, combed back from either side of her forehead and ears, gives her face an oval appearance. A vertical black line stresses the line between the arched eyebrows. On their heads, the princess and her ladies-in-waiting wear headcloths extending down over their shoulders.

110

This beauty from an album of the Ottoman Sultan Murād III wears a cheeky cap of brocade with curls peeping out at the sides. Her gown, buttoned down below the waist, has a V-neckline with revers revealing the fastening of her shirt and is tied around the hips with a brightly colored sash. The calf-length gown reveals trousers of a dazzling hue.

111

It was nothing unusual for women to smoke the hookah. This young Persian of 1673/74 is wearing a coquettish head-dress with a flower and a feather, a shaped patterned jacket of hip length over a low-belted gown, and brightly patterned trousers gathered at the ankles. She wears pearl ornaments around her face, at her wrists and ankles, over her forehead, and above her belt.

112

*The miniaturist has surrounded this semi-
nude with garlands of flowers and strips
of lettering. With her small breasts and
round hips, this lady represents the ideal
of beauty not only of the Persian and
Turkish poets but also of the Arab bards
of the Middle Ages.*

This Persian lady of the seventeenth century has wrapped her filmy veil over the back of her head. Over her pointed red slippers with their tiny heels, she is wearing colored trousers and a long, yellow shirt-like gown. She has tucked in the end of the long-sleeved overgown which is tied with a cloth below the waist. She has a two-row pearl necklace around her neck, a diadem over her forehead, and small bunches of pearls as buttons. The sash coquettishly drawn through the belt has a large brooch pinned to it.

114
*A wall tile conveys an impression of the
ideal beauty of seventeenth-century Iran.
Eyebrows joined above the nose curve high
above black almond-shaped eyes. She has
corkscrew curls on either side of her face.*

115

This Mogul lady has made herself comfortable in an easy chair. She wears the Mogul fashion of the sixteenth century, before Indian influence became apparent: a long, shirt-like gown reaching down to her feet and gathered in at the waist and between the breasts, a high cap, not unlike a hennin, decorated with a plume of feathers and pearls, a patterned scarf around her shoulders, and a ring on the thumb of her right hand. Instead of a stone, it is set with a little mirror which was preferred by the ladies of the time. She has discarded her red slippers.

116

This bottle, skillfully carved and ground from a piece of rock crystal in Egypt during the Fātimid period, was probably made originally for scattering rose water. It is believed that it came to Germany with the dowry of Theophano of Byzantium and was subsequently converted into a reliquary in Lower Saxony. Ornamentation of gold and precious stones was added to the top, neck, and base of the bottle, and reveals a rare appreciation of the original style.

117

This Persian bracelet of soft gold with bird and cone ornamentation recalls the art of the Sassanid period.

35. Un Seigneur Mahometan avec une femme qui s'embrasse

118
This Mogul lady from the first half of the eighteenth century is wearing fine pearl ornaments around her neck, wrists, and upper arms, at her ears and on her forehead, and under her nose. The tips of her fingers are dyed with henna. Her princely lover is also wearing a lot of jewelry.

This Mogul girl feeds a bird with a
graceful movement of her hand. Her
headgear resembles a turban, and her
breasts shine through the close-fitting
upper part of her costume. Over her
narrow trousers, she wears a wide skirt
of elegant, semi-transparent material,
with lenghtwise stripes, which reaches
down to her feet.

120

The fairy tale of Tobias, originating from the philosophical and didactic literature of the Near East, was given a literary presentation in the Biblical Apocrypha and was very popular throughout the Near and Middle East.

In this Indian miniature, where Persian influence is still apparent, Tobias has become an angel to whom the painter has given the appearance of a beautiful young woman. She is wearing a trouser-dress of a magnificent pattern and with wide legs, pearl pendants in her ears, close-fitting necklaces, and strings of pearls around her feet. Her imaginary headdress is probably what the artist considered appropriate for an angel.

122
These rings, characterized by fine chased work and set with stones of rose-colored agate or red jasper, may have belonged to a married couple.

123
Long, golden ear pendants such as these ornate examples were worn by Persian ladies in the tenth century and also later, as evidenced by miniature paintings.

124
This necklace from twelfth-century Egypt features beautiful filigree work, in which amethysts are set, and droplet-style pendants holding tiny pearls. On the crescent over the center pendant is an Arabic inscription which means "lasting respect."

121
This ivory miniature from about 1860 shows the Empress Zinat Mahall of Delhi. Masses of jewelry with pearls and precious stones ornament her hair, ears, neck, arms, and hands.

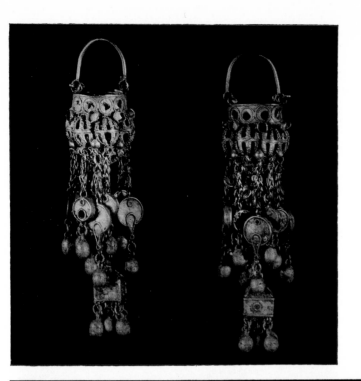

125
*European influence is evident in ladies'
fashions in the first half of the nineteenth century during the Qājār period
in Iran. Wide skirts were worn with
tailored jackets that had a deep pointed
neckline; bright little caps with a
pretty scarf attached at the back sat
on wavy hair.*

bans by the king's permission. On the turban is a valuable aigrette, surrounded by pearls and precious stones. This is extremely becoming, and makes them look very graceful. . . . During entertainments, such as balls and such-like, there are dancing-women who have the same privilege." [*Ibid.*] This shows the regard in which dancers were held at Court.

The love of jewelry was closely associated with the love of luxurious clothes. Both men and women in the Islamic countries paid a great deal of attention to complementing the splendor of their clothes with the right jewelry. Sometimes they indulged this inclination to excess. In *Thousand and One Nights* it is said of Zubayda, wife of Hārūn ar-Rashīd, that she "could scarcely walk under the weight of her jewelry and dresses." [164, I, 325]

In the Book of Customs by Ibn al-Washshā, it is written that fashionable ladies liked to wear close-fitting necklaces of fermented cloves or long cords of costly camphor or ambergris pearls over their collars. (This predilection for perfumes will be examined later on.) Long chains of sweet-smelling cloves are still sold in the *sūq* of the Kurd town of Sulaymaniyya in Northern Iraq, and short necklaces of the small white *ful* blossoms—probably a species of narcissus—may be bought in Cairo. They have an excitingly sweet scent, which clings for a long time to the skin and cloth.

Ibn al-Washshā lists other jewelry favored by the ladies of Bagdad of his time. They include link chains and pierced amulets to which tassels of braided gold or silken thread were attached. Among the precious or semiprecious stones were the black obsidian, pure rock crystal, genuine pearls, corals, amber, and all kinds of corundum. The women decorated their head coverings, of whose shape nothing is now known, with pearls and jewels, and they embroidered their headbands with silk and gold. They wore signet rings in which brilliantly colored precious stones—like rubies, emeralds, and sapphires were embedded. The etiquette of the time, however, prevented a lady from wearing rings of silver, enamel, or iron with carnelian, turquoises or garnet stones. Only men or female slaves could wear such rings.

In a text of the eleventh century, a desirable and prosperous singing girl of Bagdad is reported to have worn a rosary of Shi'rite ambergris and sandalwood from Maqāsir, carved in the shape of large pearls and worth a thousand dinar. Her jewelry is lauded in rhyming prose: "The jewel on her breast flashes like lightning in clouds dark, like in the night the lamp's spark, like flowers in full bloom in the meadow of spring or in the June sky's nightly blue the Pleiades' ring. Her bangles shine like the half-moon the same, her anklets like rings of flame." [18, 53]

Trade in jewelry was of considerable importance in the Middle East of the Middle Ages. Rubies came from India and the Yemen, pearls from Southern Iran and the coast of Oman, corals from the coasts of the Red Sea, sapphires from Ceylon, emeralds from Egypt, and ivory and gold dust from Abyssinia and East Africa. Precious stones, as was apparent from the Book of Customs, were also subject to the whims of fashion. Diamonds, now regarded as the most precious of precious stones, were used only for drilling and as poison in Khorasan and the Land of the Two Rivers around 1000 A.D. Wealthy people used them to commit suicide. The most valued stones of this time were sapphires, emeralds, and rubies; pearls were also highly valued. By the twelfth century, however, rubies were so common, even among the lower strata of the population, that more prosperous citizens used only the large specimens, making them into salve boxes, beakers, and the like. Chardin relates that a Persian lady of the middle of the seventeenth century might pin aigrets of precious stones on her head or to her headband, that she might wear a collar of pearls extending from underneath the chin to the ears, and that she often wore on the left nostril a ring that hung down like an earring and had two pearls and a ruby on the lower edge. It was especially the slaves and children of the wealthy who wore these rings. The Persian ladies of Isfahan, however, did not pierce the nose. The ladies also ornamented themselves with loose bangles of precious stones. Gold or pearl necklaces hung down on the breast, and were held there by golden perfume boxes, studded with jewels. Young girls mostly wore only narrow golden bracelets fastened with a precious stone. [30, IV, 44 ff.]

When the Mogul Empire was at the peak of its power and outward glory, the ladies also wore an exceptional amount of jewelry. In the past, two pearls and a pendant in the ear had sufficed, but now the ears were ornamented with more pearls and several small rings at the edge. In addition to bangles on the upper arm, wide golden bracelets bordered with pearls were worn at the wrists and circlets at the ankles.

Manucci says that the jewelers were kept busy at the Mogul Court of 1700. "The best and the most costly of their productions are for the king's person, the queens, and the princesses. The latter pass the time in examining their jewels and showing them to others." As a physician, he had access to the imperial harem, where he observed that the ladies, when they sent for him, had their ornaments and jewels fetched "solely as an opening for a conversation." He reports that the princesses not only had strings of pearls around the neck and over the bosom but also wore bunches of pearls decorated with jewels over their forehead, diadems as earpendants, armlets and bracelets, rings on their fingers, belts of gold studded with precious stones, trouser strings with bunches of pearls at the ends, rings and strings of pearls at their ankles. "All these princesses own six to eight sets of jewels, in addition to some other sets of which I do not speak, worn according to their own fancy." [108, II, 339 ff.]

From about 1750, the Mogul ladies began to wear nose rings. They later adopted the pearl necklaces crossed over the breast worn by Rajput women.

Fig. 118 shows that extravagance of ornamentation of the late Mogul period was not exclusively the privilege of the ladies, since jewelry was also worn by men of high rank. Even Ibn al-Washshā describes rings worn by the men of Bagdad around 900. Gold was not favored, since according to Islamic traditions, Mohammed had forbidden the wearing of gold rings by men.

Of course, only the really wealthy could afford such expenditures. As early as the tenth century, there are reports that less prosperous women borrowed jewels and ornaments from the jewelers so as not to be outdone by their more prosperous sisters.

At various times, rulers attempted to impose a kind of social discipline on their subjects. Tavernier, a French goldsmith and jeweler, who was in Persia on several occasions between 1631 and 1665 at the time of Shah Abbās II, relates that often a courtier who had an income of seven to eight *tomān* per year would spend four to five *tomān* on clothes. Abbās II did nothing about this, unlike his forefather, Shah Abbās I (1587–1629), who once ordered a courtier "to be given so many strokes on the soles of his feet that he gave up the ghost a few days later"; the courtier had worn golden stockings which he could not afford on his pay. [165, I, 275]

Unfortunately, relatively little of this profusion of jewelry has survived. On that which still exists, certain motifs, such as birds, trees of life, and the shape of the half-moon or crescent, are found time and again. The bird motif is found even in the pre-Islamic Persian jewelry of the Sassanid period. People also liked to inscribe benedictions for the wearer; these could be either displayed prominently or carefully concealed.

It may be supposed that women—not only women, of course, but nevertheless predominantly women—have always and everywhere attempted to give their natural beauty added attractiveness in accordance with the ideal of beauty at the time. The basic condition for this in the Islamic countries was the thorough cleansing of the body after every form of bodily contamination specified in Islamic law.

The public baths were also visited after journeys, after long illnesses, and, quite simply, for the pleasure of a sociable activity. Only the extremely wealthy could afford to install baths in their own houses. A seventeenth-century European view of this frequent bathing is conveyed by the French jeweler Tavernier: "They have a different idea of washing, which is prescribed by law, namely, to take a bath after they have approached their women, and some of them are so superstitious that they go to the baths almost every day." [165, I, 273 b]

The cosmetic procedures carried out in the bath included thorough rinsing with cold water, perspiring in a room filled with hot steam, soaping, and rubbing down or a massage. The hair was undone, washed, rubbed with rose or orange blossom water, and braided again in plaits. Men and women had their body and pubic hair removed in the baths. For this, the skin was rubbed with *nūra*, a kind of cream or salve of quicklime and arsenic trisulphate. After being allowed to take effect for a short time, it had to be washed off, rapidly, together with the hairs, since frequent use roughened the skin. For the skin care that followed, use was made of an ointment of rice, barley, broad-bean or chick-pea flour, which had been blended with rose or myrtle water. The women also underwent a quite painful treatment for the removal of facial down and hair on the legs; a mixture of thick syrup and turpentine was applied to the skin, allowed to dry, and then peeled off with the hairs.

One was considered untidy if body hair was not removed. An Arab author slanders a singing girl with verses that begin: "She has a pudenda which is as prickly as the face of a Khazar lout." [62, 77] Lesbians in Bagdad of the eighth century did not shave the pudenda.

Since expressive dark eyes pretty much define the ideal of beauty in Islamic countries even up to the present century, and as the eyes were the only part of a veiled woman's face that could be seen, eye make-up was of considerable importance. Blackening the edges of the eyes was the custom even in the Egypt of the Pharaohs. Here, as later in the Islamic countries, antimonite (antimony sulfide) or galena was used for this purpose. The Arab designation for this is *al-kohl* (a word which the sixteenth-century physician Paracelsus arbitrarily applied to the spirits of wine and which is known to us today as alcohol). In Persia, the blackening agent was called *Isfahāni* or *Surma* after the place where it was found.

The physician Russell was obviously allowed to see something of the make-up secrets of the Syrian women of his time, since he describes how it was applied: The powdered *kohl* was placed on a short, smooth probe of ivory, wood, or silver. "The probe being first dipt in water, a little of the powder is sprinkled on it; the middle part is then applied horizontally to the eye, and the eyelids being shut upon it, the probe is drawn through between them, leaving the inside tinged, and a black rim all around the edge." [142, I, 111] Iraqi women of the present day still make up their eyes in this manner. Russell also reports that the women used to dye their eyebrows black with *khatat*, a decoction of equal parts of oil and bruised oak-apples, to which sal ammoniac, burnt copper, and henna leaves were subsequently added, but that this was no longer in fashion.

Incidentally, *kohl* was also used by men, and the eyes of newborn babies were treated with it, since it was considered to have medical properties.

Many sources state that men dyed their hair and their beards, since they did not like white hair. Even the first Khalif Abū Bakr is said to have dyed his hair red with henna. Black hair was generally regarded as most desirable, and black dye, made from woad leaves or pomegranate peel, for instance, was used for this purpose.

Henna was used by men and women in the Arab countries, Persia, Turkey, and Mogul India for centuries to lend a reddish color to the palms of the hands or just the finger tips, fingernails, and toenails. For this, henna was dried, pulverized, and mixed with pomegranate or lemon juice or sometimes just with water to obtain a paste. The parts to be dyed were then rubbed with the paste in the evening and a cloth bound over them. In the morning, the cloth was removed, and the henna fell away as dust. [173, II, 89 ff.] In some regions, flower patterns were drawn with henna on the hands and feet. However, in the nineteenth century it was only among the lower strata of the population that henna was still in use in Turkey as a dye for the hands and feet.

The author of the Arab Book of Marriage of the eleventh century, from which passages have already been quoted before, records a whole series of formulas for cosmetics, with the assertion that the use of these preparations could enhance the sexual attractiveness of women. In a society in which polygynous marriages were possible, a relatively large number of women in the harems of the wealthy often lived in a state of isolation, which made them dependent on one another but which also led to a very strong sense of competition. In his Book of Marriage, this Syrian physician provides formulas for making straight hair curly and curly hair straight as well as for dyeing the hair black or red. He also mentions cleansing agents, at least some of which are probably still being used by the cosmetics industry, such as rice flour, barley flour, and almond flour, borax, and fish oil. However, recalling the European "muck apothecary" of the Middle Ages, he also knows of sophisticated mixtures in which natural substances and others are blended to produce astonishing effects. Thus he mentions a cosmetic that "gives the face a bright and radiant rosy hue and causes freckles and tetter to disappear, eliminates traces of leprosy, smallpox, scars, and all black spots so that one brother would no longer recognize the other when he has used it for seven days." He then lists a complicated mixture of peeled cherries, grapevine roots, saffron, candy, gum arabic, bat's urine, boiled bran water, human milk, egg white, almond oil, fig juice, dried

and powdered sea onion, celandine, peppermint, chick-pea flour, milk vetch, rice flour, pistachios, Roman mustard, Armenian borax, and, for binding, water, oil, and egg white. [8, 27 ff.] He also quotes formulas for teeth-cleaning agents and for mouth-odor pastilles.

Whereas most of us today try to achieve the ideal of a slim figure and more or less silently regret giving up many a favorite dish, this text has the following to say: "Since a man likes a woman to be fat and plump for he then experiences, when he sleeps with her, a pleasure which he does not have with a thin woman, I mean, a slight woman, we list here foods which make a delicate woman fat, make her flesh firm, give her skin a clear color and enable her to win the favor of her husband when she always eats them." [8, 60 ff.] Among the fattening substances named by the author are mixtures of various kinds of nuts with honey. Foods rich in calories were also taken by women when they went to a public bath.

Finally, there are formulas for deodorants and scents with the note: "The cosmetics which we have named so far are of no use if pleasant smells are lacking." [8, 76] The liking for pleasant smells, which the people of the Middle East have always had, is legendary. It would seem to be based on a highly developed sense of smell, and reflects a certain degree of civilization. The Islamic traditions record that Mohammed had Ā'isha rub his beard with sweet-smelling *ghāliya* salve. Even Herodotus calls Arabia the land most blessed with pleasant smells. The Koran, *Sura* 56 : 89 (88), speaks of Paradise not only as the "Garden of Delight" but also of "an evening breeze and fragrance." Islamic religious law exhorts the faithful to perfume themselves on Friday, the sabbath of the Moslems, but a woman should not do so when she goes to the mosque. The same applies to the period of mourning prescribed by law after the death of her husband. Frankincense was burned in the mosques on days of prayer, but the mosques were also perfumed. It is thus related that the mother of the Abbāsid Khalif al-Moqtadir (908–932) had the Ka'ba in Mecca and the Holy Rock in the Dome of the Rock (Mosque of Omar) in Jerusalem perfumed with *nadd*, a mixture of musk and ambergris, every Friday. [183, 424]

At receptions given by the Khalifs and the great men of the Empire, the rooms were scented with aloe, camphor, saffron, and rose water. Frankincense was also burned. Of the Mogul Emperor Akbar, it is reported by his friend and minister, Abu l-Fazl: "His Majesty is very fond of perfumes, and encourages this department from religious motives." [6, 73] Tavernier relates that in seventeenth-century Persia visitors were offered pipes with aloe wood. Prior to this, however, they were offered rose water in vessels of gold or silver, depending on the rank of the guests, with which to wash face and hands. They then dried off the water by bending over aloe smoke, whose scent clung to the hair and the beard.

The principal constituents of perfumes were musk—Mohammed is said to have termed it the best of all essences—camphor, aloe, ambergris, and saffron. Other aromatic substances included spikenard, cloves, sandalwood, nutmeg, roses, cinnamon, cardamom, a series of other vegetable substances, and the secretion of the civet cat.

Even at a relatively early date, however, perfumes were synthesized. A treatise on perfumes by a famous Arab scientist of the ninth century contains formulas for imitating these precious essences, which can be sold "for good money without anyone noticing the deception." [186, 2 ff.]

The perfumed ointments *nadd* and *ghāliya*, mixtures of musk and ambergris or ambergris, musk, and aloe, were held in particularly high esteem. The books of formulas state that special variations were produced for illustrious historical personalities and that the formulas became increasingly more sophisticated in the course of history.

Like necklaces of camphor and cloves and shirts perfumed with ambergris, *ghāliya* salve was a popular gift for the singing girls of Bagdad from their admirers in 900 or thereabouts. It was dark in color, and, like musk and ambergris, was customarily used in an amorous pastime, namely, the writing of verses on the forehead or cheeks of singing girls and slaves. The singing girls also used it for sealing their love letters, while the boy-girls already referred to employed *ghāliya* for painting mustaches on their faces.

However, by then, in contrast to earlier periods, it was regarded as a characteristic of the demimonde, since Ibn al-Washshā calls it the perfume of the singing girls and the homosexual pleasure-boys.

Some perfumes are reported to have been invented by women, who either evolved them for their own use or were commissioned by others to do so. Nūr Jahān, the clever and attractive wife of the Mogul Emperor Jahāngīr, is said to have invented a kind of rose essence with which she won the admiration of her Imperial husband. [108, I, 163 f.]

French and English perfumes are now sold in the Islamic countries to those who can afford them. There are, of course,

still shops where the classic perfumes of the Middle East are sold, but these are generally in parts of the city frequented by tourists. They are designed to cater to those who wish to take home with them something of the atmosphere of the Orient in the shape of a dearly bought phial of lotus, sandalwood, or aloe perfume.

Development in the Islamic world has been marked for about 150 years by a process which has not run its course without contradictions; the process of displacing old traditions by innovations from outside. For about two generations this has also made itself felt, though in varying degrees in the individual countries, through women's clothes, it having shown itself earlier in men's clothes. Yet here once again dress only emphasizes social differences. Only the upper class in most Islamic countries has followed the international fashion trends. In Iraq there is even an attempt to create an haute couture which is also very strongly based on pre-Islamic dress of the Land of the Two Rivers. Women from the petite bourgeoisie and urban proletariat, and women from the country still wrap themselves in their black cloaks which are called *milāya* in Egypt, *abāya* in Iraq, *chādor* in Iran, and *charshaf* in Turkey. White cloaks are widespread in North Africa. It is not unusual, however, to meet young girls, for example in Bagdad, who wear denim skirts under their *abāya*. In Orthodox Islamic Libya even the female television announcers appear in *milāyas*, however, there is no obligation to wear a veil. It is said of young Saudi Arabian women who have to wrap themselves up when in their strongly Orthodox homeland that they already change their traditional clothing for skin tight jeans and tight pullovers in the plane when travelling abroad. Yet these are only external manifestations of a process which we will go into further at the end. In this we will only be able to give an insight into the development and problems of women's liberation which have arisen against the respective historical backgrounds and which have not been able to be satisfactorily resolved to this day. A claim to completeness can and should not be made. We wish to concentrate on the Near East. North Africa, Pakistan, and Afghanistan are extensively, if not totally, excluded as there was no material at our disposal.

"Tear away the veil!"

Tear away the veil, woman of Iraq,
Unveil yourself for life needs reforms.
Tear it away, burn it, do not hesitate,
It has only given you false protection!

[188, 335]

This was the appeal of the Iraqi poet Jamil Sidqi az-Zahāwi to his countrywomen in the first quarter of the twentieth century. As early as the second half of the nineteenth century, the veil, for enlightened intellectuals in some countries of Islam, became the symbol of the exclusion of women from public life and from practically all forms of education, trends that had increased markedly in the period of the decline of the Islamic world.

Toward the end of the eighteenth century, the countries of the Middle East were politically, economically, and culturally at low ebb. In this state, they presented an attractive prize for the colonial powers, England, France and, to some extent, Tsarist Russia (with regard to Iran and Turkey), which were seeking to expand their spheres of economic and political influence. The first contacts with Western Europe, such as the journey by a small group of Turkish politicians to France in 1720, the later activities of European specialists in some Oriental countries, and, above all, Napoleon's expedition to Egypt in 1798–1801 made it terrifyingly clear to enlightened politicians and a small intellectual elite just how backward their countries were in comparison with the highly developed civilization and technology of Western Europe. They realized that the only way to resist the expansionist aims of the powers of Western Europe was to adopt the foundations of Western civilization and use them to their own advantage. This was considered to be quite compatible with the original principles of Islam, whose openmindedness toward new knowledge in the first Islamic centuries was recalled. A start was made with military and administrative reforms, since the politicians were primarily concerned with preserving their power. Nonetheless, study groups from Turkey and Egypt, at French universities to begin with, established contact with new educational principles and other aspects of European society. The ideas of the French Enlightenment and the French Revolution and such concepts as nationalism, constitutionalism, and democracy penetrated the Middle East. Schools and the first universities were founded on European

models, and European teachers were recruited. The report on his journey to France written by the Egyptian Rifā'a Bey shows the great impact the social position of French women made on Islamic intellectuals, although, of course, he describes only the middle class, with whom he had the most contact. He had accompanied the first Egyptian study group to Paris where they stayed from 1826 to 1831, and his report reveals the differences between the two worlds, particularly the virtual ignorance of the one, the Orient, about the other, Europe. Rifā'a Bey tells his countrymen that Frenchwomen not only travel unaccompanied but also pursue scientific interests. In France, he comments, the saying that man's beauty lies in his understanding while woman's is in her speech did not apply, since understanding, talent, perception, and knowledge were also expected of women. He finds that French women "are equal to the men in all things." [135, 89] To an Oriental accustomed to an extremely patriarchal family structure, Western forms of politeness appear highly suspicious: "In many things the men are the slaves of the women." [135, 59] Although this devout Moslem finds it necessary to criticize the morals of Frenchwomen, he says that a woman's virtue does not depend on whether she is veiled or not but on her education and certain other factors, mostly of mental nature. Rifā'a Bey was subsequently to become one of the first Egyptians to advocate that girls should also be given an appropriate school education.

For centuries, the countries of Islam had believed that they were superior to all other lands, and in the Golden Age of the Khalifat this had not been very far from the truth. The religion of Islam was considered to be the reason for this superiority. Now that it had to be acknowledged that the civilization and technology of Western Europe had reached a higher level of development, people were nevertheless still convinced that Islam was the best of all religions, although they did not deny the fact that rethinking was needed and many things had to be seen from a different angle.

The Egyptian modernist Mohammed Abduh, who was the Grand Mufti of Egypt from 1899 until his death in 1905 and who emphasized time and again that Islam was the most rational of the world religions, in the last decades of the nineteenth century also undertook a reinterpretation of the Koran in which, for instance, he wished polygyny to be considered as an historical and social question and noted that Islam did not recommend it as an absolute but only under certain historical and social conditions.

The publicist Qāsim Amin (1865–1908), who had been one of Abduh's pupils at the Islamic Az'har University, published in 1899 a book entitled *The Liberation of Woman*. The author stresses that the degradation of women in Islamic countries, which had increased in the course of the centuries, did not have its origin in Islam but had been absorbed from the views and customs of peoples who had subsequently become Moslems. This opinion throws light on the emergence of Arab nationalism. According to Qāsim Amin, respect for women and equality of the sexes are basic principles of Islam. He refers to the early days of Islam when one of Mohammed's wives, Umm Salama, accompanied him on various expeditions and tended the sick and the wounded, whereas in contemporary Islam women were not permitted to perform such humanitarian services. Amin sees the real reason for the low social status of women in the political absolutism which prevailed for centuries in the Orient, leading to abuse of power and to corruption of the individual. Since everyone corrupted in this way endeavored to tyrannize those in close contact with him and dependent on him, women, as the weaker sex, had been victimized. He argues that a free society can be established only when all its members are free. The lower social position of women as well as patriarchal tyranny as affirmed by convention did not justify, ipso facto, its continuance. Women had a right to education, a share in social life and the practice of a profession, since they were no less human beings than men. The verses in the Koran, which had subsequently been quoted to justify the obligation to wear a veil as well as those referring to polygyny and *talāq* needed to be interpreted differently and had to be understood in the context of the age in which they had first appeared. Qāsim Amin's book was violently attacked. Two years later, he published a slightly revised version entitled *The New Woman*, which once again underlined his views.

A few decades earlier, a start had been made on giving women a chance to obtain an education. In 1873, the Egyptian Khedive Ismā'il opened the first school for girls in Cairo. He also issued instructions that the pupils were not to wear their veils when leaving the house. But this effort was apparently premature, since young Egyptian women had not yet been adequately prepared for such a measure.

The first college for the training of women teachers was opened in Turkey in 1863, the idea being to prevent upper-class families from bringing foreign women into the country for the education of their daughters. As early as 1893—at a time of harsh political tyranny under Sultan Abdulhamid—women were permitted to attend lectures at the Medical Faculty of Istanbul University, while from 1899 they were allowed to pursue a regular course of medical studies. (This was not possible in Germany either until 1899.) Admittedly, it was an urgent necessity in Turkey because only a few women in the Islamic countries of that time would allow themselves to be treated by a male physician.

A decree on general compulsory education was enacted in October, 1913, which, although it could not be implemented everywhere, did provide—and this was really a sensation—for coeducation for boys and girls up to the age of twelve. Even nowadays, this is still not customary in every Islamic country. Also in October, 1913, a women's university was founded at Istanbul, but its curriculum was closer to that of a secondary school. Regular courses for women at Istanbul University began in February, 1914.

In Iraq, the first girls' school was opened in 1899, in Iran not until 1917. The difference in the speed with which such innovations were introduced in the various Islamic countries depended very largely on their political situation. Iraq, for instance, like Syria and the Lebanon, was a Turkish province until the end of the First World War, whereas Egypt under the Khedives enjoyed relative independence until it was occupied by Great Britain in 1882.

On March 19, 1919, the Turkish Minister of Education opened the first lectures for women at the Philosophical Faculty of the University of Istanbul. The first lecture halls for joint use by men and women students were opened in 1921, but the young girls were still separated from their male classmates and were permitted to lift their veil only while attending lectures. In Egypt, the first women began university studies in the mid 1920's.

The Egyptian novelist Nagīb Mahfūz, gives us in his book *Reflections* an impression of the relationship between men and women students in Egypt a few years later:

The women students of 1930 were few in number, not more than ten. Most of them were characterized by the harem. They dressed discreetly, wore no jewelry or make-up, and sat by themselves in the first row of the lecture room as if they were in the women's compartment of the tram. We did not greet each other, nor did we talk together. When a question had to be asked or a book borrowed, this was done cautiously and shyly, and it did not happen secretly either, but attracted attention and led to gossip and aggressive comments. [107, 160]

The University of Teheran was not founded until 1935. In 1938 by decree of the Shah women were allowed to study and were also given access to professions and even posts in the government that had previously been barred to them. As early as 1928, financial assistance had been made available for some upper-class women for studies abroad.

In 1922, the first Turkish woman physician opened her practice in Istanbul, the first Turkish woman lawyer appeared on the scene in 1927, the first woman judge in 1930, and the first woman prosecutor in 1932. But in Egypt, for example, it is still not permitted for women to be either judge or public prosecutor. In 1937, the first Iraqi woman received the degree of Doctor of Medicine at the University of Beirut, but it was only in 1960 that an Iraqi woman won a doctorate in Chemistry—and this was at a foreign university. In 1979, the first three Iraqi women lawyers were appointed judges.

Let us return once more to the veil. In 1910, a young Turkish woman attracted attention by daring to have herself photographed. For women who were not allowed to show themselves in public without a veil, this was certainly not an everyday event. At about the same time, young educated women in Turkey began to leave the house unveiled. In Egypt, on the other hand, young girls did not put aside the veil until the mid 1920's. In Iran, it was a sensation even in the late summer of 1928 when the police chief of Teheran visited a café in a summer resort in the company of his veiled wife—even today the traditional Arab coffeehouses are reserved exclusively for men. A few weeks after the daring appearance of Teheran's police chief, men were seen walking side by side with their veiled wives in the street or, for instance, riding in an open carriage to the cinema, although men and women continued to sit there in separate sections. A European observer reports that at this time in Teheran two or three women and half a dozen schoolgirls went unveiled in the streets. It was also then that the women's compartments disappeared from the public transportation system, something that had been done in Turkey a few years earlier. In 1936 the then Shah of Iran introduced a law forbidding the wearing of veils, but many women were still so bound by tradition that the law had to be revoked in 1941. Customs practiced for centuries cannot be terminated from one day to another at the stroke of a pen. On the contrary, a fairly long process of education is needed, not only for the women but also for the men.

In addition the legal position of women was not in any way changed by this law; neither at this time nor at any later period could one speak of equal rights between men and women in Iran. After 1941 most women from the lower urban population classes put the *chādor* on again. Clothes from the West were characteristic of the upper class.

As late as 1943, Sultan Mohammed of Morocco astonished his entire people when he presented his daughter Ā'isha to the nation without a veil. At a session of the All-India Women's Conference at Lahore in January, 1931, in which women of all creeds took part, the chairwoman of the Reception Committee welcomed the guests. Her words were broadcast over loudspeakers, but she herself sat behind a screen, concealed from view in the same way as the noble ladies of the Islamic Middle Ages had sometimes taken part in negotiations from behind a curtain.

The *milāya, abāya, chādor, charshaf,* or veil also offered women protection. When progressive Egyptian women took part in the uprising of 1919, the *milāya* enabled them to hide weapons. This was, incidentally, the first great opportunity for Egyptian women to demonstrate that they wanted to participate in the political struggle of the country. Iranian women carried weapons under their *chādor* in the riots that occurred at the end of 1978.

Nowadays women are veiled who in bygone centuries did not wear the veil since, according to the social group to which they belonged, the veil would have been a hindrance when working, so, for example, peasant women or women of the proletariat of provincial towns. Obviously this is a reaction against the upper classes of society with their westernized way of life. While at the beginning of the emancipation development the struggle against the veil and against traditional Islamic dress was a main point, today in several Islamic countries retrogressive trends can be observed.

Women's organizations play an important role in the struggle for women's political rights and for legal reforms in the Islamic countries. In Turkey, the first women's clubs and societies were formed even before the First World War. In Iraq, the first women's organization was founded in 1924 and was led by the sister of the poet az-Zahāwī, quoted at the beginning of this chapter. This was only a year after the first women's political organization came into existence in Egypt.

To begin with, the principal aim of the Egyptian organization was to win the right to vote as the most important basic political right of women. In actual fact, this aim was not achieved until after the Egyptian Revolution of 1952, namely in 1956. In the first Egyptian constitution following complete political independence that year, it was declared that all citizens, men and women, had the same rights. In 1957, the first two women entered the Egyptian Parliament as elected representatives, and in the parliamentary period of 1964–1968, there were eight women members.

In Turkey, where the sentence, "The religion of the realm is Islam," had already been dropped by constitutional amendment on April 8, 1928, women were given the franchise in three stages: in 1930 for the town councils, in 1933 for the

Councils of Elders, and in 1934 for the National Assembly. Seventeen women deputies, including 14 teachers, were elected for the first time in Turkey in February, 1935. In contrast to this, there were only three female deputies still in the Turkish National Assembly in 1950.

In Pakistan and Syria, women have had the right to vote since 1954, in Iran since 1963; since the mid sixties, they have also taken part in elections in Algeria, Tunisia, Morocco, Iraq, and the Lebanon. In this same period, women have from time to time been made ministers in some Islamic countries; so far, women have headed the Ministry of Social Affairs (Egypt) and the Ministries of Education and Higher Education (in Iran before 1978, in Iraq, and in Afghanistan since the revolution).

The women's organizations furthered, and are still furthering, education for women, especially for those levels of the population which till now have been characterized by the highest percentage of illiteracy; that is, village inhabitants and lower classes in the towns. However, it is precisely among the rural population that literacy is progressing at only a slow rate, in Iran, for instance, from 1 percent in 1956 to 3.6 percent in 1966. Between 1960 and 1970 the percentage of female illiterates in the Arab countries decreased by 5 percent (to 85 percent), that of male illiterates, however, by 10 percent (to 60 percent). [144a, 52]

The women's organizations also provide information on hygiene and endeavor—often in the face of great resistance from the women concerned—to encourage family planning. In addition, they hold courses, for example, on various kinds of needlework and typewriting, thus preparing women for a commercial activity.

By reason of the taboos that still prevail concerning the mixing of the sexes, women in Islamic countries continue to prefer certain professions. Graduates are mainly employed as teachers in girls' schools, as professors on women's faculties, which are still to be found in universities of Islamic countries, and as doctors, for the most part only as gynecologists and pediatricians. Women with a medium level of education work, for example, as nurses in women's and children's wards and only fairly recently with male colleagues as administrators or laboratory technicians as well. In factories in Egypt, Syria, and Iraq, the author often saw departments exclusively reserved either for men or women workers. The reason given for this was the mostly conservative attitudes of the lower strata of the population, who had not yet had a modern education; fathers, it was said, would refuse to send their daughters to work in a factory where they would mix freely with male co-workers. It was also suggested that separation of the sexes was a first step in persuading women of this class to work at all outside the house.

A Moroccan, who took her doctor's degree at an American university in 1974, wrote in her thesis that in Morocco a girl who had to go out to work was regarded as being on the lowest step of the social ladder. The ability of women to remain apart from public activities was still the privilege of the wives of wealthy men. It was true, she wrote, that many men, because of unemployment in the country, were unable to feed their families adequately, but to allow a woman to work outside her own house and, in addition, under the supervision of other men gave them, in the traditional view, the feeling of being a pimp. [114, 185] Surplus labor in many countries, such as Morocco, Tunisia, Egypt, and Turkey, considerably cuts down the possibilities of women to liberate themselves by taking up a work outside the house.

Some fields of activity, which are now largely reserved for women in Central Europe, such as domestic service and retail trade, are still the domain of men in Islamic countries or, at most, of foreign women. It probably seems strange only to Westerners when in Bagdad, for instance, in one of the little shops of the *sūq*, we see a young woman, wrapped in an *abāya*, buying the sheerest of underclothes from a male clerk.

The women's organizations have also called for reforms in family law in the countries of Islam, a demand that is still current. In some Islamic countries, such as Libya (since 1971), Saudi Arabia (since its foundation), and recently Pakistan and Egypt as well, the *shari'a* is still in force in unchanged form, and later additions have even been removed. Other states have relaxed some of the restrictions.

Most countries do still adhere to the *shari'a* over-all, but in a form that includes new elements. In this way, an effort is being made to obtain legislation that is in harmony both with Islam and with the needs of modern life. To begin with, the approach was eclectic; that is, to adopt from each school of law those principles that seemed most suitable for the present time. The aim here is to convey a brief idea of those modifications that have been introduced.

As already mentioned, Turkey adopted Swiss civil law, practically word for word, on October 4, 1926. It was the only Islamic country to make a clean break with the *shari'a*. However, introduction of the obligatory civil marriage ceremony has shown that a body of law cannot simply be transplanted to a country where it has no tradition. To the present day, the Turkish rural population has clung to the form of marriage performed by the *imām*, the prayer leader, although the law does not permit this ceremony even to be performed if not preceded by a civil ceremony. The marriage ceremony performed by the *imām* still permits polygyny and *talāq* (the repudiation of the wife). One result of the conflict between the old and the new was that between 1933 and 1974 the Turkish Government was obliged to pass a total of six "am-

126
The women in their black milāyas *stand
out in the busy crowd in the* sūq *or market
in the little streets of central Cairo.*

127
Nude studies, such as this by the Iraqi sculptor Khaled El-Rahhal, are still relatively rare in the art of the Islamic countries.

128
*The Iraqi sculptor Mohammed Ghani
symbolizes women wrapped in the* abāya
as a corpse in a coffin.

129
*It is only in the modern art of the Islamic
countries that attention was also paid to
the peasant population.*

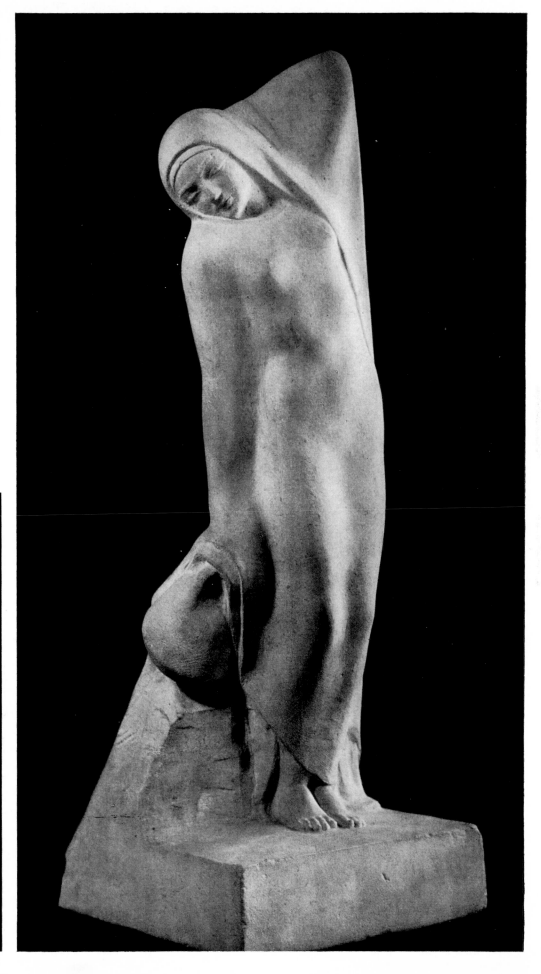

130
Modern women in the big cities of many Islamic countries have put aside their veils.

Changes have also taken place in the lives of Egyptian countrywomen. Nevertheless, progress is slower in the traditional structure of the village than in urban society.

132
Modern art of the Arab countries utilizes advanced techniques, too.

133
Some artists in the Arab countries are returning to the ancient tradition of using Arabic lettering as a decorative element with its message as part of the picture. The Syrian Burhan Karkutli places three dark-eyed and graceful girls in the Arab word for "God," Allah, the last letter of which ends in a stylized head decorated with an almond-shaped eye. The words beneath it repeat the message of the artist: "O God, how beautiful their eyes are!"

134
This Yemenite mother protectively cuddles her child while in the background an Arab horseman gallops over a tall house of the kind often found in towns of the Yemen.

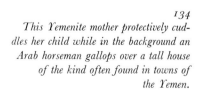

135
The grinding of corn with primitive utensils is still one of the hardest tasks that have to be done by women.

136
The peasant women of Upper Egypt still gracefully balance their loads on their heads.

Following page:
137
Women painters are no longer a rarity in many Islamic countries. The inspiration of this painting by Battul El-Fukaiki of Iraq was the story of "The Land of the Sad Oranges" by the Palestinian Ghassan Kanafani.

nesty laws," recognizing, in particular, the legitimacy of the children born from such unions. Nonetheless, it is hoped that the civil ceremony will gradually be accepted by the whole population.

The only Islamic country, apart from Turkey, that has officially prohibited polygyny is Tunisia. The law was passed there in 1956, and it also required the agreement of both partners to the marriage. Here, too, the implementation of this law was apparently difficult, since in 1964 it was found necessary to state again that a marriage is invalid if contracted by a person who is already married. Anyone attempting to contract such a marriage would be punished by law.

The Turkish law of 1917, which continued to recognize polygyny although the wife had to agree to a second marriage by her husband, remained in force until the 1950's in Syria, the Lebanon, Jordan, and Iraq, which had previously been ruled by Turkey, even though it was superseded in Turkey itself in 1926. In Iran, by amendment of 1959, the husband also has to prove to the court that he is financially able to maintain a second wife. It may be assumed that the agreement of the first wife is obtained without much difficulty when she is economically dependent on her husband; that is, when he can put pressure on her. In actual fact, however, polygyny is nowadays an exception in the more advanced Islamic countries, at least in the towns.

Another innovation introduced in many Islamic countries is the prescription of a minimum age for marriage, mostly 18 years for the husband and 16 years for the wife. In an amendment of 1959 to Tunisian family law, this was raised to 20 and 17 years respectively, and in Iran, in the summer of 1974, to 20 and 18 years respectively. The reason for this was clearly the desire to control the population explosion since, according to traditional Islamic views, at least in the lower strata of the population, the status of a woman still depends on the number of children, especially sons, she has borne. On the other hand, in Iraq, the family law supplement of February, 1978, permitting the marriage of 15-year-olds in exceptional cases when the judge agrees, is considered to be taking account of reality.

Some legislation, in Tunisia and South Yemen, specified that the wife, when she is able to do so, has to contribute to the upkeep of the household together with the husband. According to the *shari'a*, she is not obliged to do so. In South Yemen, each of the two partners must provide for the upkeep when the other is unable to do so. This means that the wife is no longer regarded as a helpless creature in need of protection for whom the husband must take responsibility.

The right that some schools of law give the father or guardian to force a girl who is under age to contract a marriage has also been eliminated in countries with a modified *shari'a*. In the Iraqi family law supplement of February, 1978, drastic punishment is prescribed for anyone attempting this, a sign that such marriages still take place in rural districts.

Limits are set to the arbitrary divorcing of the wife by the husband in Algeria and South Yemen, for example, following modifications of the family law. In countries with a modified *shari'a*, the wife has more rights than in the past for demanding divorce by a court of law, for example, when physical or mental illness affects the marriage, when the husband does not contribute to the upkeep of the family, when the wife is the victim of cruelty or unbearable treatment, when the husband is absent for a long time, and, in Iraq after the last supplement of 1978, when the husband is unfaithful.

Most Islamic countries, however, still make no provision for the adequate support of divorced women, but they can keep their children for a longer time than that stipulated in the *shari'a*.

By the way, the return to the original Islam, as is demanded for example similarly by Libya and Saudi Arabia, can also be understood in various ways. This then includes in Libya equal rights in school and professional education for girls and boys, to a certain extent also coeducation, and opens new, as yet unknown professional opportunities up to women. In Saudi Arabia, however, the first school for girls was not opened before 1959.

The patriarchal family structure in Islamic countries is disintegrating, but only very gradually. Among the upper classes of the towns, in particular, it is now rare for a family group to live together. Nevertheless, it is still unusual for a young unmarried woman, even a university graduate, to live alone and not with her immediate relatives. How greater freedom will affect the crime and suicide rates among the female population of the Islamic countries, which have remained very low till now, is unknown.

Even for the somewhat older generation of university graduates, many fathers still consider it self-evident that they should find the right husband for their daughter despite the changes that are taking place—and these changes will be even more marked in the future—as a result of the increasing amount of coeducation at the universities.

Many young men still expect their bride to be a virgin. Latifa az-Zayyāt, professor at the Ayn-Shams University in Cairo, refers to the sexual confusion of young Egyptian girls of the mid 1950's in her novel *The Open Door*, published in 1960:

Our mothers understood their situation. We, however, we are lost. We do not know whether or not we still belong to the harem, whether love is forbidden or permitted. Our family says 'forbidden', but the government radio broadcasts love songs day and night. Books urge a girl: 'Go, you are free!' But if she believes this, she will be unhappy since her reputation is then lost and sullied by shame. [189, 71]

Incidentally, this novel is a sharp protest against the patriarchal family and the custom of having parents seek husbands and wives for their children, mostly on the basis of social status, without regard to the feelings of the young people. It is made quite clear that women in particular fall apart emotionally in such marriages. As against the rigid social convention that puts a woman's life entirely under the control of her father and husband, the author demands a woman's right to individual liberty and self-determination in her own country.

When an unmarried Moslem girl has a baby, both she and the child are stigmatized. Not only is she rejected by her family and society, it can even happen in rural areas that a close male relative will kill the girl for having brought shame on the honor of the family, the most precious thing that it has.

As late as 1973, an Egyptian authoress wrote in her book, published in Beirut under the title *The Arab Woman and the Backward Conventional Society*, that many women hesitate between a traditional life, restricted to home and children, since it is simple, undemanding, and familiar, and the kind of life they came to know during their studies. She wrote that they feel torn between the world of emancipation and meeting their responsibilities personally and the world of the harem with their reliance on others. Incidentally, this writer attacks Islam, since it always supplies arguments for the opponents of women's emancipation. [69, 9]

Nevertheless, when visiting relatively advanced Arab countries such as Iraq, Syria, or Egypt, one often has the impression, at least in well-educated circles, that the woman of the family is sometimes the "power behind the scenes," exercising a strong influence on the opinions and decisions of her husband. The fact that in the lower strata of the population and especially in rural districts there still exists a very conventional attitude to the role of women in family and society is demonstrated by a Master's thesis submitted to the University of Bagdad in 1970. The author had organized a poll in the district of Diyala, northeast of Bagdad, in which, for instance, only 30 percent of the lower strata (68 percent of the upper strata) answered "no" to the question of whether a girl's education should focus exclusively on preparation for marriage. Only 15 percent of the lower strata (80 percent of the upper strata) favored votes for women. Only 10 percent of the lower strata (78 percent of the upper strata) considered that a woman could successfully act as ambassador to a foreign country. [7]

It can be inferred from realistic works of modern Egyptian writers like Abderrahmān ash-Sharqāwi or Nagīb Mahfūz, for example, that among the younger peasant women some are shaking off the fetters of the past, a past in which the female fellah was valued only as cheap labor. For an Egyptian landowner of the first half of the twentieth century, a woman laborer's wage for a twelve-hour day was less than the amount of money required for keeping a donkey for one day, only half that required for a mule, and only a quarter of that needed for a cow.

It is of interest that in countries profoundly marked by a strong ideology as the countries belonging to the Islamic world, traditionalists and advocates of progress alike use the ideology itself as the basis of their arguments for and against change. For example, a few weeks before the Egyptian Revolution, on June 11, 1952, a commission of scholars of the Islamic Az'har University at Cairo issued a *fetvā*, a religious legal opinion, in which it rejected the right of women to vote and be elected, arguing that the *shari'a* gave only men the right to exercise public functions and that at the election of the first Khalif Abū Bakr the electoral body had consisted exclusively of men. In his book, *Treat the Women well!*, published in Cairo in 1975, Shalabī, Director of the Department for Islamic Propaganda and Culture at the Faculty for Religious Fundamentals of the same university, inveighs against the Arab women's movement, which imitates European women and demands prohibition of polygyny, thus attacking the word of Allah and the revealed religion. With reference to the "emotional nature" of women and their weakness, he justifies *talāq*, polygyny, and separation of the sexes. [145] This was not the only example of such literature which could be seen in Cairo bookshops in the spring of 1977.

Most Islamic countries are therefore in a state of upheaval which affects to a great degree also the situation of the woman in family and society. Of course the development differs in the individual countries and does not always run a true course. As a result of a superficial westernization, felt by many to be disappointing, a trend is nowadays to be observed even among members of the upper classes toward a conscious return to old Islamic traditions. The present development in Iran is without doubt the most striking in this regard. From the measures taken by the Shah regime in connection with the emancipation of women, mentioned on the last pages, the idea may have been planted that Shah Reza Pahlavi had carried out a very progressive policy in this field. Doubtless the efforts of the Shah regime to modify family law and to improve the position of women in Iran was a part of its show-piece projects. They encompassed, however, only a tiny upper class and only seem to have been of use to this class. It was members of just this class, however, who unscrupulously made themselves rich at the expense of the rest of the population and was, as a result, hated by them. Thus in Iran, but also in other Islamic countries, though less obviously, for example, in Tunisia [20a, 141 ff.], for years in Algeria [20a, 159 ff.], the emancipation of women based on the western model was seen to be closely connected with the failures of western colonial and imperial policy and therefore rejected by many. But also in Turkey, the striving for secularization which Atatürk wanted to achieve in the twenties and thirties of this century could not be fulfilled to the extent planned. In the return to Islam there is in many Islamic countries today a search for the power to overcome the complicated development of the present time. But we have seen especially from the position of women which varied and partially contradictory aspects Islam has embraced in the course of its development.

Women, as we have already learned, had rights in the early period of Islam which were later taken from them. However, in the Islamic world, there have always been women who knew how to exploit their role in the social, political, and cultural life of their time. At present, in the more advanced Islamic countries, there are many women who have assumed the position they deserve not only in the family but also in scientific, political, and especially cultural affairs. Women artists and authors are no longer a rarity, and among women educators—especially those of the older generation—there are some who are more impressive than their male colleagues precisely because they had to overcome obstacles the men did not. It remains to be seen what the future will bring. Which tendencies will, in the long run, prevail depends very much on the political and economic situation of the respective Islamic country, as well as the psycho-social factors.

Appendix

Select Bibliography

Abbreviations

HO   *Handbuch der Orientalistik*
MW *Muslim World*
N. S. *Neue Serie (New Series)*
WI   *Die Welt des Islams*

1. Abbott, N. *Aishah the beloved of Mohammed*. Chicago, 1942.

2. —. *Two queens of Baghdad*. Chicago, 1946.

3. —. "Women and the state in early Islam." In *Journal of Near Eastern Studies* 1/1942, pp. 106 to 126, 341–368.

4. 'Abd ar-Rāziq, A. *La femme au temps des Mamlouks en Égypte*. Paris, 1974.

5. Abū l-Faraǧ al-Iṣfahānī. *Kitāb al-Aġānī*
   a. Vols. 1–20, Būlāq, 1285. Vol. 21, edited by R. Brünnow, Leiden, 1305.
   b. Vols. 1–16, al-Qāhira, 1927 to 1961.

6. Abū l-Faẓl 'Allāmī. *The Ain-i Akbari*. Vol. I. Translated by H. Blochmann. Calcutta, 1873.

7. Akram, I. I. Al-ittiǧāhāt al-iǧtimā'iyya as-sā'ida fī ba'ḍ qiṭā'āt al-muǧtama' al-'irāqī naḥwa markaz al-mar'a fī l-muǧtama'. Risālat Māǧistār. Bagdad, 1970.

8. Amdja, K. *Das Buch der Aufklärung über die Geheimnisse der Eheschliessung 2. Teil (Kitāb al-iḍāḥ nin asrār an-nikāḥ des Aš-Šīrāzī)* [sic!] Medical thesis. Erlangen-Nuremberg, 1976.

9. Anderson, N. *Law reform in the Muslim world*, 2nd edition. London, 1976.

10. Andrae, T. *Islamische Mystiker*. Stuttgart, 1960.

11. al-Anṭākī, D. Tazyīn al-aswāq fī aḫbār al-'uššāq. Beirut, 1973.

12. al-'Aqqād, 'A. M. Aṣ-Ṣiddīqa bint aṣ-Ṣiddīq. al-Qahira, 1943.

13. Arberry, A. J. *The poems of al-Mutanabbī*. Cambridge, 1967.

14. Arnold, T. W. *Painting in Islam* (reprint). New York, 1965.

15. Ashtor, E. *A social and economic history of the Near East in the Middle Ages*. Berkeley et al., 1976.

16. 'Aṭṭār, Farīd ad-Dīn. The Tadhkiratu l'-auliyá of Shaykh Farídu d-din 'Aṭṭár, Vols. 1, 2. Edited by R. A. Nicholson. Persian Historical Texts 3, 5. London, Leiden, 1905, 1907.

17. Authors, team of. *Geschichte der Araber*, Vols. 1–4. Berlin 1971 to 1974.

18. al-Azdī, M. b. A. Ḥikāyat Abī l-Qāsim al-Baġdādī. Edited by A. Mez. Heidelberg, 1902.

19. al-Batlūnī, Š. "Kitāb tasliyat al-ḫawāṭir fī muntaḫabāt al-mulaḥ wa-n-nawādir." In A. Fischer. *Arabische Chrestomathie aus Prosa-Schriftstellern*, 6th edition. Leipzig, 1953.

20. Bebel, A. *Die Frau und der Sozialismus*, 9th edition. Stuttgart, 1891.

20a. Beck, L. and N. Keddie (editors). *Women in the Muslim world*. Cambridge, Mass., London, 1978.

21. Bertel's, E. E. *Nisami i Fusuli*. Moscow, 1962. (Bertel's, *Izbrannye trudy*).

22. Blachère, R. "Les principaux thèmes de la poésie érotique au siècle des Umayyades de Damas." In *Annales de l'Institut d'Études Orientales de la Faculté des Lettres de l'Université d'Alger* 5/1939–1941, pp. 82–128.

23. Boyce, A. S. "Moslem women in the capital of Persia." In *MW* 20/1930, pp. 265–269.

24. al-Buḫārī. Kitāb al-ǧami' aṣ-ṣaḥīḥ. Vols. 1–3, edited by L. Krehl. Leiden, 1862–1868. Vol. 4, edited by T. W. Juynboll. Leiden, 1907/1908.

25. Bürgel, J. C. *Drei Hafisstudien*. Bern/Frankfort on the Main, 1975. (Schriften d. literar. Gesellschaft Bern 11).

26. —. "Love, lust, and longing: Eroticism in early Islam as reflected in literary sources." In Marzot, A. L. al-S. (editor). *Society and the Sexes in Medieval Islam*. Malibu, Calif., 1979, p. 81–117.

27. Bulliet, R. W. *The patricians of Nichapur: A study in medieval social history*. Harvard Middle Eastern Studies 16. Cambridge, 1972.

28. Cahen, C. *Der Islam I. Vom Ursprung bis zu den Anfängen des Osmanenreiches*. Fischer-Weltgeschichte, Vol. 14. Frankfort on the Main, 1968.

29. *The Cambridge History of India*, Vol. 4. "The Mughul period." Planned by W. Haig; edited by R. Burn. Cambridge, 1937.

30. Chardin, J. *Voyages du Chevalier Chardin en Perse et autres lieux de l'Orient*, Vols. 1–10. Paris: L. Langlès, 1811.

31. Chehata, C. "L'évolution moderne de droit de la famille en pays d'Islam." In *Revue des Études Islamiques* 37/1969.

32. Cooper, E. *The harim and the purdah*. Studies of Oriental women (reprint). Detroit, 1975.

33. ad-Darbandī, 'A. S. Al-mar'a al-'irāqiyya al-mu'āṣira. Ǧ. 1, 2. Bagdad, 1968, 1970.

34. Derenk, D. *Leben und Dichtung des Omaiyadenkalifen al-Walīd Ibn Yazīd*. Islamkundl. Untersuchungen, Vol. 27. Freiburg, 1974.

35. Dietrich, E. "Eine arabische Eheurkunde aus der Aiyūbidenzeit." In *Documenta Islamica Inedita*. Berlin, 1952, pp. 121–154.

36. Dilger, K. "Ziviltrauung und religiöse Eheschliessung in der Türkei." In *WI N.S.* 17/1976/1977, pp. 194–206.

37. Drewes, G. W. J. "The beginning of emancipation of women in the Arab world." In *Nederlands Arabische Kring 1955–65*. Leiden, 1966, pp. 47–66.

38. Duda, H. W. *Ferhād und Schīrīn. Die literarische Gestaltung eines persischen Sagenstoffes*. Monografie Archívu orientalního, Vol. 2. Prague, Paris, Leipzig, 1933.

39. Edib, H. *Memoirs*. New York, London, 1926.

40. *The Encyclopedia of Islam*, new edition, Vol. 1–4. Leiden, London, 1960–1978.

41. *Enzyklopädie des Islams*, Vols. 1–4 and Supplementary Volume. Leiden, Leipzig, 1913 to 1938.

42. Fahmy, M. *La condition de la femme dans la tradition et l'évolution de l'Islamisme*. Paris, 1913.

43. Firdausī. *Šāh-nāma*, Vol. 1, edited by E. Bertel's. Moscow, 1960.

44. Fück, J. W. "Die Religion des sunnitischen Islams." In *HO*, 1st Section, Vol. 8, 2nd Paragraph. Leiden, Cologne, 1961, pp. 405–448.

45. Fyzee, A. A. *Outlines of Muhammedan Law*, 2nd edition. London et al., 1955.

46. Gätje, H. *Koran und Koranexegese*. Zurich, Stuttgart, 1971.

47. Ǧahāngīr. *The Tūzuk-i-Jahāngīrī or Memoirs of Jahāngīr*. Edited by H. Beveridge. Translated by A. Rogers. Vols. 1, 2. Oriental Translation Fund Series 19, *N.S.* 22. London, 1909, 1914.

48. al-Ǧāḥiẓ: Pellat, C. *Arabische Geisteswelt*. Selected and translated texts of al-Ǧāḥiẓ. Zurich, Stuttgart, 1967.

49. —. *Ṯalāṯ rasā'il*. Edited by J. Finkel. al-Qāhira, 1344/1926.

50. al-Ǧāḥiẓ (Pseudo-al-Ǧāḥiẓ). *al-Kitāb al-musammā bi-l-maḥāsin wa-l-aḍdād*. Edited by G. V. Vloten. Leiden, 1898.

51. Ǧāmī. *Mewlana Abdurrahman Dschami: Kitāb-i Yūssuf wa-Zulaiḫā. Joseph und Suleicha*. Romantic historical poem, translated by V.v. Rosenzweig. Vienna, 1824.

52. Gaudio, A. *La révolution des femmes en Islam*. Paris, 1957.

53. al-Ġazālī. *Ghazali's book of counsel for kings (Naṣīḥat al-mulūk)*. Translated by R. C. Bagley. London, 1964.

54. —. *Von der Ehe. Das 12. Buch von al-Ġazālī's "Neubelebung der Religionswissenschaften"*. Translated and explained by H. Bauer. Islamische Ethik, No. 2. Halle, 1917.

55. Di Giacomo, L. *Une poétesse andalouse du temps des Almohades: Ḥafṣa bint al-Ḥājj ar-Rukūnīya*. Paris, 1949.

56. Gibb, E. J. W. *A history of Ottoman poetry*, Vols. 1–5. London, 1900–1909.

57. Giffen, L. A. *The theory of profane love among the Arabs*. London, New York, 1971.

58. Goetz, H. "The history of Persian costume." In A.V. Pope, P. Ackerman. *A survey of Persian art*, Vol. 3. Oxford et al., 1939, pp. 2227–2256.

59. —. "Kostüm und Mode an den indischen Fürstenhöfen der Grossmoghulzeit." In *Jahrbuch d. asiat. Kunst*, 1924, pp. 67–101.

60. Goldziher, I. *Muhammedanische Studien*, Vols. 1, 2. Halle, 1889/1890.

61. Granquist, H. *Marriage conditions in a Palestinian village*, Vols. 1, 2. Helsingfors, 1931, 1935.

62. Grotzfeld, H. *Das Bad im arabisch-islamischen Mittelalter*. Wiesbaden, 1970.

63. Grunebaum, G. E. von. "Avicennas Risāla fī l-ᶜIšq and höfische Liebe." In *Kritik und Dichtkunst*. Wiesbaden, 1955.

64. —. *Der Islam II. Die islamischen Reiche nach dem Fall von Konstantinopel*. Fischer-Weltgeschichte, Vol. 15. Frankfort on the Main, 1971.

65. —. *Medieval Islam*, 2nd edition. Chicago, 1953.

66. Haddad, T. *Kitāb nuzhat al-aṣḥāb fī muᶜāšarat al-aḥbāb fī 'ilm al-bāh*. Part 1, Paragraphs 6–8. Edited, translated, and revised text. Medical Thesis. Erlangen/Nuremberg, 1976.

67. al-Hamaḏānī. *Die Maqāmen des Hamaḏānī*. Translated from the Arabic by O. Rescher. Leonberg, 1913.

68. Ḥamdī, A. M. *Muᶜaddāt at-taǧmīl bi-Matḥaf al-Fann al-Islāmī*. al-Qāhira, 1959.

69. al-Ḥammāš, S. *Al-mar'a al-ᶜarabiyya wa-l-muǧtamaᶜ at-taqlīdī al-mutaḥallif*. Beirut, 1973.

70. *Handwörterbuch des Islam*. Edited by A. J. Wensinck and J. H. Kramers. Leiden, 1941.

71. Heffening, W. "Zur Geschichte der Hochzeitsbräuche im Islam." In *Beiträge z. Arabistik, Semitistik u. Islamwissenschaft*. Leipzig, 1941, pp. 386–422.

72. Hell, J. "Al-ᶜAbbās Ibn al-Aḥnaf, der Minnesänger am Hof Hārūn ar-Rašīds." In *Islamica* 2/1926, pp. 271–307.

73. Hickmann, H. "Die Musik des arabisch-islamischen Bereichs." In *HO*, Section 1, Supplementary Volume 4. Leiden, Cologne, 1970.

74. Hoeltich, F. H., and Waltz, J. C. *Quaestio. Foemina non est homo videbunt publicè in Auditorio JCtorum à D. XIV. Decembris Anno 1672. Nunc recusa*. Wittebergae, 1678.

75. Hoenerbach, W. "Zur Charakteristik Wallādas, der Geliebten Ibn Zaidūns." In *WI N.S.* 13/1971, pp. 20–25.

76. Hume, E. C. "Woman's part in modern movements in India." In *MW* 22/1932, pp. 361–372.

77. Ibn ᶜAbd Rabbihi. *Kitāb al-ᶜiqd al-farīd*. Edited by A. Amīn, I. al-Abyārī, ᶜA. Hārūn. Ǧ. 6. al-Qāhira, 1949.

78. Ibn Abī Ṭāhir Ṭaifūr: *Kitāb balāġāt an-nisā'*. Beirut, 1972.

79. Ibn Dāwūd. *Kitāb az-zahra. The first half*. Edited by A. R. Nykl with I. Tuqan. (The Oriental Institute of the University of Chicago. Studies in ancient oriental civilization, No. 6.) Chicago, 1932.

80. Ibn Ḥair Allāh al-ᶜUmarī. *Kitāb ar-rauḍa al-faiḥā' fī tawārīḫ al-nisā'*. Edited by R. M. as-Samarrā'ī. Bagdad, 1966.

81. Ibn Ḥallikān. *Kitāb wafayāt al-aᶜyān wa-anbā' abnā' az-zamān*. Ǧ. 1–3. Būlāq, 1299.

82. Ibn Ḥanbal, A. *Musnad*. Ǧ. 1–6. Miṣr, 1313.

83. Ibn Ḥazm al-Andalusī. *Das Halsband der Taube. Über die Liebe und die Liebenden*. Translated from the Arabic by M. Weisweiler, 4th edition. Leiden, 1942.

84. Ibn Hišām. *Kitāb sīrat rasūl Allāh li-bn Isḥāq*, Vols. 1, 2, edited by F. Wüstenfeld. Göttingen, 1858, 1860.

85. Ibn Qayyim al-Ǧauziyya. *Kitāb aḫbar an-nisā'*. Beirut, n. d.

86. —. *Rauḍat al-muḥibbīn wa-nuzhat al-muštāqīn*. Edited by A. ᶜUbaid. Damascus, 1930.

87. Ibn Saᶜd. *Kitāb aṭ-ṭabaqāt al-kabīra*, Vols. 1–9, edited by E. Sachau et al., Leiden, 1904–1921.

88. Ibn as-Sā'ī. *Nisā' al-ḫulafā' al-musammā ǧihāt al-a'imma al-ḫulafā' min al-ḥarā'ir wa-l-imā*. Edited by M. Ǧawād. al-Qāhira, 1960.

89. Ibn al-Waššā'. *Kitāb al-muwaššā*. Edited by R. R. Brünnow. Leiden, 1886.

90. Jäschke, G. "Die Frauenfrage in der Türkei." In *Saeculum* 10/1959, pp. 360–369.

91. Jorga, N. *Geschichte des osmanischen Reiches*, Vols. 1–5. Gotha, 1908–1913.

92. Juynboll, T. W. *Handbuch des islamischen Gesetzes*. Leiden, Leipzig, 1910.

93. Kaḥḥāla, 'U. R. *A'lām an-nisā' fī 'ālam al-'Arab wa-l-Islām*. Ǧ. 1–5. Damascus, 1959.

94. Kai Kā'ūs b. Qābūs. *Kitāb-i naṣīḥat-nāma maᶜrūf ba-Qābūs-nāma*. Edited with commentary by S. Nafīsī. Teheran, 1342.

95. Kohn, S. *Die Eheschliessung im Koran*. London, 1934.

96. Kračkovskij, I. "Die frühgeschichte der erzählung von Mačnūn und Lailā in der arabischen literatur." Translated into German by H. Ritter. In *Oriens* 8/1955, pp. 1–50.

97. Kremer, A. von. *Culturgeschichte des Orients unter den Chalifen*, Vols. 1, 2. Vienna, 1875, 1877.

98. *Kitāb-i Kulṯūm-nāma. Customs and manners of the women of Persia and their domestic superstitions*. Translated by J. Atkinson. London, 1832.

99. Lane, E. W. *Sitten und Gebräuche der heutigen Aegypter*, Vols. 1–3. Translated from the English by J. T. Zenker. Leipzig, n. d.

100. Le Brun, C. *Voyages de C.L.B. par la Moscovie, en Perse et aux Indes Orientales*, Vol. 1. Amsterdam, 1718.

101. Lens, A. R. de. *Pratique des harems marocains: sorcellerie, médecine, beauté*. Paris, 1925.

102. Levy, R. *The social structure of Islam*. Cambridge, 1957.

103. Lichtenstädter, I. "Das Nasīb in der altarabischen Qaṣīde." In *Islamica* 5/1932, pp. 17–96.

104. —. *Women in the Aiyām al-'Arab*. London, 1935.

105. Littmann, E. *Kairiner Volksleben*. Leipzig, 1941.

106. Maher, V. *Women and property in Morocco*. Cambridge, 1974.

107. Maḥfūẓ, N. *al-Marāyā*. al-Qāhira, n. d.

108. Manucci, N. *Storia do Mogor or Mogul India 1653–1708*, Vols. 1–4. Translated by W. Irvine. Indian Text Series 1. London, 1907–1908.

109. al-Maqqarī. *Kitāb nafḥ aṭ-ṭīb min ġusn al-Andalus ar-raṭīb*, Vols. 1, 2. Edited by R. Dozy, G. Dugat et al. Leiden, 1855, 1860.

110. el-Masry, Y. *Le drame sexuel de la femme dans l'Orient arabe*. Paris, 1962.

111. Massignon, L. "Der gnostische Kult der Fatima im schiitischen Islam." In *Eranos-Jahrbuch*, edited by O. Fröbe-Kapteyn. Zurich, 1939, pp. 161–173.

112. al-Mas'ūdī. Murūǧ aḏ-ḏahab, Vols. 1–9. Texts and translation by C. B. de Meynard and P. de Courtelle. Paris, 1861–1877.

113. Mayer, L. A. *Mamluk costume*. Geneva, 1952.

114. Mernissi, F. *The effects of modernization of the male-female dynamics in a Muslim society: Morocco*. Ph. D. thesis, Brandeis University, 1974.

115. Mez, A. *Die Renaissance des Islams*. Heidelberg, 1922.

116. Minhāǧ ad-Dīn. Ṭabaqāt-i Nāṣirī, Vols. 1, 2. Translated by G. Raverty. London, 1881.

117. Montague, M. W. *The complete letters*, Vol. 1. Edited by R. Halsband. Oxford, 1965.

118. Morier, J. *A second journey through Persia, Armenia, and Asia Minor*. London, 1818.

119. Munaǧǧid, S. Al-ḥayāt al-ǧinsiyya ʿinda l-ʿArab. Beirut, 1958.

120. al-Muttaqī, ʿA. Muntaḫab kanz al-ʿummāl. In the margin of A.Ibn Ḥanbal: Musnad. Miṣr, 1313.

121. Nafzāwī. *Scheik Nefzaui: Der blühende Garten. Die arabische Liebeskunst*. Translated by J. Wilkat. Munich, 1966.

122. Niẓāmī. *Leila und Madschnun*. Transl. by R. Gelpke. Zurich, 1963.

123. Nuwairī. Nihāyat al-arab fī funūn al-adab. Ǧ. 2. al-Qāhira, n.d. (Turāṯunā)

124. Nykl, A. R. *Hispano-Arabic poetry*. Baltimore, 1946.

125. Olearius A. *Offt begehrte Beschreibung Der Newen Orientalischen Reise*. Schleswig, 1647.

126. —. *Vermehrte Moscowitische und Persianische Reisebeschreibung. Zum Andern mahl herausgegeben*. Schleswig, 1656.

127. Paret, R. *Zur Frauenfrage in der arabisch-islamischen Welt*. Veröffentl. d. Orient. Seminars d. Univ. Tübingen. Stuttgart, Berlin, 1934.

128. —. *Muhammed und der Koran*. Stuttgart, 1957.

129. Pellat, C. *Le milieu baṣrien et la formation de Ǧāḥiz*. Paris, 1953.

130. Polak, J. E. *Persien. Das Land und seine Bewohner*. Parts 1, 2. Leipzig, 1865.

131. Prigmore, C. S. *Social work in Iran since the White Revolution*. Alabama, 1976.

132. Ragai (Shafik), D. *La femme et le droit religieux de l'Égypte contemporaine*. Paris, 1940.

133. ar-Rāǧib al-Iṣfahānī. Kitāb muḥāḍarāt al-udabā' wa-muḥāwarāt aš-šuʿarā' wa-l-bulaǧā'. Ǧ. 2. al-Qāhira, 1870.

134. Reintjens, H. *Die soziale Stellung der Frau bei den nordarabischen Beduinen unter besonderer Berücksichtigung ihrer Ehe- und und Familienverhältnisse*. Bonn, 1975.

135. Rifāʿa Bey aṭ-Ṭahṭāwī. Taḫlīs al-ibrīz ilā talḫīṣ Barīz au ad-dīwān an-nafīs bi-iwān Bārīs. Būlāq, 1849.

136. Ritter, H. *Über die Bildersprache Niẓāmīs*. Studien z. Gesch. u. Kultur d. Islam. Orients, Heft 5. Berlin, Leipzig, 1927.

137. —. *Das Meer der Seele*. Leiden, 1955.

138. Rodinson, M. *Mohammed*. Harmondsworth, 1971.

139. Roe, T. *The embassy of Sir Thomas Roe to India 1615–1619*, 2nd edition. Edited by W. Foster. London, 1926.

140. Rosenthal, E. I. J. *Political thought in medieval Islam*. Cambridge, 1958.

141. Rossi, E. "La sultana Nur Banu moglie di Selim II (1566–1574) e madre di Murad III (1574 to 1595)." In *Oriente Moderno* 33/1953, pp. 433–441.

142. Russel, A. *The natural history of Aleppo*, Vols. 1,2. 2nd edition. London, 1794.

143. Sābā, ʿI. Ġazal an-nisā'. Beirut, 1953.

144. as-Saḫāwī. Aḍ-ḍau' al-lāmiʿ li-ahl al-qarn at-tāsiʿ. Ǧ. 12. al-Qāhira, 1355.

144a. Šajdullina, L. I. *Arabskaja ženščina i sovremennost'*. Moscow, 1978.

145. Šalabī, R. Istauṣū bi-n-nisā' ḫairan. Naẓariyyat al-Islām fī šu'ūn al-mar'a. al-Qāhira, 1975.

146. Schacht, J. (editor). *G. Bergsträssers Grundzüge des islamischen Rechts*. Berlin, Leipzig, 1935.

147. Schack, A. F. von. *Poesie und Kunst der Araber in Spanien und Sizilien*, Vols. 1, 2. Stuttgart, 1877.

148. Schimmel, A. *Mystical dimensions of Islam*. Chapel Hill, 1975.

149. —. "Der Islam im Rahmen der monotheistischen Weltreligionen." In A. Mercier (editor). *Islam und Abendland*. Bern, Frankfort on the Main, 1976, pp. 9–27.

150. Schregle, G. *Die Sultanin von Aegypten. Šaǧarat ad-Durr in der arabischen Geschichtsschreibung und Literatur*. Wiesbaden, 1961.

151. Schwarz, P. *'Umar Ibn Abi Rebīʿa. Ein arabischer Dichter der Umajjadenzeit*. Leipzig, 1893.

152. Serjeant, R. B. "Material for a history of Islamic textiles up to the Mongol conquest." In *Ars Islamica* 9/1942, pp. 54 to 92.

153. Smith, M. *Rābiʿa the mystic and her fellow-saints in Islam*. Cambridge, 1928.

154. Sourdel-Thomine, J., and Spuler, B. *Die Kunst des Islam*. Propyläen-Kunstgeschichte Vol. 4. Berlin, 1975.

155. Spies, O. "al-Muǧulṭā'īs Spezialwerk über "Märtyrer der Liebe"." In W. Heffening and W. Kirfel (editors). *Studien zur Geschichte und Kultur des Nahen und Fernen Ostens. P. Kahle zum 60. Geburtstag*. Leiden, 1935, pp. 144–155.

156. Spies, O. and Pritsch, E. "Klassisches islamisches Recht." In *HO*, 1st Section, Supplementary Volume 3. Leiden, Cologne, 1964.

157. Spuler, B. *Iran in frühislamischer Zeit*. Ak. d. Wiss. u. Lit. Veröff. d. Orient. Kommission, Vol. 2. Wiesbaden, 1952.

158. Stern, G. *Marriage in early Islam*. London, 1939.

159. Stigelbauer, M. *Die Sängerinnen am Abbasidenhof um die Zeit des Kalifen al-Mutawakkil*. Theses of Vienna University. Vienna, 1975.

160. Sundermann, W. (editor). *Lob der Geliebten. Klassische persische Dichtungen*. Paraphrased by M. Remané. Berlin, 1968.

161. as-Suyūṭī. Kitāb al-īḍāḥ fī 'ilm an-nikāḥ. No place, n.d. (Lithograph).

162. aṭ-Ṭabarī. Ta'rīḫ ar-rusul wa-l-mulūk, 2nd edition. Edited by M. A. Ibrāhīm. Ǧ. 1–10. Miṣr, 1969.

163. at-Tauḥīdī. Kitāb al-imtāʿ wa-l-mu'ānasa, 2nd edition. Edited by A. Amīn and A. az-Zain. Ǧ. 2. al-Qāhira, 1953.

164. *Die Erzählungen aus den Tausendundein Nächten*, 3rd edition. Vols. 1–6. Translated into German by E. Littmann. Leipzig, n.d.

165. Tavernier, J. B. *Beschreibung Der Sechs Reisen/welche J.B.T. in Türckey/Persien und Indien/innerhalb viertzig Jahren/durch alle Wege/die man nach diesen Länderen nehmen kan/verrichtet*. Parts 1–4. Translated by J. H. Widerhold. Geneva, 1681.

166. Timm, K. and Aalami, S. *Die muslimische Frau zwischen Tradition und Fortschritt*. Berlin, 1976.

167. *Tuti-Nameh oder Das Papageienbuch*. Translated from the Turkish by G. Rosen. Leipzig, 1956.

168. Ullmann, M. "Die Medizin im Islam." In *HO*, 1st Section, Supplementary Volume 6, Paragraph 1. Leiden, Cologne, 1970.

169. Uluçay, Ç. "The harem in the XVIII. century." In *Akten d. 24. Int. Orientalisten-Kongresses München*. Wiesbaden, 1959, pp. 394–398.

170. Vadet, J. C. *L'esprit courtois en Orient dans les cinq premiers siècles de l'hégire*. Paris, 1968.

171. —. "Une personnalité féminine du Ḥiǧāz au Ier/VIIe siècle: Sukayna, petite-fille de ʿAlī." In *Arabica* 4/1957, pp. 262–287.

172. Vagabov, M.V. *Islam i ženščina*. Moscow, 1968.

173. della Valle, P. *Eines vornehmen Römischen Patritii Reiss-Beschreibung in unterschiedliche Theile der Welt*. Geneva, 1674.

174. Walther, W. "Altarabische Kindertanzreime." In *Studia Orientalia in mem. C. Brockelmann*. Wiss. Ztschr. Martin-Luther-Univ. Halle-Wittenberg 17/1968, No. 2/3, pp. 217 to 233.

175. Watt, W. M. *Muhammad at Mekka*. Oxford, 1953.

176. —. *Muhammad at Medina*. Oxford, 1956.

177. Weisweiler, M. *Von Kalifen, Spassmachern und klugen Haremsdamen*. Düsseldorf, Cologne, 1963.

178. Wellhausen, J. "Die Ehe bei den Arabern." In *Nachr. v. d. kgl. Ges. d. Wiss. u. d. Georg-August-Univ. zu Göttingen 1893*, No. 11, pp. 431–481.

179. Wensinck, A. J. *A handbook of early Muhammadan tradition*. Leiden, 1927.

180. Werner, E. and Markov, W. *Geschichte der Türken*. Berlin, 1978.

181. Westermarck, E. *Wit and wisdom in Morocco*. London, 1930.

182. White, C. *Häusliches Leben und Sitten der Türken*, Vols. 1, 2. Edited by A. Reumont. Berlin, 1844, 1845.

183. Wiedemann, E. "Aus Nuwairis Enzyklopädie. Über Parfüms." In *Archiv f. d. Gesch. d. Naturwiss. u. d. Technik*, Vol. 6. Leipzig, 1913, pp. 418–426.

184. —. "Über Parfüms und Drogen bei den Arabern." In *Beiträge z. Gesch. d. Naturwiss.*, 56. Sitz. ber. d. Physikal.-Med. Sozietät in Erlangen, Vol. 48. Erlangen, 1916, pp. 329–339.

185. *Wunderbare Erlebnisse, seltsame Begebnisse. Arabische Erzählungen*. Translated by H. Wehr. Berlin, 1962.

186. Ya'qūb b. Isḥāq al-Kindī. Kitāb kīmiyā al-'iṭr wa-t-taṣ'īdāt. Translated by K. Garbers. Abh. f. d. Kunde d. Morgenlandes 30. Leipzig, 1948.

187. Youssef, N. H. *Women and work in developing societies*. Westport, Conn., 1974.

188. az-Zahāwī, Ğ. Ṣ. Al-lubāb. Bagdad, 1928.

189. az-Zayyāt, L. Al-bāb al-maftuḥ. al-Qāhira, 1960.

About the Illustrations

1 *Abū Zayd and al-Ḥārith arrive in a village.*
Miniature by Wāsiṭī from: Ḥarīrī, Maqāmāt. Bagdad, dated 635 (1237). Size of page 36.5 × 29.4 cm. Bibliothèque Nationale, Paris, MS. arabe 5847, f. 138 r.

2 *Conquest of a city.*
Miniature in the style of Tabriz, around 1300. 37.2 × 29 cm. Orientabteilung der Staatsbibliothek Preussischer Kulturbesitz, Berlin (West), MS. Diez A fol. 70, f. 7 r.

3 *Page of the Koran.*
From a fragment of the Koran in Kūfic lettering. Eighth century. Size of page 55 × 63 cm. Forschungsbibliothek Gotha, MS. orient. A 462, f. 2 r.

4 *A woman worshiper.*
Tin relief, fragment, Seljūq, twelfth/thirteenth century. Height 10.6 cm. Staatliches Museum für Völkerkunde, Munich, Cat. No. 36-19-54

5 *Bahrām Gūr with the Princess of the Green Pavilion.*
Miniature from: Amīr Ḥusrau Dihlavī, Ḥamsa. Iran, School of Shiraz, probably between 1590 and 1600. 14 × 13 cm (without dome). Orientabteilung der Staatsbibliothek Preussischer Kulturbesitz, Berlin (West), MS. or. fol. 1615, f. 210 r.

6 *Prince Humāy and Princess Humāyūn in the garden.*
Miniature from a work by Hvaǧū-i Kirmānī. Herat, first half of fifteenth century. 29.4 × 17.9 cm. Musée des Arts Décoratifs, Paris, In 3727.

7 *Noah's ark.*
Miniature from: Isḥāq an-Nīšā-pūrī, Qiṣaṣ al-anbiyā'. Iran, School of Shiraz, last quarter of sixteenth century. 13.9 × 10.5 cm. Orientabteilung der Staatsbibliothek Preussischer Kulturbesitz, Berlin (West), MS. Diez A fol. 3, f. 23 r.

8 *Isfandiyār kills a sorceress.*
Miniature from: Firdausī, Šāhnāma. Iran, School of Isfahan, dated 1014 (1605). 24.3 × 14 cm. Deutsche Staatsbibliothek, Berlin, MS. or. fol. 4251, f. 478 v.

9 *Scene before the gate of a city.*
Miniature from the Jahāngīr Album. India, 1617/18. Size of pages 53.5 × 40 cm. Orientabteilung der Staatsbibliothek Preussischer Kulturbesitz, Berlin (West), Libr. pict. A 117, f. 14 r.

10 *Abū Zayd and his wife before the qāḍī of Tabriz.*
Miniature by Wāsiṭī from: Ḥarīrī, Maqāmāt. Bagdad, dated 635 (1237). 20 × 26.7 cm. Bibliothèque Nationale, Paris, MS. arabe 5847, f. 21.

11 *Abū Zayd, disguised as a woman, tries to sell his son as a slave.*
Miniature by Wāsiṭī from: Ḥarīrī, Maqāmāt. Bagdad, dated 635 (1237). Size of page 36.5 × 29.4 cm. Bibliothèque Nationale, Paris, MS. arabe 5847, f. 105.

12 *Prayer niche (mihrāb).*
Wood. From the mosque of Sayyida Roqayya. Egypt, Fāṭimid period, middle of twelfth century. Height 210 cm, width 111 cm, depth 54 cm. Islamic Museum, Cairo, Inv. No. 446.

13 *Stone tablet with Arabic lettering.*
From the mosque of the Marjāniyya Madrasa. Bagdad, fourteenth century. Height 146.5 cm, width 195.5 cm. Iraqi Museum, Bagdad, A 9874.

14 *Mosque of Bībī Khānum.*
Samarkand, fifteenth century.

15 *Mohammed's first meeting with Khadīja.*
Miniature from: Isḥāq an-Nīšāpūrī, Qiṣaṣ al-anbiyā'. Iran, around 1560. Chester Beatty Library, Dublin, MS. 231, f. 253.

16 *The birth of Christ according to the Koran.*
Miniature from: Isḥāq an-Nīšāpūrī, Qiṣaṣ al-anbiyā'. Iran, around 1560. Chester Beatty Library, Dublin, MS. 231, f. 225.

17 *Entrance to the harem of a palace.*
Miniature from an album of Murād III. Bukhara style, sixteenth century. 21.1 × 12.6 cm. Österreichische Nationalbibliothek, Vienna, Cod. Mixt. 313, f. 29.

18 *Adam and Eve being driven out of Paradise.*
Miniature from: Fuẓūlī, Ḥadīqat as-suʿadā'. Turkey, end of sixteenth century. Size of page 31 × 21 cm. Bibliothèque Nationale, Paris, Suppl. turc 1088, f. 9 v.

19 *The Queen of Saba on the throne.*
Miniature from: Niẓāmī, Maḫzan al-asrār. Iran, middle of sixteenth century. 35.2 × 21.1 cm. Bibliothèque Nationale, Paris, Suppl. pers. 1956, f. 1.

20 *Sūfī preaching from the pulpit.*
Miniature from: Ḥusain Baiqarā, Maǧālis al-ʿuššāq. Iran, middle of sixteenth century. 11.1 × 10 cm. Bodleian Library, Oxford, MS. Ouseley Add. 24, f. 55 v.

21 *Stoning of an adulterous pair.*
Miniature from: Qiṣṣa-i Amīr Ḥamza. India, probably end of fifteenth century. 10 × 15.8 cm. Orientabteilung der Staatsbibliothek Preussischer Kulturbesitz, Berlin (West), MS. or. fol. 4181, f. 11 r.

22 *Celebration in the palace of Emperor Akbar at the birth of Prince Salīm.*
Miniature from: Abū l-Faẓl, ʿAin-i Akbarī. Delhi, late sixteenth century. Chester Beatty Library, Dublin, MS. 3, f. 143 v.

23 *Storage jar.*
Clay, unglazed. Iraq, thirteenth century. Height 83 cm, greatest circumference 212 cm. Iraqi Museum, Bagdad, A 5497.

24 *Figurines.*
Clay, with reliefs. Iraq, Wasit, thirteenth century. Height 24 and 23.5 cm. Iraqi Museum, Bagdad.

25 *Nursing Woman.*
Faïence, lustre-painted. Iran, Kashan, thirteenth century. Islamic Museum, Cairo.

26 *Scene from* Kalīla wa-Dimna.
Book page with miniature. Syria, second quarter of fourteenth century. Size of page 29.4 × 22.5 cm. Bibliothèque Nationale, Paris, MS. arabe 3467, f. 61.

27 *Laylā and Majnūn at school.*
Book page with miniature. Iran, Shiraz, dated 984 (1576). Size of page 41 × 27 cm. Museum für Islamische Kunst, Staatliche Museen Preussischer Kulturbesitz, Berlin (West), Inv. No. I 14/62.

28 *Cradle.*
Gold inlaid with jewels. Turkey, seventeenth century. 103 × 57 cm. Topkapi Saray Museum, Istanbul, Inv. No. 2/680.

29 *The birth of Rustam.*
Miniature from: Firdausī, Šāh-nāma. Iran, School of Isfahan, dated 1014 (1605). 24.5 × 14.5 cm. Deutsche Staatsbibliothek, Berlin, MS. or. fol. 4251, f. 180 v.

30 *A scene from a Bedouin camp.*
Miniature by Mīr Sayyid 'Alī probably from a Ḥamsa of Niẓāmī. Iran, Tabriz, around 1540. Two parts stitched together, each 13.8 × 19.4 cm. Fogg Art Museum, Harvard University, Cambridge, Mass., Gift of John Goelet, Inv. No. 1958 75 a–b.

31 *The Iranian King Jamshīd teaches his subjects the various crafts.*
Miniature from: Ṭabarī, Ta'rīḫ. Iran, dated 874 (1470). Chester Beatty Library, Dublin, MS. 144, f. 20.

32 *Tahmīna comes into Rustam's room.*
Miniature from a *Shāh-nāmeh* manuscript, which is ascribed to the patronage of Iskandar Sulṭān. Iran, Shiraz or Isfahan, around 1410. 21 × 10.9 cm. Fogg Art Museum, Harvard University, Cambridge, Mass., Gift of Mrs. Elise Cabot Forbeo (Ralph E.), Mr. Eric Schroeder, and the Annie S. Coburn Fund, Inv. No. 1939. 225.

33 *Popular celebration watched by a prince and his harem.*
Miniature from: Firdausī, Šāh-nāma. Iran, probably School of Mashhad, around 1570. 18.8 × 9.7 cm. Orientabteilung der Staatsbibliothek Preussischer Kulturbesitz, Berlin (West), MS. or. fol. 189, f. 12 r.

34 *In the bazaar.*
Miniature from: Ḍarīr, Siyar-i Nabīy. Turkey, dated 1003 (1594/5). Chester Beatty Library, Dublin, MS. 419, f. 310 r.

35 *Doctor in the harem.*
Miniature from: 'Alī Čelebī, Humāyūn-nāma. Turkey, end of sixteenth century. 22 × 12 cm. Topkapi Saray Museum, Istanbul, Ḥaz. 843, f. 163 v.

36 *Zāl on his way to Rūdābeh.*
Miniature from: Firdousī, Šāh-nāma. Iran, School of Isfahan, dated 1014 (1605). Deutsche Staatsbibliothek, Berlin, MS. or. fol. 4251, f. 167 v.

37 *Bowl.*
Rock crystal with gold and jewels. Iran, seventeenth century. Musée du Louvre, Paris.

38 *Ladies preparing a picnic in the country.*
Miniature from: Amīr Ḫusrau Dihlavī, Ḥamsa. Iran, around 1575. 19.6 × 12.5 cm. Bodleian Library, Oxford, MS. Elliott 189, f. 192 r.

39 *Zāl fetches his bride, Rūdābeh.*
Miniature from: Firdausī, Šāh-nāma. Iran, probably Shiraz, dated 1002 (1593). 19.5 × 15.5 cm. Deutsche Staatsbibliothek, Berlin, MS. Diez A fol. 1, f. 72 v.

40 *Bahrām Gūr and Āzādeh hunting.*
Miniature from: Amīr Ḫusrau Dihlavī, Ḥamsa. Iran, School of Shiraz, probably between 1590 and 1600. 17 × 13 cm. Orientabteilung der Staatsbibliothek Preussischer Kulturbesitz, Berlin (West), MS. or. fol. 1615, f. 198 v.

41 *Lamentation at the bier of Rustam and Zavāra.*
Miniature from: Firdausī, Šāh-nāma. Iran, School of Isfahan, dated 1014 (1605). 24.5 × 14.5 cm. Deutsche Staatsbibliothek, Berlin, MS. or. fol. 4251, f. 519 v.

42 *Carpet.*
India, late sixteenth century. 2.23 × 1.75 m. Museum of Fine Arts, Boston.

43 *Harem.*
Miniature. India, end of seventeenth century. 32 × 21.5 cm. Museum für Indische Kunst, Staatliche Museen Preussischer Kulturbesitz, Berlin (West), Cat. No. MIK I 5055.

44 *Emperor Akbar crosses a river with his harem.*
Miniature from: Iqbāl-nāma-yi Ǧahāngīrī. India, seventeenth century. 13.3 × 28.3 cm. Free Library of Philadelphia, Lewis MS. 44, f. 18 r.

45 *Woman milking.*
Miniature by Mu'īn. India, beginning of seventeenth century. 19.3 × 12.7 cm. Staatliche Museen, Berlin, Islamisches Museum, Inv. No. I 6756.

46 *Mogul lady with maidservants in the garden of the harem.*
Miniature. India, end of seventeenth century. 21 × 13.7 cm. Staatliche Museen, Berlin, Islamisches Museum, I 4597, f. 25.

47 *Court scenes.*
Miniature. India, probably middle of eighteenth century. 77.5 × 38.7 cm. Schloss Schönbrunn, Vegetin-Room, west wall.

48 *Scene from a mosque.*
Miniature by Bihzād from: Sa'dī, Bostān. Khorasan, dated 893 (1488/9). 21.5 × 15.7 cm. National Library, Cairo, Adab Fārisī 22, f. 26.

49 *A lady in discussion with a sheikh.*
Miniature. Iran, 1658. 18.5 × 11 cm. Museum des Kunsthandwerks, Leipzig, Inv. No. B 11.10c.

50 *The goldsmith, Hasan, is freed from the prison tower by his wife.*
Miniature from: Amīr Ḫusrau Dihlavī, Ḥamsa. Signed Hāšim. India, School of Jahāngīr, around 1610. 16 × 10. 8 cm. Deutsche Staatsbibliothek, Berlin, MS. or. fol. 1278, f. 147 v.

51 *Mohammed with his daughter, Fāṭima, and his wives, Ā'isha and Umm Salama.*
Miniature from: Ḍarīr, Siyar-i Nabīy. Turkey, dated 1003 (1594/5). Chester Beatty Library, Dublin, MS. 419, f. 40 v.

52 *Footbath.*
Miniature. Iran, post-Īl-Khānid period between 1340 and 1370. 31.7 × 25.7 cm. Orientabteilung der Staatsbibliothek Preussischer Kulturbesitz, Berlin (West), MS. Diez A fol. 70, f. 16.

53 *Man before a princess with attendants.*
Miniature from: Ṣadaqa b. Abī l-Qāsim Šīrāzī, Kitāb-i Samak-i 'Iyār. Iran, Inǧū style, 1330 to 1340. 11 × 11.4 cm. Bodleian Library, Oxford, MS. Ouseley 379–81, Vol. I, f. 119 r.

54 *Metal basin of Atabeg Lūlū of Mosul for a princess, detail.*
Iraq, middle of thirteenth century. Diameter 61.5 cm, height 7 cm. Staatliches Museum für Völkerkunde, Munich, Cat. No. 26 - N - 118.

55 *Bowl.*
Faïence. Iran, Ray (?), late twelfth century. Diameter 23 cm, height 8.8 cm. Smithsonian Institution, Freer Gallery of Art, Washington, No. 38,12.

56 *Seated princess with bouquet.*
Miniature. Iran, Tabriz style, around 1540. 39.7 × 28 cm. Fogg Art Museum, Harvard University, Cambridge, Mass., Gift of John Goelet, Inv. No. 1958. 60.

57 *Royal couple with servants.*
Painting on silk. Herat, early fifteenth century. 21.6 × 30.1 cm. Metropolitan Museum of Art, New York, Inv. No. 57.51.24.

58 *Tīmūr's family rides out from Samarkand to meet him.*
Miniature from: Šaraf ad-Dīn Yazdī, Ẓafar-nāma. Iran, Shiraz style, around 1533. 13 × 13 cm. India Office Library, London, Pers. MS. Ethé 175 (I.O.137), f. 368 v.

59 *Suhrāb takes the helmet off Rūdābeh who is disguised as a warrior.* Miniature from: Firdausī, Šāh-nāma. Iran, School of Isfahan, dated 1014 (1605). 24.5 × 14 cm. Deutsche Staatsbibliothek, Berlin, MS. or. fol. 4251, f. 227 r.

60 *Court scenes.* Lid of a lacquer-painted mirror-box. Iran, seventeenth century. Metropolitan Museum of Art, New York, Gift of Lily Place, 1921, Inv. No. 21.114 a.

61 *Afrāsiyāb's wives beg Kay Khosrou for mercy.* Miniature from: Firdausī, Šāh-nāma. Iran, School of Isfahan, dated 1014 (1605). 24.5 × 14 cm. Deutsche Staatsbibliothek, Berlin, MS. or. fol. 4251, f. 425 v.

62 *An old woman complains to Sultan Sanjar of injustice.* Miniature from: Niẓāmī, Ḥamsa. Herat, probably Maḥmūd Muḏahhib or one of his pupils (sixteenth century). Metropolitan Museum of Art, New York, Gift of Alexander Smith Cochran, 1913, Inv. No. 13.228.7.

63 *Candlestick.* Brass with silver inlays. Egypt, Ayyūbid, middle of thirteenth century. Height 34 cm. Islamic Museum, Cairo, Inv. No. 15 121.

64 *Decorative strips.* Ivory. Egypt, eleventh/twelfth century. 36.1, 40.6 cm, 5 cm. Museum für Islamische Kunst, Staatliche Museen Preussischer Kulturbesitz, Berlin (West), Inv. No. I 6375.

65 *The young lute player.* Miniature. Turkey, between 1640 and 1650. 22 × 12.4 cm. Bibliothèque Nationale, Paris, MS. arabe 6076, f. 2.

66 *Troop of tumblers.* Miniature. India, eighteenth century. 27 × 17.7 cm. Museum für Indische Kunst, Staatliche Museen Preussischer Kulturbesitz Berlin (West), Cat. No. MIK I 5070.

67 *Scene from an Indian harem.* Miniature. India, end of eighteenth century. 34 × 44.6 cm. Museum des Kunsthandwerks, Leipzig, B 19.2.

68 *Vāmiq and Shakardukht playing polo.* Book page with miniature from: Mīrzā Ibrāhīm Kirmānī, Vāmiq wa-Aẕrā. North Indian provincial style, around 1800. 13 × 12 cm. Orientabteilung der Staatsbibliothek Preussischer Kulturbesitz, Berlin (West), MS. or. quart. 1158, f. 99 r.

69 *Pen case.* Brass with gold and silver inlays. Probably Iran, 1281. Length 19.7 cm. British Museum, London, Inv. No. 916-235. *The same, detail.*

70 *Girl writing.* Miniature in Isfahan style, around 1600. 13.5 × 9 cm. India Office Library, London, Johnson 13-4.

71 *Court scene.* Lacquer-painted bookcover, signed Sayyid-i 'Alī. Nawā'ī, Dīwān. Iran, Tabriz, Safavid, around 1550. 24 × 14.5 cm. British Library, London, MS. Or. 1374.

72 *Humāy and Humāyūn in their love-nest.* Miniature from: Ḫwāǧū-i Kirmānī, Ḥamsa. Iran, Herat, dated 823 (1420). Size of face 23.6 × 15.7 cm. Staatliche Museen Berlin, Islamisches Museum, I 4628, p. 645.

73 *Love scene.* Miniature by Ustāḏ Muḥammadī. Iran, around 1575. 17.9 × 9 cm. Museum of Fine Arts, Boston, Francis Bartlett Donation, Inv. No. 14.588.

74 *Pair of lovers.* Miniature by Mu'īn Muṣawwir. Iran, dated 1098 (1689). 19.2 × 10.5 cm. Walters Art Gallery, Baltimore, Inv. No. 10 690.

75 *Warqa kills her lover's rival by thrusting a lance into his back.* Miniature from: Warqa wa-Gul-šāh. Iran, Mongolian, first half of thirteenth century. 6 × 17.7 cm. Topkapi Saray Museum, Istanbul, Ḥazine 841, f. 22 r.

76 *Zāl climbs into Rūdābeh's pavilion.* Miniature from: Firdausī, Šāh-nāma. Iran, Shiraz, between 1590 and 1595. 40 × 26 cm. British Library, London, MS. Add. 27257, f. 44 v.

77 *The black-eyed Talha kills another suitor.* Miniature from: Ḍarīr, Siyar-i Nabīy. Turkey, dated 1003 (1594/5). Chester Beatty Library, Dublin, MS. 419, f. 91 v.

78 *Bahrām Gūr with the Princess of the Sandalwood-colored Pavilion.* Miniature from: Amīr Ḥusrau Dihlavī, Ḥamsa. Iran, School of Shiraz, probably between 1590 and 1600. 13.4 × 13.4 cm (without dome). Orientabteilung der Staatsbibliothek Preussischer Kulturbesitz, Berlin (West), MS. or. fol. 1615, f. 226 r.

79 *Wine bottle with figurative design.* Green faïence. Iran, Isfahan ware, seventeenth century. Walters Art Gallery, Baltimore, Inv. No. 48.1120.

80 *Two men kneel before a lady.* Miniature by Muḥammad Yūsuf al-Ḥusainī. Iran, around 1630. 24.5 × 14.2 cm. Pierpont Morgan Library, New York, M 386, p. 15.

81 *Bottle with figurative design.* Faïence. Iran, seventeenth century. Height 22.3 cm. Hetjens-Museum, Düsseldorf, Inv. No. 12 161.

82 *Couple of lovers.* Miniature attributed to Muḥammad Qāsim. Iran, Isfahan, around 1660. 13 × 21.5 cm. Fogg Art Museum, Harvard University, Cambridge, Mass., Inv. No. 1950.130.

83 *The wedding night of Mihr and Nāhīd.* Miniature from: 'Aṣṣār, Mihr wa-Muštarī. Bukhara, School of Bihzād, dated 1523. 26.5 × 16.8 cm. Smithsonian Institution, Freer Gallery of Art, Washington, Inv. No. 32.8, p. 341.

84 *Couple of lovers.* Miniature, signed Riẓā-i 'Abbāsī. Iran, dated 1039 (1630). 18.1 × 11.9 cm. Metropolitan Museum of Art, New York, Francis M. Welch Fund, 1950, Inv. No. 50.164.

85 *Bahrām Gūr with the Princess of the Yellow Pavillion.* Miniature by Ṭālib from: Niẓāmī, Ḥamsa. Iran, dated 1077 (1666). Size of page 27.2 × 19 cm. British Library, London, MS. Add. 6613, f. 165 v.

86 *Fitna carries the cow on her shoulders.* Miniature from: Ibn 'Imād, Rauḍat al-muḥibbīn. Iran, dated 1582. 15.7 × 8.5 cm. Free Library of Philadelphia, Lewis Oriental MS. 78, f. 24 v.

87 *Two lovers on the harem terrace.* Miniature. India, middle of eighteenth century. 21.4 × 14 cm. Staatliche Museen Berlin, Islamisches Museum, I 4599, f. 19.

88 *Tāj Mahall in Agra, gate.* 1630–1648, erected by Shah Jahān as a tomb for his favorite wife, Mumtāz Mahall.

89 *Shīrīn in the garden looking at Khosrou's picture.* Miniature from: Niẓāmī, Ḥamsa. Iran, dated 968 (1561). 20.7 × 18.7 cm. Bibliothèque Nationale, Paris, MS. suppl. pers. 1956, f. 32 v.

90 *Khosrou catches sight of Shīrīn bathing.*
Miniature from an anthology for Prince Baisonqūr. Iran, Shiraz 823 (1420). 29 × 20 cm. Museum für Islamische Kunst, Staatliche Museen Preussischer Kulturbesitz, Berlin (West), Inv. No. I 4628, p. 23.

91 *Ferhād carries Shīrīn and her horse.*
Miniature by Riżā-i 'Abbāsī from: Niẓāmī, Husrau wa-Šīrīn. Iran, Isfahan, dated 1042 (1632). Victoria and Albert Museum, London, Inv. No. 364-1885, f. 138 r.

92 *Shīrīn visits Ferhād.*
Miniature from: Amīr Husrau Dihlavī, Hamsa. India, Lahore 1597/8. 22.7 × 14.7 cm. Walters Art Gallery, Baltimore, Inv. No. 10.624, p. 59.

93 *The wedding of Khosrou and Shīrīn.*
Miniature probably by Mahmūd Muḏahhib or one of his pupils from: Niẓāmī, Hamsa. Herat, dated 1524/5. Metropolitan Museum of Art, New York, Gift of Alexander Smith Cochran, 1913, Inv. No. 13.228.7, f. 104 v.

94 *Khosrou and Shīrīn in discussion with a sage.*
Miniature from: Niẓāmī, Hamsa. Iran, dated 848/9 (1444/5). 16.3 × 10.6 cm. University Library of Manchester, Rylands MS. 36, f. 88 v.

95 *Carpet with scenes from Laylā and Majnūn.*
Kerman or Kashan, sixteenth century. 3.75 × 2.70 m. Musée des Arts Décoratifs, Paris, Inv. No. 106/5.

96 *Majnūn is brought in chains to Laylā's tent.*
Miniature by Mīr Sayyid 'Alī from: Niẓāmī, Hamsa. Iran, Tabriz, dated 1539–1543. 32 × 18.2 cm. British Library, London, MS. Or. 2265, f. 157 v.

97 *Majnūn dies at Laylā's grave.*
Miniature by Bihzād from: Niẓāmī, Hamsa. Iran, around 1495. Size of page 24 × 17.5 cm. British Library, London, MS. Or. 6810, f. 144 v.

98 *Laylā and Majnūn in Paradise.*
Miniature from: Niẓāmī, Hamsa. Iran, Herat 1449/50. Metropolitan Museum of Art, New York, Gift of Alexander Smith Cochran, 1913, Inv. No. 13.228.3 MS. 6, f. 181 v.

99 *The first meeting of Yūsuf and Zulaykhā.*
Miniature from: Ğāmī, Haft Aurang. Iran, about 1570. 29.1 × 23.8 cm. Bodleian Library, Oxford, MS. Elliott 149, f. 182 v.

100 *Yūsuf and Zulaykhā surrounded by pictures of their love.*
Miniature from: Ğāmī, Yūsuf wa-Zulaihā. Iran, about 1570. 21.5 × 11.5 cm. National Library, Cairo, Adab Fārisī 45 m, f. 91 v.

101 *Jug with handle, narrow opening, and low foot.*
Glazed clay, lustre-painted. Iran, Seljūq period, early thirteenth century. Height 18 cm, diameter 14.8 cm. Smithsonian Institution, Freer Gallery of Art, Washington, Inv. No. 29,9.

102 *Shallow bowl.*
Glazed clay, lustre-painted. Egypt, Fātimid period, eleventh century. Diameter 40 cm. Islamic Museum, Cairo, Inv. No. 14 923.

103 *Reigning couple on throne with servants.*
Miniature. Mongolian, School of Tabriz, around beginning of fourteenth century. 18.3 × 25.8 cm. Orientabteilung der Staatsbibliothek Preussischer Kulturbesitz, Berlin (West), MS. Diez A fol. 71, f. 48.

104 *Star tile with woman's picture.*
Faïence. Iran, Kashan, middle of thirteenth century. Width 20 cm. Hetjens-Museum, Düsseldorf, Inv. No. 1941/39.

105 *A lady's jewel box.*
Ivory carving. Spain, Madīnat az-Zahrā, around 962. Length 13 cm, width 8.5 cm, height 8.5 cm. Victoria and Albert Museum, London, Inv. No. 580-1910.

106 *Flask.*
Glass. Egypt, tenth century. 6 cm, 3.4 cm. Museum für Islamische Kunst, Staatliche Museen Preussischer Kulturbesitz, Berlin (West), Inv. No. I 2339.

107 *Abū Zayd preaching in front of men and veiled women in Ray.*
Miniature by Wāsitī from: Harīrī, Maqāmāt. Bagdad, dated 634 (1237). Size of page 36.5 × 29.4 cm. Bibliothèque Nationale, Paris, MS. arabe 5847.

108 *Portrait of Ziyā' Sultāna.*
Miniature, signed Qudrat Allāh. Iran, Qazvin style, end of sixteenth century. 21.7 × 14.6 cm. Bibliothèque Nationale, Paris, MS. arabe 6076, f. 8 v.

109 *Shāpūr introduces Ferhād to Shīrīn.*
Miniature from: Niẓāmī, Husrau wa-Šīrīn. Iran, School of Tabriz, early fifteenth century. 27.3 × 16.5 cm. Smithsonian Institution, Freer Gallery of Art, Washington, Inv. No. 31.34, p. 59.

110 *Kneeling girl.*
Miniature from an album of Murād III. Turkey, sixteenth century. 18.4 × 11.7 cm. Österreichische Nationalbibliothek, Vienna, Cod. Mixt. 313, f. 33.

111 *Young woman smoking the hookah.*
Miniature by Mu'īn Muṣawwir. Iran, dated 1084 (1673/4). 20 × 10.2 cm. Topkapi Saray Museum, Istanbul, Hazine 2142, f. 12 r.

112 *Recumbent seminude.*
Miniature from an album of the Emir of Bukhara. Sixteenth century. 13.5 × 22.8 cm. Pierpont Morgan Library, New York, Inv. No. 386-5.

113 *Expensively attired lady with veil.*
Miniature. Iran, seventeenth century. 21.2 × 14 cm. Museum des Kunsthandwerks, Leipzig, B 11.11.

114 *Wall tile with woman's head.*
Clay, glazed. Iran, early seventeenth century. Museum für Islamische Kunst, Staatliche Museen Preussischer Kulturbesitz, Berlin (West), Inv. No. I 7/71.

115 *Mogul lady.*
Miniature, signed Maddhū Hurd. India, sixteenth century. Musée Guimet, Paris, Inv. No. 3619 Hc.

116 *Bottle.*
Rock crystal, cut and engraved. Egypt, Fātimid period, approx. tenth century. Height 17 cm. Halberstadt Cathedral, Inv. No. 49.

117 *Bracelet.*
Gold. Iran, Daylam, tenth/eleventh century. Diameter 7.8 cm, width 3.7 cm, weight 192.5 g. Walters Art Gallery, Baltimore, Inv. No. 57.1921.

118 *Lovers at the window.*
Miniature. India, first half of eighteenth century. 21 × 13.2 cm. Staatliche Museen Berlin, Islamisches Museum, Inv. No. I 4593, f. 26.

119 *Mogul girl with bird.*
Miniature. India, middle of eighteenth century. 18 × 9.8 cm. Staatliche Museen Berlin, Islamisches Museum, Inv. No. I 4594, f. 15.

120 *The angel Tobias.*
Miniature, signed Husain. India, sixteenth century. Musée Guimet, Paris, Inv. No. 3619 Ha.

121 *Empress Zinat Mahall from Delhi.*
Ivory miniature. India, around
1860. 10.8 × 7.6 cm. Staatliches
Museum für Völkerkunde, Munich, Inv. No. 1186.

122 *Rings.*
Gold with rose-colored agate or
red jasper. Egypt, Mamlūk
period. Height 2.9 cm, 2.7 cm,
weight 7 g. Benaki Museum,
Athens, Inv. No. 1890/91.

123 *Pair of ear pendants.*
Gold. Iran, Nishapur, tenth cen-
tury. 8 cm, 1.9 cm. Museum für
Islamische Kunst, Staatliche Mu-
seen Preussischer Kulturbesitz,
Berlin (West), Inv. No. I 57.71.

124 *Necklace with three pendants.*
Gold with pearls and semiprecious stones. Egypt, twelfth
century. Length 24 cm. Islamic
Museum, Cairo, Inv. No. 13749.

125 *Couple of lovers with maidservant.*
Lacquer-painted lid. Iran, first
half of nineteenth century.
29.1 × 19.3 cm. Museum für
Völkerkunde, Leipzig, WAS 690.

126 *In the* sūq.
Joussif Kamel (Egypt). Oil on
canvass. 100 × 100 cm. Museum
of Modern Art, Cairo.

127 *Young girl.*
Khaled El-Rahhal (Iraq). Wood.
Museum of Modern Art,
Bagdad.

128 *Women in the* abāya.
Mohammed Ghani (Iraq).
1964/6. Wood. Height 25 cm.
Privately owned.

129 *On the Nile.*
Mahmoud Mukhtar (Egypt).
1928. Marble. Mukhtar Museum,
Cairo.

130 *Two women on the balcony.*
Zeinab El-Siginy (Egypt). Oil on
canvass. 70 × 100 cm.
Museum of Modern Art, Cairo.

131 *In the Rif.*
Salah Taher (Egypt). Oil on
canvass. 50 × 60 cm.
Museum of Modern Art, Cairo.

132 *Young girl.*
Joussif Firansis (Egypt). 1970.
Wood, oil on canvass, 40 × 50 cm.
Museum of Modern Art,
Cairo.

133 *On the beauty of their eyes.*
Burhan Karkutli (Syria). 1975.
Lithograph. 50 × 70 cm.

134 *Mother with child.*
Fuad Al-Futaih (Yemen). 1974.
Silk-screen. 70 × 50 cm. Prop-
erty of the artist.

135 *Girls grinding corn.*
Khaled El-Jader (Iraq). 1976.
Oil on canvass. Property of the
artist.

136 *Women from Ghurna near Luxor.*
Shalabi (Egypt). 1941. Oil on
canvass. 50 × 60 cm.
Museum of Modern Art, Cairo.

137 *The Land of the Sad Oranges.*
Battul El-Fukaiki (Iraq). Oil on
canvass. Museum of Modern
Art, Bagdad.

Text Illustrations

p. 21 *Female hunter.*
Reconstructed mural from a
Khalif's palace in Samarra,
ninth century. After:
Herzfeld, E. *Die Wandmalereien
von Samarra.* Berlin, 1927.

p. 36 *Calligraphic illuminated page with
the* basmala.
Iran, seventeenth century.
Staatliche Museen, Berlin,
Islamisches Museum.
After: Kühnel, E. *Islamische
Schriftkunst.* 2nd ed., Graz,
1972.

p. 44 *Bridal procession.*
Turkey, seventeenth century.
After: Taeschner, F. *Alt-
Stambuler Hof- und Volksleben.*
Hanover, 1925.

p. 48 *Woman crushing corn.*
Miniature from an Indian
manuscript, probably by a Per-
sian painter, sixteenth century.
British Library, London, MS.
Or. 3299. After: Lewis, B.
(editor) *The World of Islam.*
London, 1976.

p. 71 *Dancer.*
Miniature, India, eighteenth
century, signed Kamāl Hileh.
Louvre, Paris, Inv. No. 3619.

p. 81 *Obverse and reverse of the Sultana
Shajarat ad-Dorr's dinar.*
Egypt, thirteenth century.
British Museum, London. After:
Schregle, G. *Die Sultanin von
Ägypten.* Wiesbaden, 1961.

p. 83 *Mogul princess on the throne.*
Miniature, India, eighteenth
century. 9.7 × 6.4 cm.
Staatliche Museen, Berlin,
Islamisches Museum, Inv.
No. I 4601, f. 18.

p. 116 *Bahrām Gūr and Āzādeh hunting.*
Ceramic tile relief, lustre-
painted. Iran, Kashan,
thirteenth century. Islamic
Museum, Cairo, Inv. No. I
11090.

p. 117 *Laylā and Majnūn have fainted
with love.*
Miniature from: Niẓāmī,
Ḥamsa. South Iran, middle of
the fifteenth century. 3.7 ×
8 cm. Deutsche Staatsbibliothek, Berlin, Ms. Sprenger
1475, f. 128r.

p. 146 *Young woman making her toilet.*
Miniature, Turkey, around
1710. 16.2 × 11 cm. Topkapi
Saray Museum, Istanbul.
After: Stchoukine, I. *La pein-
ture turque d'après les manuscrits
illustrés.* IIe partie. Paris,
1968.

p. 147 *Lady with maidservant on the way
to bathe.*
Turkey, seventeenth century.
After: Taeschner, F. *Alt-
Stambuler Hof- und Volksleben.*
Hanover, 1925.

Sources of Illustrations

Cover: Velvet brocade decorated with female figures. Iran, seventeenth century. Museum des Kunsthandwerks, Leipzig.

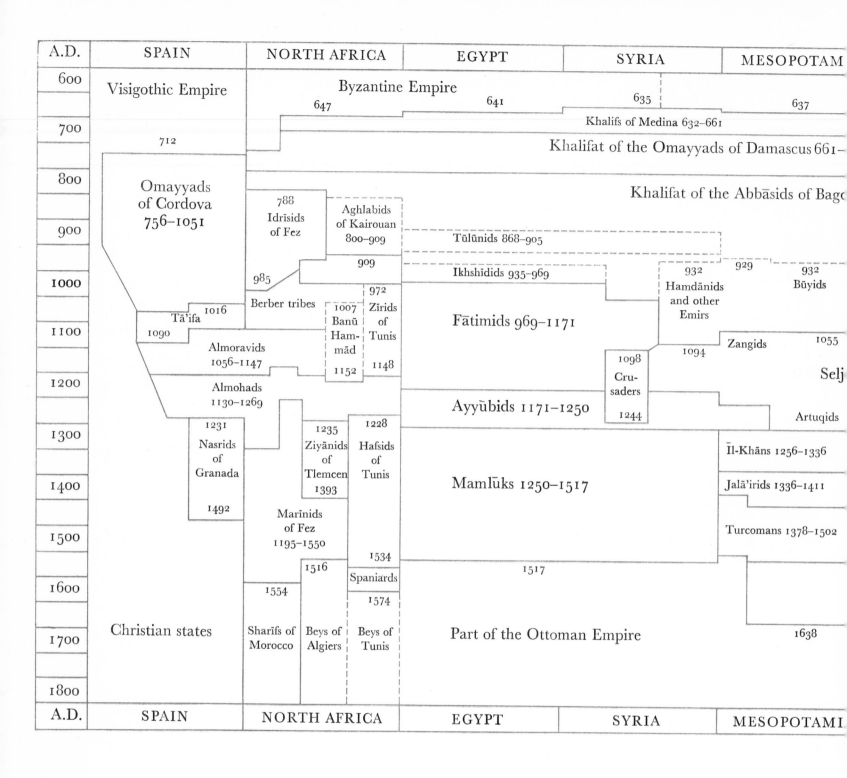

A.D.	SPAIN	NORTH AFRICA			EGYPT	SYRIA	MESOPOTAM
600	Visigothic Empire	Byzantine Empire			641	635	637
		647					
700	712				Khalifs of Medina 632–661		
					Khalifat of the Omayyads of Damascus 661–		
800	Omayyads of Cordova 756–1051	788 Idrīsids of Fez	Aghlabids of Kairouan 800–909		Khalifat of the Abbāsids of Bag		
900					Tūlūnids 868–905		
		985	909		Ikhshīdids 935–969	932 Hamdānids and other Emirs	929 932 Būyids
1000		Berber tribes	1007 Banū Ham-mād	972 Zīrids of Tunis	Fātimids 969–1171		
1100	Tā'ifa 1016 1090					1094	Zangids 1055
	Almoravids 1056–1147		1152	1148		1098 Cru-saders	Selj
1200	Almohads 1130–1269				Ayyūbids 1171–1250	1244	Artuqids
1300	1231 Nasrids of Granada	1235 Ziyānids of Tlemcen 1393	1228 Hafsids of Tunis		Mamlūks 1250–1517		Īl-Khāns 1256–1336
1400							Jalā'irids 1336–1411
	1492	Marīnids of Fez 1195–1550					Turcomans 1378–1502
1500				1534	1517		
			1516	Spaniards			
1600		1554		1574			
1700	Christian states	Sharīfs of Morocco	Beys of Algiers	Beys of Tunis	Part of the Ottoman Empire		1638
1800							
A.D.	SPAIN	NORTH AFRICA			EGYPT	SYRIA	MESOPOTAMI

ARABIA

HIJĀZ (Mecca and Medina):
Khalifs and Arabian Sharīfs

YEMEN (Southern Arabia):
Khalifs and Arabian dynasties,
1174–1536 Ayyūbids, Rasūlids
and others, since 1536
Ottomans and Imāms of San'a

Chronology of Islamic Dynasties

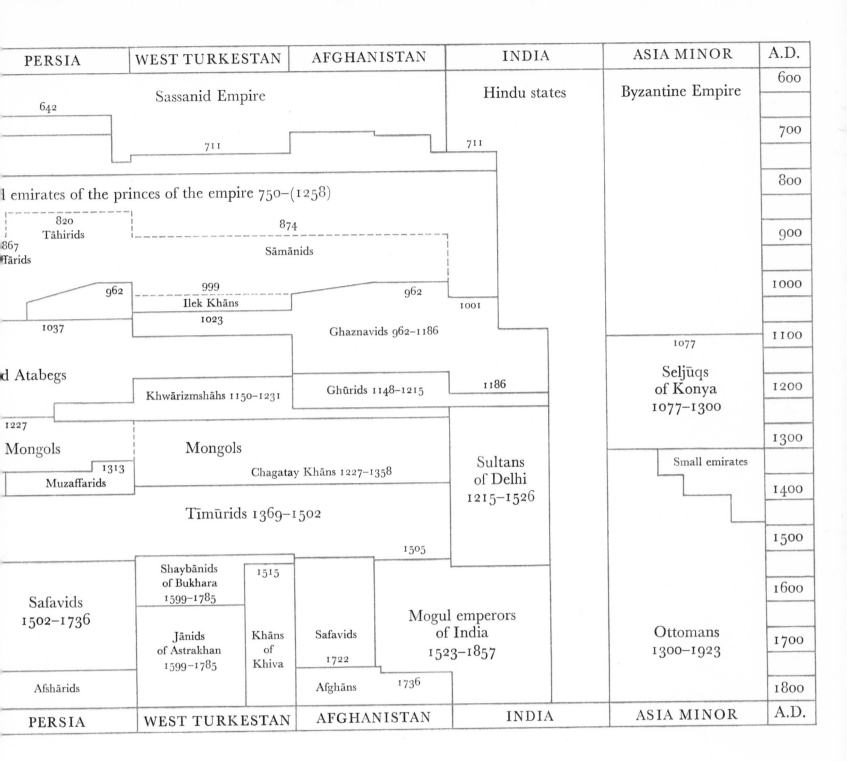

PERSIA	WEST TURKESTAN	AFGHANISTAN	INDIA	ASIA MINOR	A.D.
					600
	Sassanid Empire		Hindu states	Byzantine Empire	
642					700
	711		711		
					800
l emirates of the princes of the empire 750–(1258)					
820		874			900
Tāhirids					
867		Sāmānids			
ffārids					1000
962	999	962			
	Ilek Khāns		1001		
1037	1023				1100
		Ghaznavids 962–1186		1077	
d Atabegs				Seljūqs of Konya 1077–1300	1200
	Khwārizmshāhs 1150–1231	Ghūrids 1148–1215	1186		
1227					1300
Mongols	Mongols		Sultans of Delhi 1215–1526	Small emirates	
1313	Chagatay Khāns 1227–1358				1400
Muzaffarids					
	Tīmūrids 1369–1502				1500
		1505			
	Shaybānids of Bukhara 1599–1785	1515			1600
Safavids 1502–1736			Mogul emperors of India 1523–1857		
	Jānids of Astrakhan 1599–1785	Khāns of Khiva	Safavids 1722	Ottomans 1300–1923	1700
Afshārids			Afghāns 1736		1800
PERSIA	WEST TURKESTAN	AFGHANISTAN	INDIA	ASIA MINOR	A.D.

SICILY

up to 830 Byzantine, 830–1070
Aghlabids and Fātimids,
1070–1194 Normans, later
Hohenstaufen, Anjou, Aragon
and others

VOLGA STATES

up to thirteenth century Khāns
of the Khazars and Bulgars
1236–1558 Mongol Khāns of the
Golden Horde and rivals

CRIMEA

1420–1783 Giray Khāns

BALKANS

under Ottoman rule from
end of fourteenth or fifteenth
century to nineteenth century

HUNGARY

1541–1699 under Ottoman
rule

Index